Better Than Any Dream

Better Than Any Dream

A Personal Memoir

Paul F. Miller, Jr.

To order additional copies of this book, contact:
Xlibris Corporation
1-888-795-4274
www.Xlibris.com
Orders@Xlibris.com
27848

CONTENTS

CHAPTER TWO

CHAPTER THREE

CHAPTER FOUR

CHAPTER FIVE

CHAPTER SIX

CHAPTER SEVEN

CHAPTER EIGHT

CHAPTER NINE

CHAPTER TEN

I dedicate this book
To my mother and father, Katharine Thompson Miller and Paul Fetterolf
Miller, who got me here in the first place and instilled in me solid values.

To my dear wife, Ella Warren Miller, who has made it such a joy to be here.
To my children, Winky, Kathy, and Buzz, who have given me all the right
reasons to enjoy parenthood.
And to my grandchildren, Ryan, Jake, Maggie, Tor, Paul, and Livia,
who give me faith that some of me will continue to be here for a long while!

One of my favorite pictures of Warren, Caneel Bay, St. John, 1977

PREFACE

I almost discarded the idea of writing these memoirs. I thought it was the height of conceit to believe anyone would possibly be interested. But then I remembered how much I enjoyed my father's tales of his youth, college, and early business years—stories of his life before I knew him as his son. Now, many years later, I wish I had, in his own words, his story—his joys and sorrows, his successes and failures, his friendships, his marriage to my mother, and his feelings about his children.

Thus, I think of this work as being primarily for my children and grandchildren. I hope that many years from now, they will be pleased that I wrote it. My family has always come first by a wide margin, and I am proud of that. Even though there are many pages in these memoirs devoted to family and friends, I hope a few others who have known me only in career capacities will find it interesting.

Regardless, it also turned out to be immensely satisfying for me. I found that, as Ben Franklin observed in his autobiography, the writing of it was the next best thing to living one's life again.

The forcing of one's memory can produce remarkable results. As I edited and reedited my own words, my mind was jarred into recalling events and people that were stored in some remote recess of my brain. Indeed, not only did I remember them but I also tasted and savored them with a smile on my face and in my heart.

In looking through press clippings, I noticed one that referred to me as the boy wonder of Philadelphia's financial community. As I say in these memoirs, I walked into a talent vacuum that was created, especially in the financial world, by the Great Depression and World War II. In the financial world of today, I might be only an average talent in a field of thousands.

Perhaps wisdom increases with age. Or maybe the caution that comes with experience makes it appear that way. I made very good personal decisions early in my life, such as choosing the right mate, buying the right house, choosing a good career, and founding a business. But in business and other associations it was, as I grew older and gained more experience, that I made more confident and better decisions. I also spoke my convictions with less reticence after noticing how often I regretted not speaking out earlier and more forcefully on issues facing the businesses and institutions where I was involved.

People who know me as an investor and founder of a successful investment-management business may be puzzled that I have chosen to write more about my personal thoughts on such subjects as religion and philosophy than I have on investing. It was only at the last moment that I decided to write a brief section about investing. I did not want this to be a "how to" book. Perhaps that will come later. Besides, I regard myself as a competent but not a great investor.

My life has been better than any dream that I might have had as a young man. I have enjoyed good fortune and good health. My moments of disappointment, sorrow, and unhappiness have been very rare. I have been particularly blessed with a happy marriage to my closest friend and lover for fifty-one years. I cannot imagine having existed without her. She has always been ready with guidance and advice, and compliments or constructive criticism. Her mental capacities and common sense have cut through the fog on many problems and issues that I have faced. I am totally dependent on her. Her love and loyalty have been complete and unconditional as has been mine for her.

*   *   *

Special thanks are due to Mary Ann Meyers, Ginny Amsler, former business partners, and family members who have given me advice and help with this book.

CHAPTER ONE

Growing Up

Doubled Up

In late 1931, when I was four years old, our family of three was forced by the Great Depression to "double up" with my maternal grandparents. Doubling up was a phenomenon repeated millions of times across America in the early 1930s. We moved from a small rented twin house in Cynwyd Estates to my grandparents' very modest twin house about three miles away.

The crash of 1929 and the Depression that followed had decimated my parents' assets and income. As a stockbroker during the 1920s, Dad had done quite well. But by 1931, at the age of thirty-two, he was in debt and earning almost nothing. He could no longer pay the rent for our house.

Mother was thirty-one and pregnant with my sister Mary Anne, who would be born in April of 1932. Only ten years earlier, when Dad was a senior at Penn, she had met him on a blind date arranged by one of his fraternity brothers.

Family History

Dad was an only child from Hazleton, Pennsylvania, a town on the edge of the anthracite coal region of the state. His father was freight stationmaster for the Pennsylvania Railroad in Hazleton. My paternal grandparents were reared on neighboring farms by the Millers and the Fetterolfs, fourth-generation German American families. He was one of seven children, and she was one of six.

I have traced the Fetterolf family back to a shepherd born in 1604 in Dortel, Germany. His great-grandson, Johann Federolf (it was variously spelled *Federoff*, *Fetherolf*, and *Fetterolf*), arrived in America in 1730.

I have tried to trace the Millers but have succeeded only back to my great-grandfather in Berks County, Pennsylvania, in the 1840s. The records are simply too full of Millers, Mullers, and Muellers to trace accurately. I believe they changed the spelling from *Muller* to *Miller* in the early 1800s.

On my mother's side, Grandmother Thompson, nee Lillian Mary Jenkins, was one of four children of Edward John Jenkins and Mary Anne Harris. Edward and Mary Anne emigrated from London, England in the 1860s after the Civil War. Edward taught mathematics and French at the Episcopal Academy, then located on Pine Street in Philadelphia.

My other great-grandparents—Andrew Thompson and his wife, Katharine Mills— came from Ireland in the 1850s while in their twenties. Census records show that he was a drayman in Philadelphia. That corroborates the family story that had him pulling a merchant's cart for a living. I believe they had four children, one of whom was my grandfather, William Andrew Thompson.

Grandfather Thompson, known to us as "Ahla," was an anthracite coal dealer. Grandmother Thompson, "Nana," was a trained nurse. My mother, Katharine Mills Thompson, was the first of their three children, born on September 19, 1900.

While they were far from being part of the world of Philadelphia society, they were admirers of it, speaking in almost reverent tones about the Biddles, Cadwaladers, and Morrises. They judged anyone coming from the roughneck coal region of Pennsylvania as "not suitable" as a prospective son-in-law.

Dad had always regarded his family as strong country stock and could not comprehend his prospective in-laws' attitude toward him. They had no reason to be haughty. They were both first-generation Americans, the children of English immigrants. Neither one was college educated.

On January 2, 1923, only seven months after Dad's graduation from Penn, he and Mother eloped and were married in the Church of the Holy Trinity on Rittenhouse Square in Philadelphia. Once the deed was done, his new in-laws rather graciously accepted him. Perhaps because of their belated welcome, he always carried a small grudge against the Thompson family. It was very difficult for him to swallow his pride, admit that the Great Depression had beaten him, and accept the offer from my grandparents to share their house.

I told friends that they could identify my grandparents' house by the two life-sized hunchbacked glass cats that were on the peak of the roof, facing each other. It was not an unattractive house. The exterior was a gray stone masonry with large green-shuttered windows. Large bay windows graced both the dining room and the bedroom above it.

We were to live there for the next eleven years.

Life at 145 Montgomery Avenue

The house had only one bathroom that served seven of us: Mother's youngest brother, my uncle Bill, who had graduated from Penn in 1929 and still lived at home; my grandparents; and the four of us. Our family lived on the third floor in two small uninsulated rooms. My sister and I shared a slanted-ceiling room with one dormer window, and Mother and Dad were in the other. On the stairway landing outside our bedroom doors was a large storage closet where camphor-sprinkled clothes were kept. The closet had no light, and we would use it for hide-and-seek and other games. When my sister was five or six, I would hide there and jump out to scare her as she came up the stairs.

Hot summer months were unbearable, and hissing steam radiators worked overtime to keep us warm in winter. On very hot nights in summer, we cooled off by taking drives in our 1935 Chevy through the nearby wooded countryside, with all the windows down. There was a place in Gladwyne called Devil's Dip where the road's course was almost U-shaped. Dad would yell, "Hold on to your hats," and then we would scream as he accelerated downhill so we would feel the "Gs" from the sudden change to going uphill. (Devil's Dip has now been filled in and has lost its thrill.)

Despite the cramped quarters, I have some very pleasant memories of the house. There was a landing at the bottom of the stairs that was two steps up from both the living room and the kitchen that was off to one side. A curtain on a rod could be closed to mitigate drafts from the stairwell. It made a marvelous stage on which we could perform, singing or acting in plays that we invented. I remember coming down the stairs on Christmas morning and being made to wait excitedly behind the closed curtain until the Christmas tree was lit, and the surrounding pile of gifts was ready for the most effective presentation.

Behind the kitchen was a long unheated pantry/laundry where perishables could be kept cool and where clothes were washed by hand on a washboard. In the winter, while we had to worry about freezing temperatures, it was a place to drop cooked candy mints onto a cold marble surface, a place we headed to sneak a treat or two. Nana Thompson always let us help in the kitchen, particularly while she was making cakes and cookies. Nana was usually generous with the leavings, and we were always given the bowls and spoons to lick.

The yard was small, but there was a separate garage and hardened dirt driveway where we had a basketball court. There was a shed attached to the side of the garage that was variously used as a doghouse and the headquarters for the secret club formed by me and the other boys in the neighborhood. In those days, we burned our paper trash. It amounted to only a small fraction of what we generate today, and we had an old oil drum that served as an incinerator. There were several nice trees, a small flower garden, and a sandbox that eventually served as a home for my captured box turtles that were fed lettuce and garden worms. While I watched with fascination, they ate the worms like spaghetti, squeezing all the innards out of one end. In time, I would also keep caged garter snakes in the sandbox.

In summer, we put up a green and white awning to protect the covered porch from the sun. There was a comfortable glider as well as several cushioned wicker chairs. I remember the coolness of the porch and the hours I spent reading while enjoying the gentle movements of the glider. There was also an open section of the porch that faced the street. Traffic was light and quiet on Montgomery Avenue in those days, and we often ate lunch or dinner there, believing it was the height of luxury.

Only the other half of the twin house separated us from the local firehouse: the Union Fire Association. The fire siren was exactly at the level of our bedroom and only one hundred feet away. It was deafening when it blew, but we learned to sleep through it. The firehouse provided us with excitement as we watched the local volunteer firemen respond to the siren with their screeching brakes, run into the firehouse, don their firefighting garb, and speed out on the fire engines, hanging on to the rear while bells clanged and sirens whistled. There was a blackboard at the rear of the firehouse where the location of the fire was noted. After I learned to ride a bicycle, I would often follow the engines to the fires.

The walls of the firehouse had a series of prints of the adventures and misadventures of the Darktown Fire Company, stereotyped caricatures of an all-black fire brigade. They were humorous then but would be considered blatantly racist today. Upstairs was a room where kids were not allowed. It was a recreation room for the firemen, most of whom were volunteers from the neighborhood. I knew most of them as fathers of friends or from everyday associations with local merchants. It was a place that was effectively a club, a haven strictly for men, a place where they could play billiards, drink beer, and be profane.

Parents and Grandparents

Nana Thompson was a jolly, loving stout woman who loved to laugh contagiously and often saw humor where others might not. She loved her grandchildren with a marvelous tenderness. In retrospect, her presence was like having a second mother in the house, one who was usually more permissive and loved doing something "special" for us.

Ahla Thompson was a quiet, very deliberate person who seemed to do everything in slow motion. He ate at half the speed of others at the table while we stayed seated until he finished slowly chewing his food. My dad was fond of saying that Ahla had two speeds. Then he would imitate his father-in-law moving slowly and then his father-in-law moving very fast. The joke was that the two speeds were identically slow. Ahla often spoke through his wife who would let us know "what your grandfather thinks." To have a family of three, about to become four, join them in their small house must have been difficult for them as well. Economic conditions were also hurting them; he was having increasing difficulty getting customers to pay their bills. He was sixty-one, and she was fifty-nine at the time.

I remember nothing about my grandmother Miller. She died in 1931, before my memory stopped registering. Grandfather Miller, also called Ahla, we saw very infrequently, and my memories of him are hazy.

My mother and father were near-perfect parents. They instilled values with diligence and natural ease and were devoted to us. During school years, they attended every event of note even if we were only minor participants. They were friends to our friends and made them feel very comfortable in their company. This held true from kindergarten through college and beyond.

Mother was a very pretty woman, just a shade over five feet tall, blonde haired, had a long waist, and nicely built. Dad referred to her as being "short in the poop." (Our daughter, Winky, inherited Mother's build.) She was good-humored, mild-mannered, relatively quiet, and very even tempered and polite. While she had not gone to college, she read widely and was always informed and interested in politics and the world's affairs. I was always proud of her.

Dad was more complex. Very quick-witted and intelligent, he had a furious temper. It was often unpredictable as to when he would lose it. When it happened, we all cowered, but once it was over, it was over. He never carried his fury further. He was dark and handsome, gregarious, very masculine in his mannerisms and his tastes, popular with his peers and his children's friends, and very entertaining company. He would often reminisce about his youth and have us in stitches with some of his tales, many of which involved his mother. I particularly remember his telling of coming home from school one day to find his bedroom floor studded with nails. It was his mother's retribution for his never hanging up his clothes. "Now," she said, "you can't miss a nail to hang them on."

Dad loved telling and listening to jokes. Often he would tell off-color jokes in front of us, only to be admonished by his wife as he winked at us mischievously.

Dad had been an excellent student at Hazleton High School and had hoped to be valedictorian. The highest honors, however, went to a girl who had always been his academic rival, and he was salutatorian. The girl was Bernadine Boogner, an improbable name that was always popping up and was frequently invoked in various humorous episodes of our family life.

Early Memories

I have very hazy memories of the time prior to my sister's birth, an event that does have real clarity. I remember praying for a baby sister and the day she was brought home from the hospital.

The summer after Mary Anne was born, we somehow afforded a small rental cottage for two weeks in Ocean City, New Jersey. I have very clear memories of that summer. My baby sister seemed to sleep most of the time. Dad took me on my first fishing expedition for black bass off a bridge on the bay. I also had my first taste of independence when Dad let me out of the car to walk three blocks alone on the beach to our cottage.

Kindergarten began that fall. In good weather, I walked the three quarters of a mile through an attractive upper middle-class neighborhood where most of my friends lived to the Cynwyd Elementary School. It was housed in a square two-story brick building that still stands today. It was the same school my mother's two brothers, Ed and Bill, had attended and was across an athletic field from the antique Merion Academy where Mother went to grammar school for the early grades.

My memories of grammar school are very vivid, including the distinct odors of disinfectant in the hallways and the lingering smell of sour milk in the lunchroom (and in my thermos bottle). I remember all the teachers and can picture them and name them chronologically. It was a good school, as I would come to appreciate in my later academic life. Fundamentals of math, reading, and grammar were drilled into us. The school had strong discipline. When we changed classrooms, we marched two abreast. In fact, we learned all the marching commands in gym class so that I was well prepared for Boy Scouts and the marching band that would come later.

In the morning, boys would enter the school building by one side entrance and girls by the opposite side. Each afternoon we were dismissed to bugle calls played by sixth graders followed by a Sousa march played on a windup Victrola by the front door. When I reached sixth grade, I became the bugler. Classrooms were dismissed in sequence, and we marched in step down the hall and out the door.

We would arrive well before school started in the morning to shoot marbles or flip war cards to try to add to our collections. The cards, which came in bubblegum packs, were very gory pictures of the Sino-Japanese War. From a line about four feet from a wall, you flipped or sailed your card. The boy whose card was closest to the wall collected all the other cards. To win marbles, you had to hit them with your shooter so they touched the wall.

After school was a time for pickup games of baseball or football or crack-the-whip. One of the several concussions I suffered as a child resulted from my being at the tail end of the whip and being thrown in the air to land on my head.

Truancy, Crime, and Mischief

I was an attentive child, learned to read easily and well, and was a good but not brilliant student. I was also well behaved, which, in hindsight, makes one experience seem unlikely.

My close friend, Ike Kershaw, talked me into playing hooky in second grade. We simply walked away from school at lunchtime with no intention of returning that day. It was a very cold winter day, and we had no plan. Our first stop was an underground hut that had been built on an empty lot by the older neighborhood boys. It was simply a large hole in the ground covered by boards and a piece of metal with dirt piled on top. We were hidden but shivering with cold. I had a better idea. We would go to the shed attached to our garage that was used as a doghouse. Taking all the neighborhood shortcuts so we wouldn't be noticed on a sidewalk, we arrived at the shed.

We had given no thought to how school officials and parents might react to our disappearance. The infamous Lindbergh kidnapping had occurred three years earlier, and the trial of the alleged perpetrator was underway. Parental nervousness was high and widespread.

Thus, my mother was on the phone with Esther McKeon, the school principal, while we were hiding in the shed. They were both extremely upset. The telephone was located on a landing of our stairs where there was a window looking over the backyard and the garage area. As Mother was having the frightening conversation with Ms. McKeon, who had been her grammar-school teacher, she saw a red-mittened hand reach out of the shed's door and pull it closed. Within minutes, we were driven back to school, given a stern lecture, and punished by having to sit without talking on hard wooden chairs outside the principal's office for a week. Thus ended my life as a truant except for one day as a senior in high school when a few of us decided to take the local train into Philadelphia to see the matinee at the Troc Burlesque Theater. But more of that later.

At the age of seven, I received a solid lesson in honesty. My parents had taken me shopping at the local Woolworth's five-and-ten-cents store. I asked Dad to buy me a whistle I had seen. He flatly refused, and when his head was turned, I picked one up and stuffed it in my pocket. Not being an intelligent crook, when we were home, I took the whistle outside and blew it. Dad stormed out of the house, grabbed me by the shirt, and dragged me inside. Both Dad and Mother sat me down, lectured and wagged their fingers at me, and wondered aloud how long it would take for the police to arrive. What might they do to me? After an appropriate interval, they packed me in the car and made me return the whistle, acknowledging to the saleslady that I had stolen it. Thus ended my criminal career.

While I was far from being a troublemaker, several memories of mischievous behavior come readily to mind. I was intrigued by gunpowder after reading about it in a science book. There was a source that I knew about: the shotgun shells my grandfather kept in the garage for his occasional hunts for pheasant. One day I cut open about a half-dozen shells and emptied them of their gunpowder. Taking it to my bedroom in a glass dish, I fashioned a fuse from paper and fed it into the dish, then lit the fuse, and waited. I wasn't disappointed. With a gigantic *whoosh,* the powder ignited in a cloud of intense black smoke. Obviously, I couldn't hide the deed. I ran from the room, choking on smoke that permeated the house. My confession was quickly given and was accepted by Dad but accompanied by considerable profanity.

The Great Depression

The Great Depression pervaded our lives and the lives of our friends in ways that my grandchildren would not imagine. We lived on very little money. My grandfather's coal business was being hurt both by customers being unable to pay their bills and by the growing use of fuel oil. And of course, the securities business was almost dead through 1935, at which time there was a two-year rally followed by another bear market in 1937.

There was no real recovery until the Second World War. So we economized. A new refrigerator was a major event in 1935. We paid for it by putting quarters into a box hooked up to the electric line. No quarters, no electricity for the fridge! We ate the plainest of meals, and leftovers were carefully utilized. An ice-cream cone was a very infrequent treat. One day I was given a nickel to spend at the drugstore soda fountain that was a block away. It was a hot evening, and as I left the store, I tripped and sent the ice cream flying out of the cone. Near tears, I picked it up and continued licking, ignoring the collection of sidewalk dirt on it. To this day, when I have a vanilla ice-cream cone, the tiny black specks of vanilla remind me of that evening long ago.

I was seven before I ever saw a movie. An older boy who lived next door was allowed to take me to *Mutiny on the Bounty* at our local theater, where I would usher a few years later. It was an afternoon I will never forget, complete with a nickel's worth of penny candy.

A new bicycle was delayed for several years beyond when many of my friends learned to ride. When I finally got my Silver King bike with balloon tires, one of the first all-aluminum models, I felt unshackled.

Except for the 1932 sojourn in Ocean City, family vacations were unknown until later in the decade. A new pair of pants (all winter we wore corduroy knickers that smelled when they were wet) was a once-a-year treat. But despite the Depression, my sister and I never felt deprived. I was old enough to understand that things weren't always like this; that better times might be ahead. As a family, we had fun, laughing at Dad's stories and songs; listening to radio programs such as *Jack Armstrong*, *Tom Mix*, *Gangbusters*, and *The Shadow*; playing games; and enjoying the physical closeness that was our lot. I realized we did not have the money that some of my friends did, but I also could see that some were worse off. Except for the occasional toy that I couldn't have (I especially yearned for a six-dollar Charlie McCarthy ventriloquist dummy), it did not really matter greatly to me.

Allergies and Camp Ocean Wave

When I was nine in 1937, I was shown a different world through summer camp. But that story has a preface.

In 1936 I was riding in our car—Mother was driving and she was turning in a tight circle in my grandfather's coal yard. The car door flew open, and I was dumped in the coal dirt, which filled a bad cut on my right knee. I was taken to our family physician who lived directly across the street from the coal yard. He was Thaddeus Mongomery, who specialized in obstetrics and gynecology and had delivered both my sister and me. He would later deliver our first child in 1956. Many years later, he would marry my "aunt" Betty, one of the closest childhood friends of my mother, and would live to age ninety-four. He gave me a tetanus shot to which I had a severe reaction, developing a terrible case of hives and a shortness of breath. I began to suffer from continuing allergies, including asthma that was to have an important bearing on my next seven years.

The most immediate and most traumatic result was that our English setter, Bruce, was taken away to a farm after I was shown to be allergic to dog hair and dander. It was terrible coming home from school one afternoon to be told that Bruce was gone. He had been a real pal to me, walking partway to school with me in the morning and meeting me in the afternoon. Before that, we brought a cat into the family, so we were not "petless." Her name was Tinkerbell, and she was the first cat in a long succession that continued until poodles took over forty years later.

One beneficial result of being an asthmatic was that I was sent to summer camp: Camp Ocean Wave in Avalon, New Jersey. The objective was to remove me from the pollen-laden atmosphere farther inland. But the problem of financing summer camp was formidable. It was solved with the help of our minister, Richard T. Lyford, at the Church of St. Asaph in Bala, Pennsylvania. He nudged a wealthy parishioner to help, for which I will always be grateful. I learned this only some years later after my benefactor had died. I was able to relate the story to one of his sons and thank him.

My gratitude is only partly because I escaped allergies for the summer. More importantly, I was transferred to a completely new world where I could start anew without all the baggage that a child accumulates with his friends in school and neighborhood life. Not that I had an unpleasant life at home, but both metaphorically and literally, I was usually one of the last boys chosen for a pickup baseball game. I was quite small and puny and far from being a natural athlete.

In this new environment, I was a leader, not a follower; more popular than I had ever been; more athletic than I had thought; and had a great group of friends. The experience provided me a large jump in self-confidence, one of several that would occur over the next sixteen years.

Camp Ocean Wave was a genuine seashore experience. We lived in pyramid tents nestled among giant sand dunes on an uninhabited stretch of lovely beach between Avalon and Stone Harbor. Ocean swimming was a nude activity. It was there I learned to body surf, sail, shoot, and swim. The camp was an educational experience in other ways mainly by engaging in bull sessions on our families, sex, religion, and even politics. My parents and sister were regular weekend visitors, which gave them a nice respite from the heat of the city.

Initially, in 1937 and 1938, Camp Ocean Wave was well attended and quite good, although as the war approached, it began to fall on hard times. My last year there was 1942 when the shore was blacked out, the beaches were patrolled, and we could see and hear explosions offshore as German submarines took their toll on coastwise shipping.

School progressed satisfactorily for me though not brilliantly. Asthma caused a high rate of absence. Attacks were frequent during the night and were quieted by Dad bringing me a shot of whiskey that eased the wheezing and put me to sleep. That was in my tenth and eleventh years, and I have wondered since what people might have thought smelling liquor on my breath in class the next morning.

Reading and Uncle Bill

I believe that I was saved from mediocrity in school by my love of reading. During summer months and over weekends, I was a regular visitor at the local library that was two blocks from home. My memories of the library are vivid, particularly in the heat of summer when the interior seemed so cool. I thought the musty odor emanating from shelves of books was so very pleasant that today, when I enter a library and encounter that same odor, I have instant flashbacks to those summer days.

My reading was encouraged by my uncle Bill Thompson who lived with us for the first few years we were doubled up. Bill was a gentle-mannered, reddish-haired bachelor with a roundish face that was always very full colored. His degree from Penn, in 1929, was in architecture, but he had been denied that profession by the Depression. He had a midlevel job with the Pennsylvania Railroad and had developed a fascination with trains and train travel, perhaps because he had an employee pass. He took me on several train excursions through Civil War country and succeeded in interesting me in history, travel, and photography, as well as reading. Some of my favorite Christmas gifts came from him as carefully selected books on history, and historical novels. Several of these are still in my library. I spent hours with him in a makeshift basement darkroom, learning how to develop, print, and enlarge black-and-white photographs. He also taught me what little I know about chess.

Uncle Bill, a thirty-six-year-old bachelor at the time of Pearl Harbor, was drafted and put in the Transportation Corps from 1943 to 1946. He then came back from France to work again for the Pennsylvania Railroad in Atlanta and Boston. He never married. He died suddenly and unexpectedly at the age of forty-five of an aneurysm when I was a senior at Penn. He was a good friend and an important influence on me.

More Depression and Sickness

My parents, although subdued by the Great Depression, seemed relatively happy—a happiness that was sporadically interrupted by my father's temper usually unleashed at Mother. I hasten to say that he was never abusive; he simply got mad. They were attentive and at times almost obsessive parents. While my sister and I always felt very close to them, both of us had some difficulty establishing our independence from Mother when the time came to do so.

They endured difficult circumstances in our house with one bathroom and six other people. Privacy was rare. Mother seemed to be ill often; I remember hearing her retching in the middle of many nights.

In the late 1930s, perhaps 1938, she became very ill with what was diagnosed as "sleeping sickness." I don't know what it would be called today—perhaps encephalitis. She was bedridden for many weeks and would sleep for days at a time. It could have been some form of depression that we know more about these days than we did in the 1930s.

Dad claimed that the sickness left a permanent mark on her; that she was never again as alert as she had been before. My sister and I did not notice any difference, although we later wondered whether it was a partial cause of the mental deterioration she suffered beginning in her late sixties. Physically, despite a double mastectomy when she was in her forties, she was strong and lived until a month before her eighty-fourth birthday.

Dad was almost never sick but was felled by a thug who struck him on the head, fracturing his skull, when he was thirty-nine. It happened when I was with him at a local firemen's fair. We were walking along the midway when Dad fell to the ground, bleeding. Our first thought was that a part had flown off the nearby Ferris wheel. Other people saw a man run away from the scene and heard another voice shouting that he had hit the wrong man. We never found the culprit or discovered his motive. This event occurred on the heels of Mother's illness and was the proverbial straw on the camel's back. I now believe that both Mother and Dad went through bouts of depression in those years. It was the culmination of a decade that had been terrible for them.

Politics and Intolerance: Dad Gets a Push

My parents both became devoted fans of Franklin Delano Roosevelt because he was attempting to change the system that seemed to have caused and aggravated the Great Depression. Our grandparents were both staunch Republican, and FDR was not well accepted in our home. I was one of very few children who wore a Roosevelt button to school in the 1936 Roosevelt/Landon election campaign. The Philadelphia Main Line suburbs remained strongly Republican until the 1990s.

As the '30s came to a close, Dad became progressively less enchanted with FDR and grew, as Mother said, increasingly narrow-minded, even bigoted. In the 1940 campaign, he deserted FDR for Wendell Wilkie, only to return to the fold in 1944. I remember coming home from high school one day in April 1945 to find Mother sobbing. She had just learned of Roosevelt's death.

In 1941, after listening to Dad sound like an intolerant Main Line Republican crank, Mother said to him in disgust, "Why don't you go back to school and have your mind opened?"

He had graduated from Penn almost twenty years before. However, he took her seriously. It was the beginning of a period of change that would have an immense influence on the whole family.

That Mother would have pushed him was a wonder. Her formal education had ended with high school, and she certainly had no awareness of what graduate school might offer. That he took the challenge was an equal wonder. He would have to do it part-time; he could not forgo what little income he was earning, although business had improved a bit by then.

A Generation Passes On

"Ahla" Thompson died of a sudden heart attack in 1942 at the age of seventy-two. His eccentricities had always amused us, but in the few years before he died, they had become difficult for my grandmother to handle. Dementia was obviously taking a toll on him. Nana had to sell the house because she was left with very little except the remnants of a fuel oil order-taking business. I remember that the price was $6,500 (about $130,000 in today's money), which gave her some degree of independence.

With the economy and financial markets improving after the war began, we could afford the rent for a single house only a block away. How luxurious it seemed to us! We now had two bathrooms, one of which was all mine on the third floor, complete with a ring shower over the bathtub. Appreciation of space, privacy and a sense of self-sufficiency were felt by all of us. Nana Thompson came to live with us and was a jolly, good-humored lady and fun to have. Some years later, she moved to a retirement home run by the Episcopal Diocese. She became ill with lung cancer at the age of seventy-eight and died in 1953, a year after I was married.

Our Miller grandparents, Nathan Benjamin Miller and Beulah Ann Fetterolf Miller, remained in Hazelton after Dad left for college in Philadelphia. Beulah died in 1931, and I have no memories of her. I gathered from what Dad and Mother told me that she was a very definite character, very much like Dad—fun loving, irreverent, humorous, but with a temper. Dad had been badly shaken by her death. Nate Miller remarried in 1938 to a very stout woman named Hattie who was determined to run his life. She convinced him to move to St. Petersburg, Florida, in 1940. He died there in 1943. The funeral service was in Hazelton. There was a viewing the day before the service that I well remember because it was my first look at a dead body.

After his death, I was disconnected from our upstate relatives for many years until 1974 when my sister took Dad on a trip of memories to Bloomsburg and the surrounding area that had been so familiar to him as a child. Some years after that, Warren and I—with Mary Anne and her husband, Scotty—went on a repeat trip over that route to see the church where Nate and Beulah were married, the neighboring farms where they had been reared, the graveyard that held several generations of Millers (many inscriptions in German), and another graveyard near Bloomsburg College where Nate and Beulah are buried.

Dad's Graduate-school Years

Dad enrolled at Penn to pursue a master's degree in economics, attending classes four afternoons a week from 4:00 to 6:00 PM. Our family's life was about to become quite fascinating. He was gregarious by nature and easily made friends of professors and fellow students.

The war had begun just prior to his enrollment, and the ranks of American graduate students had been thinned considerably. At Penn there were large representations from neutral nations and Chinese who had been trapped in the United States since the late 1930s. Our little house overflowed with graduate students, including Chinese, South Americans, military officers who were taking special courses at Penn, and Catholic priests who were taking graduate work. They were from all over the university with several from the Graduate School of Fine Arts architecture program. Sunday nights were established as a time to entertain these new friends and became a Miller tradition that continued for the next twenty-five years.

We were encouraged to invite our friends to these affairs and did so with regularity. We taught people from Bolivia, Uruguay, Argentina, Cuba, and China how to jitterbug in return for lessons in the rumba and tango. We sang Spanish and Latin American songs and made many good friends, some of whom would reappear in our lives many years later. The world was opened to me and my sister and our friends. The joys of those days continued through my high-school years.

Dad loved his new life. We began to talk economics at dinner and in our spare time. By the time I was sixteen, I had learned most of what I would study as a freshman taking Economics 1 in 1946. Dad's adventures in graduate school provided a greatly needed spark to our lives in those years.

It was during those years that we became closest as a family. Neither my sister nor I ever went through that awful teenage stage of not wanting their parents around. They were always an asset even in a gathering consisting exclusively of our friends. We were always included in adult table talk and were expected to participate while never being made to feel or look stupid.

A Story for a Writing Course

In the summer of 2004, I enrolled in an online writing course offered by Allearn, a consortium of Yale, Stanford, and Oxford. One of the assignments was to write a five-page story about a life-changing event. I chose to write the story related above about my mother's prodding of my father to go back to graduate school. Here it is:

A Woman's Words

On a hot, humid night in July, twelve years after the stock market crash that marked the beginning of the Great Depression, the man was sleeping restlessly in the steamy third floor bedroom of his in-laws' house. His wife of seventeen years was in a deep sleep beside him. His two children were in the room that shared the wall behind the headboard of his bed. Downstairs were his wife's parents and brother, asleep in rooms of their own.

There was one small bathroom in the modest twin house. Seven people shared it. Often his family of four was all in there together. They had to be if school and transit deadlines were to be met. His impatience was palpable on mornings when his father-in-law, a slow moving man under any conditions, took an agonizingly long time to shave meticulously with an old straight razor that he stropped for endless minutes.

The sheets were wet with his perspiration. But his discomfort was trifling compared with the bitterness within him. The past decade had destroyed his dreams; dreams built on the shaky foundation of the '20's, dreams of privacy in a home for themselves, dreams of financial independence, dreams of what he might do for his son, born shortly after Lucky Lindy's trans-Atlantic solo, and for his sweet daughter, who came five years later, in the worst year of the Depression. Dreams of having the comforts and privileges that had been denied to his parents; a father who was a railroad freight agent in a small upstate town, and a mother who had scrubbed floors and sold corsets door-to-door to earn his college tuition.

He rose from the bed and descended the stairs in barefooted silence to the bathroom to pee. He didn't really need to pee, it was simply better than tossing in bed and dealing with his thoughts of what might have been. Afterward, he decided to go down the next flight of stairs to the cooler air of the small porch.

The dull roar of an approaching thunderstorm made him hope idly for cooler weather. Distant lightning occasionally flashed off the trunk of the huge maple tree in the yard and illuminated a small flower garden. Lighting a cigarette, he sat on the porch glider, his mind racing backwards in time.

Whose fault was it that he had sunk deeper and deeper into debt? That he had to double up with his in-laws because he couldn't pay the small rent for the tiny semidetached house he had been so proud of, the house that had given his family the privacy that every family needs to thrive? Or, that he was now dependent upon the same people who had opposed their daughter's marriage to this man from a less desirable background. Opposed him with such vehemence that the couple had to elope? And who was to blame for his college education had not having insulated him from the ravages of the business cycle? Or that his son suffered from terrible asthma and his wife seemed afflicted with chronic health problems?

"It sure as hell wasn't my fault", he whispered emphatically to himself.

He felt as if he was the victim of a huge conspiracy. The politicians, his business associates, the rich, the foreigners, the Jews, the Catholics, the niggers . . . he blamed them all. He hated them all.

"God damn them", he shouted at the maple tree, just as a clap of thunder shook the porch.

Stubbing his cigarette out in a flower pot, he stomped back up the stairs, not caring if he disturbed the sleepers.

"Don't give a shit! God damn them all", he said, almost in rhythm with his noisy footsteps on the stairway.

Gruffly throwing himself on the bed, purposely making his wife stir, he ended what had become his nightly ritual and fell asleep quickly.

Some weeks later, his wife, having at first endured his pain with sympathy, then with stoicism, found her feelings turning into a raw anger. She was a smallish woman of considerable fair complexioned beauty. She was a quietly calm person, not usually taken naturally to fits of anger. This particular evening, perhaps emboldened by a pre-dinner highball, her fury overflowed, sweeping through the room and hitting him like a tornado.

"What ails you?" she asked in anguish after they went to their bedroom.

"You have become just plain unpleasant to be with! The kids, all of us, feel that way. You are a closed-minded bigot of the worst order! Whatever happened to the nice, interesting man I married?"

Then, her voice rising in volume with each successive sentence, she began, "Always looking for someone else to blame! Moping around with that sad look on your face! Wake up! Look inside yourself! Okay, so the Depression almost destroyed us financially. Please! Don't let it destroy our lives, our marriage, and our children".

Surprised by the suddenness and uncharacteristic intensity of her pleading, he sat down, sobbing, tears cascading.

"I know", he whispered, "but what the hell can we do. I can't shake off my anger. I can't control my thoughts. Am I going nuts?"

In a voice suddenly changed to gentleness, she said, "No, you're not going nuts. I think what you need is some good, hard brain exercise. Get out of yourself and your self-pity. Why don't you go back to school and open that closed bigoted mind? Let some fresh air in."

"That's ridiculous", he said softly, I've been out of school for eighteen years. Jesus, I can't give up what little income we have to go to school, let alone pay tuition".

His wife turned away, thinking she might have said more than she should have. The conversation ended.

After a weekend of obvious agitation, the man went to work as usual, on Monday morning, For all the years of their marriage he had always called her at lunchtime. Their talk was brief; short questions and short responses.

"Anything new?"

"No, not really. Your son seems to have developed a cold. A bad cough"

"What was in the mail?"

"Nothing but bills and a postcard from your cousin."

They never sent tender or loving comments over the phone. Yet it was a contact necessary for their love. They both looked forward to the call, she always close to the phone at the expected time.

But that Monday no call came. She sat by the phone waiting, wondering, tears beginning. What had she done? Had she driven him away?

The man came home at his usual time. He was quiet, almost meditative.

"Get the kids", he said, "there is something I must tell you all together."

The little family came together, sitting in a circle, the children on the floor, fearful of what they were about to hear in their first serious family conference.

"On my lunch hour today", he began, "I took the trolley out to the university. That's why I didn't call today. There wasn't any time. I wanted to see if it was possible to go back to school. It is. I can enroll as a candidate for a master's degree in economics. I can go to class after work, 4 to 6 in the afternoon, three days a week. At that rate I can get a degree in three years, assuming I can also write a thesis in that time.

"There will be lots of reading and studying to do, and it won't be easy after a full day's work, but I'll try it. I need your help. I must have quiet in the evenings and on weekends. It'll also be a financial push, the tuition and all, but I think I can manage it."

His wife hugged him, saying, "I'm so very proud of you."

The children watched, a bit embarrassed by the length and intensity of the embrace. While they didn't fully grasp the significance of what their father had said, they sensed that something very important had just happened, something that might change their family's future.

The changes were greater than any of them might have imagined. Their dinners became lively, discussions of current events, politics, and economic systems. All in the context of what he was studying. The man talked with animated enthusiasm about his professors and fellow students, and the interesting people he met in the campus coffee shop. He explained economic laws such as The Law of Diminishing Returns, Gresham's Law, and the difference between the concepts of average returns and marginal returns, all the stuff in freshman economics courses.

The war was underway in Europe and Pearl Harbor followed. Graduate schools were quickly stripped of students who either enlisted or were drafted. Remaining students were mostly foreigners from neutral nations, especially South Americans, and some Chinese who were stranded here by the war.

Then several things occurred that brought further change. The man's father-in-law died of a heart attack, his wife's brother was drafted, business improved, the little twin house they had endured for twelve years was sold, and they rented a single home a block away. The mother-in-law, a very pleasant, humorous woman went with them. The children got their own bedrooms and now there were two bathrooms.

They began to entertain faculty and fellow students on Sunday nights. A phonograph played South American rhythms as they all learned to rumba and sing bawdy songs in Spanish. Interests in geography, philosophy, architecture, and languages, were stimulated. Serious discussions about politics, economics and the progress of the war were mixed with martini-soaked fun. Curiosity became an integral part of the family's lives.

The children were encouraged to include their friends. The sixteen year-old son taught a gorgeous Cuban architectural student to do the jitterbug and the eleven year-old daughter did the rumba with a charming mustached man from Uruguay. Chinese sang Spanish songs and the whole group learned to speak some Chinese.

A marriage may have been saved. The adults made friendships that would last a lifetime. The children experienced adults at their very best; tolerant, kind, interesting, and curious.

All because of a woman's words.

Junior High School and George W.R. Kirkpatrick

In 1939, after completing sixth grade, I moved across the athletic field from Cynwyd Elementary School and began a completely new and different experience in Bala-Cynwyd Junior High School. The building was large, new, and beautifully designed. Instead of attending from nine o'clock to three o'clock the hours were nine thirty to four, giving us a chance for a more relaxed morning but getting us home late after extracurricular activities.

It's common wisdom that the junior-high years are difficult, coinciding with the beginning of puberty. Perhaps. But my years at Bala-Cynwyd, or BC as we called it, were both enjoyable and influential. The influence was only partly academic and social. More important were the values imprinted on my friends and me by the school principal, George Washington R. Kirkpatrick.

Kirk, as we surreptitiously called him, was a no-nonsense guy with a temper. Stocky, with wavy gray-tinged hair and a handsome face, he not only promoted school spirit but he also insisted on it. He would single a person out of the crowd in the bleachers then become red-faced as he screamed at him for not cheering enthusiastically.

He would walk the sideline at a football game, exhorting the players to greater effort, and, from time to time, face the stands and whoop it up with his arms.

He was a feared disciplinarian, but never unfair. Those who deserved punishment got it. He revered academic achievement and participatory activities. Any kind of dishonesty or misbehavior was dealt with harshly, usually in front of peers. We toed the line.

I strayed badly only once. My algebra teacher, a buxom gray-haired lady named Ms. Swift, was not pleased with my work and one day ordered me to come to her after school for help. I told her I could not because I had to attend confirmation class that afternoon. It was a lie. Although I was attending confirmation class at the time, it was not on that day.

Ms. Swift's room had windows facing the athletic field, where I had stupidly gone to play touch football after school. She marched onto the field, took me by the collar, and marched me directly to Kirk's office. He gave me a thunderous and stern lecture then called my mother to come to school and hear my confession. Mother came and the confession was given. I learned some years later that as I was talking, Kirk was smiling and winking at Mother. They were in cahoots and became good friends over the course of the six years my sister and I were at BC. I cannot say I never lied again, but that experience impressed me so that my subsequent lies were small and "white" and rationalized as being justified.

I have looked retrospectively at the BC years with my sister and her husband, Scotty, Rinky Pollock (Neuhauser), and Dottie Biddle (Smith) and other friends who shared the experience. There is strong agreement that George Kirkpatrick inculcated us with integrity, loyalty, and respect for accomplishment. One of my honors some years later, when I had achieved some modest fame in business, was to be invited by Kirk to speak at a BC assembly. I had fun telling the kids what a great principal they had, and then giving an imitation of him singling out and yelling at an individual in the audience for inattention. It must have hit home because there was laughter. I looked at Kirk and saw him red-faced, not with anger but laughter.

As the first class to attend BC for all three years, we were among those who first learned the school's cheers and songs, and voted for the school's colors. Athletic and band uniforms appeared with magical alacrity on the field. I can still sing the school's alma mater and often do so with old friends.

I was still small and puny, and serious athletics, although I enjoyed them, were out of the question. The best I could do was manage the basketball team. I learned the baritone horn and played in the band all three years. My family was fond of saying, and they were right, that the horn was bigger than I was. I had played the bugle in grammar school, so I was asked to sound the colors for school assemblies as the flag was carried in. Each Memorial Day, my best friend Ike Kershaw and I were asked to play taps (I played and Ike played the echo a block away) at the World War I memorial in the center of town while the veterans stood at attention in their American Legion uniforms and saluted.

Ah, Marvelous Puberty

These were the years when hormones began to stir and I and all my friends began to notice and comment on the young breasts sprouting around us. In eighth grade I fell madly in love with a beautiful seventh-grader named Barbara Furlong. A date was a night at the local movie house followed by a milkshake at the drugstore soda fountain. A classmate, Newbury Hovde, was a rival for Barbara, and one night we both took her to the movies and each of us held one of her hands. When I was in the service I heard that she had become pregnant while still a high school senior. In those days, this was a cause for serious gossip. When I last saw her in the early 1990s, she weighed about 250 pounds.

We needed no cars. Everything we needed was within a radius of a mile and a half, so we could walk to most destinations. If necessary we could take a bus that covered the area from Bala to Ardmore, a distance of about four miles.

Most of us attended Ms. Stoddard's dancing class where we learned the waltz, polka, and fox trot. The boys' attitude toward dancing class was bored tolerance. We had to wear dark suits and ties and would all sit on one side of the room with the girls on the other side. We invented ways to collectively annoy Ms. Stoddard. One night we all decided to wear white socks under our dark trousers, and after sitting down in a row, hiked up our pant legs to show a solid row of white. Ms. Stoddard gasped and just rolled her eyes. Despite what she taught us, which we did actually use occasionally at dances, jitterbugging was the popular dance at the time. Once a week there was an after-school dance in the girl's gym where the popular records were played. I particularly recall "Elmer's Tune" and "Chattanooga Choo Choo."

I was among those boys who were slow to mature. When we began junior high, we were introduced to jockstraps and group showers after gym classes. There was a group of Italian American boys and girls in the school who provided a new experience for the very Waspy group from our elementary school. They were physically much more mature than most of us, much more rough and tumble, and spoke as if they had had sexual adventures that we hadn't even imagined. In seventh grade I felt awkward and ashamed in the locker room because I was in the small minority who had not yet grown pubic hair, let alone had the hirsute bodies of my new Italian friends.

Dad had talked to me about the facts of life and had given me a book to read, but it soon became obvious that neither the book nor the lecture covered certain subjects that the boys all whispered about. As humorous proof of both my naiveté and my physical immaturity, in seventh grade one of my friends asked me if I had tried "this" and then demonstrated masturbation. I had no idea that anybody, especially I, could do that, and in fact, I could not. My body wasn't ready and would not be for at least a year.

From that time on thoughts of sex were natural and frequent. We had bull sessions, especially in summer camp, marked by highly imaginative but inaccurate ideas. When it came to actually doing anything, we all proved very timid. It was all talk and no action.

One humorous event born of our sexual bravado occurred in ninth grade when Johnny Wynn and I briefly became peeping toms. One Friday night we climbed a tree outside Charlotte Freihofer's bedroom to watch her undress. Charlotte, a classmate, seemed to have the best-developed chest and we longed to see it. We waited on a tree limb. She began to shed her clothes, but our view was obstructed. We climbed a rose arbor on her porch, thinking that the porch roof would afford a perfect view. The arbor collapsed as we reached the roof. We were stranded and so worried that we forgot to look at what we had come to see. We jumped to the ground with little noise, no injuries, no brush with the law, and no satisfaction.

The only personal problem I had at age fourteen was that I had not grown and was only a bit over five feet tall, well behind my friends. The doctor who had been treating my asthma (which had subsided by then) was consulted. She gave me some kind of growth hormones that seemed to have no effect, and I quit taking them after a short while. But nature finally took over and I grew almost a full foot over the next eighteen months.

Pearl Harbor and the War

In September 1939, our family was spending the Labor Day weekend at Beach Haven, New Jersey, when news came that Germany had invaded Poland. We followed closely as the German War Machine blitzed across Europe. With my grandparents being first-generation British Americans, we were particularly distressed at the British disaster at Dunkirk and the London Blitz. But while the war was part of the fabric of those years, it seemed very distant and irrelevant to a thirteen-year-old. That is, until December 7, 1941.

That Sunday afternoon we were visiting Nana Thompson's sister, Aunt Edith Jenkins, in her apartment on Spruce Street in downtown Philadelphia. We heard the initial broadcast with the news of the Japanese attack on Pearl Harbor. It was one of a handful of moments that one remembers vividly, where you were and what you were doing when you heard it, like the death of FDR, the assassination of John F. Kennedy, and the terrorist attacks of September 11, 2001.

I had read widely about World War I and had devoured books with maps and pictures of the battles. I mistook the event as the beginning of an adventure. Dad quickly changed my attitude with a strong lecture about the horrors of war.

The following day we were called into assembly to listen to President Roosevelt ask Congress for a Declaration of War against Japan, Germany, and Italy. It was a somber time as we realized the magnitude of the blow Japan had dealt us. The months to come were sobering as we suffered defeats in the Philippines and the horrors of the death march of Corregidor.

At school, we turned to making model airplanes to be used for training in aircraft recognition. As boy scouts, we organized and conducted door-to-door scrap-metal collections. And of course, there were the air-raid drills. Both parents became air-raid wardens and I became a messenger, riding my bike over darkened streets, carrying make-believe messages from the firehouse to Cynwyd Elementary School.

Most of these efforts were early in the war when people wanted to do something, anything, to make them feel as if they were contributing to the war effort. Mother rolled bandages for the Red Cross. Dad, forty-two at the time, wanted badly to seek a commission and go to war, even if it were a desk job. But he was past draft age and Mother persuaded him to stay home. Both my uncles were drafted, one to the army and one to the navy. When I graduated from Bala-Cynwyd Junior High, my ambition, as listed in the yearbook, was "to become a marine."

I saved to buy books about warships and planes and became quite good at aircraft recognition. I knew the silhouettes of all the American, British, German, and Japanese planes and gained a reputation as an expert among my friends. One day a letter arrived, vaguely threatening me, and signed "Le Diablo Rouge." My parents were so concerned they reported it to the FBI. An agent visited and in an hour or so he determined that it was a hoax played by a friend and neighbor, Johnny Carver. My sole experience as a secret agent!

The war was always there in some form: food rationing, gasoline rationing, air-raid drills, war songs, gathering for the evening news on the radio, a victory garden, saving aluminum foil, newsreels and movies with a war theme. Still, there was really no hardship. We ate and slept well although, of course, families with members in combat zones were always on edge. I remember it as a time of great patriotism and community cohesion, and as a period of waiting—waiting for the next big news and waiting to grow older and go to war myself.

A large field nearby was opened to the neighborhood's use as a victory garden. Dad fast became a devotee of vegetable gardening with my help. We both worked hours growing corn, beans, tomatoes, cabbages, broccoli, beets, carrots, peppers, eggplant, and other crops in large enough quantities—both to satisfy our demand for fresh vegetables and for canning. Cellar shelves were packed with canned vegetables by summer's end. We filled huge containers with sauerkraut that were covered with only a board topped by a brick. The result was a permeating odor of sauerkraut in the cellar and kitchen. But it was the best kraut I've ever eaten, much stronger than what is available commercially. I enjoyed vegetable gardening and began a garden of my own as soon as we had land to do so. I am still vegetable gardening today on our property in New Hampshire.

A Penn Fan at Age Five

Beginning at the age of five, I was taken to Penn football games at Franklin Field in West Philadelphia. With no real competition from pro football at that time, the stadium was frequently filled to its capacity of seventy thousand. We had season seats in the end zone because the price was right. Saturdays in the fall were days with Dad. I would go with him by train to the office (the stock market was open half day on Saturdays). I knew all his office friends at F. P. Ristine & Co., who would entertain me with ticker tape, rubber bands, and paper clips. We had an early lunch at Leed's Restaurant and went by trolley to the stadium then home by train after the game. I was a rabid Penn fan, emulating Dad, and have been ever since. Penn's football stars were my heroes. I sought their autographs and still have the collection from the 1930s.

I was certainly not a notable athlete, but I discovered in summer camp, where I was free to start anew, that I was much better than I had thought. There were plenty of pickup baseball and football games, including tackle games, played on vacant lots in our neighborhood. Dad and I played catch in the yard for hours, and he coached me to become a pitcher. I tried out for baseball in junior high, but at my shrimp size did not make the team.

Lower Merion Years

My high-school classmates and I talk so much about our years at Lower Merion Senior High School, and in such enthusiastic fashion, that spouses and friends listen in amazement. One commented to Rinky Pollock (now Neuhauser) that if she were reincarnated, she hoped she could go to Lower Merion.

Graduating to Lower Merion High School was a very big deal. In eighth grade I had stopped going to Penn games and began to attend Lower Merion games. But basketball was the really big sport at Lower Merion. In 1942, LM won the state championship and went on to win it for three years in a row. School spirit overflowed, and after championship games there were immense victory bonfires.

Lower Merion years were marvelous for the most part. Our activities were quite wholesome compared to later years. Drinking was a rarity, real sex was unknown (at least by my closer friends and me), and there were no drugs. With gasoline rationing, our use of family cars was infrequent and we often took dates by public transportation or on foot. When cars seemed necessary, I depended on friends whose families had a higher ration of gasoline than mine did.

The hangouts included milkshake and jukebox places around the Main Line and occasionally we would go to a Howard Johnson's on Sixty-ninth Street in Philadelphia. The "thing to do" was to stay up until one o'clock to listen to Jan Pierce sing "The Bluebird of Happiness" while drinking a milkshake with your arm around a girl.

High school had its cliques, and I never thought I was one of the guys who were really "in," although friends told me later that I was and that they had felt the same way. We had fraternities that met once a month in someone's house, after which we would all pile into a sorority meeting. The big thing was to gorge on food, particularly hoagies. To this day I have an unqualified opinion that the Philadelphia area's hoagies are the best in the country.

Fraternity initiation was a rite we had to endure, complete with paddling and the painful experience of wearing a jockstrap soaked in wintergreen oil. I was not selected for the "best" fraternity, the one with all the athletic heroes, but our group, Delta Phi, provided me with many good and lasting friendships. Nevertheless, I was conscious of not being part of the top clique. The girls seemed to like guys who were well built, athletic, and made them laugh. I was much too skinny, not known as an athlete, and wasn't funny.

I began to play soccer as a sophomore at the urging of my friend Johnny Wynn, and was a varsity regular by the end of my junior season and a starter in my senior year. We had excellent soccer teams, winning the league championship in two of my three years. Jack Burkholder, a teammate, would become a fraternity brother, roommate, and teammate at Penn. Several Lower Merion teammates I met again as opponents when playing for Penn. One of them, Jimmy Billington, was the best high school and college goalie in the country. He went to Princeton, was a Rhodes Scholar, became a professor of history, and is now the Librarian of Congress.

I had no steady girlfriends, although I was seldom without a date for school and fraternity dances. I had a continuing crush on the two most popular girls in the class, Rinky Pollock and Dottie Biddle. They are good friends to this day and I still have a crush on them! Dad was fond of saying that I was a "sap" for women. He was right. Looking over our senior yearbook, I was chagrined to find the descriptive phrase under my name read, "Forever dame dreaming." I was always enchanted by one girl or another, although the feelings seldom seemed to be mutual. I recall my social life as very satisfying, though perhaps more so in retrospect. By the time I was a senior, I was still very skinny but over six feet tall; had won varsity letters in soccer; and was considerably more relaxed, self-confident, and at ease socially.

I was a mediocre student, receiving mostly Bs and more than a light sprinkling of Cs. I never made the honor roll and was not a member of the National Honor Society. Teachers often told me and my parents that they knew I could do better. I evidently had tested well and my work lagged considerably from what was predicted. Motivation was a problem for me. I did not have college immediately in mind, knowing that military service would probably come first. I don't remember even being aware of a choice of colleges.

My report card for junior year, which I still have, shows a D in algebra, along with three Cs and two Bs. In the comment section, it says, "Library attitude needs improvement," and then, for the following semester, "Library attitude unimproved." Farther down it reads, "Homework assignments not turned in."

While my academic successes were rare, one seems worth mentioning, because with hindsight, it appears to have been a precursor of my superior academic accomplishments in college. Toward the end of my senior year, Mrs. Madge Barber, a lovely woman with a massive bosom, assigned a research paper on English Literature.

At home we had been discussing the Industrial Revolution because Dad had been studying it in a course on the history of economic development. He led discussions on Sundays at the dinner table and in the evenings, about the economic thinking that was stimulated by the Industrial Revolution and the social upheaval caused by the accompanying migration from the English countryside to the cities.

Meanwhile, I had noticed social commentary in the literature of that period that we had been reading in school. Putting the two together, I researched more of the late eighteenth and early nineteenth century poetry and prose to seek more social criticism and commentary. The resulting paper I wrote was very good and gave me a great sense of satisfaction. But Mrs. Barber held me after class one day to say she did not believe I had written it. Having been so proud of my work, I was crestfallen. I told her the long story of how I had become interested in the subject. It must have rung true because she finally held out her hand and congratulated me. It was then I realized how good I could be if I worked hard on a subject that interested me.

The high school had several dances each year, including a reverse dance for which the girls issued the invitations, a sophomore hop, junior prom, and senior prom. The senior prom was the time when the senior class voted for a snow queen and her court. In our year, Dottie Biddle was elected snow queen, and Rinky Pollock was in her court as the runner-up. Five years later, my sister Mary Anne was elected snow queen. I was a college senior by then and remember being certain that she would win that title, given her popularity and good looks.

The school dances were big affairs held in the gymnasium with a globe plastered with many small mirrors that sprinkled light as it revolved. Many of us would spend most of a day decorating the gym with streamers of crepe paper. There was a small admission charge, but the main expense was the purchase of a corsage for your date. An orchid could cost a full day's wages. We quickly learned that the local food fair had the least expensive orchids, but you had to get there early, so I would be at the store when the doors opened on Saturday before reporting to work.

In-between these big dances, the fraternities sponsored their own dances, financed by admission charges validated by an ink stamp on your wrist. As I recall, there were four or five of these affairs a year. Each fraternity and each sorority concentrated on raising money from their dances to rent a "shore house" in Ocean City, New Jersey, for a week in June (or two weeks if you were a graduating senior and released a week early). I cannot imagine why anybody would have rented to us, although I never saw any serious damage. We got badly sunburned, had mostly nonalcoholic parties, and did our best to "make out" with the girls. Making out was very mild petting for me and most others, although more advanced success stories were rampant. We talked about "getting to first, second, or third base," and dreamt about a "home run."

Ocean City was and still is a dry, circumspect Methodist town. Ridiculously, in the 1940s, men had to wear bathing-suit tops, and the beaches were patrolled to assure compliance. We carried cutoff undershirts to don when the law approached. The town police kept a watchful eye on the large groups of teenagers who invaded each June.

At the end of my junior year, our entire fraternity was hauled off to jail for disorderly conduct. We had been very noisy, singing and blowing a trumpet from a second-floor porch, when a neighbor complained. We were put in cells for the night and brought before a magistrate in the morning. The fine was $17.70 for each of us, the current equivalent of over $200. We would not be released until we paid. But we had no money. Several boys who had escaped arrest went to the beach and organized a collection for us, and by noon, we were free. The only aftermath I remember was my father having his lawyer call Ocean City to make sure we had no permanent arrest record.

I was not the kind of boy who got in trouble often. We had several classmates who were always being penalized with after-school janitor duty for some infraction of the rules. The only specific instance I recall when I served as a janitor for a week occurred in my senior year. Six of us decided to leave school at lunchtime to go by train into the city to the Troc Burlesque Theater's afternoon matinee. Sally Rand was dancing with her fans, and Billy "Cheese and Crackers" Madge Barber was performing his comedy routine. I had been to the Troc only once before, where I saw, for the first time, a live bare-breasted woman.

The show this time was perfect in terms of teenage tastes, and we joked about it and imitated Billy Hagan going home on the train. As we drew into the Ardmore Station, we saw the vice principal, Pop Pierce, who served as the school's chief disciplinarian, waiting for us. We were marched back to school and given brooms to sweep the halls for the next five afternoons.

Working, Always Working

I always had a job, and often two or three at the same time. I never received any allowance and was completely self-sufficient from the age of fourteen. I ushered at the local movie theater, was a busboy in a local restaurant, worked in the local grocery store, cut lawns, simonized cars, helped the florist meet the peak demands of Mother's Day and Easter, and sorted mail at Christmas. During summers and Saturdays of my sophomore and junior years in high school, I was a clerk and stock boy at the local grocery store. Supermarkets were just beginning to appear, and this store was an American store, the precursor of Acme Markets. Only a block from home, it was a comfortably old-fashioned store with a butcher counter, a produce section, and high shelves that we accessed with pincers on a long pole. The pay was $27 per six day week for a workday of 8:00 AM to 6:00 PM.

Every Thursday and either Friday or Saturday night, year-round, I was a busboy at the Tavern, the best neighborhood restaurant only three doors from home. The waiters shared their tips with us, and on a good night, I would take home about $4, the equivalent of $50-$60 today.

Two nights a week, I ushered at the Egyptian Movie Theater that was a ten-minute walk away. It was a typical movie palace of that era with outlandish pseudo-Egyptian statues and paintings all over the ceilings and walls. I dressed in a typical usher's suit: black clip-on bow tie, red coat, and a vest that reeked with stale perspiration. Part of the job was stoking the coal furnace in the winter and changing the marquees when required. The pay was $1 per night and a free movie. The free movie got a bit stale after the ninth or tenth showing! More than a few friends were admitted "free" to the theater via the backstage door in return for free milkshakes at the soda fountain at King's, the local drugstore.

Graduating to the U.S. Coast Guard

As high school reached its final stages, the war became paramount to us. Several friends left school halfway through senior year to enlist. One could do that and still receive a diploma. Several members of the preceding classes whom I knew, including my fraternity brother and neighbor, Phil Hawkins, had been killed in action. Gold stars were placed in a hall of honor at school. One member of our class, Jimmy McQuiston, was killed in March of 1945, only ten weeks after enlisting in the army. He is buried in the graveyard of the Gladwyne Methodist Church.

My best friend, Ike Kershaw, the man who had played hooky with me in second grade, and I were determined to join the marine corps. In March of 1945, we went to the marines' recruiting station in Philadelphia and came home with papers for parents to sign. (Seventeen-year-olds required parental permission to enlist.) Our mothers, having heard about the heavy losses the marines suffered in the taking of various Pacific islands, refused to sign. Dad suggested the navy.

Back we went to the recruiting offices in the city. They were all bunched together in one building on Market Street. There was a coast guard recruiting poster with a picture of a landing craft going in to a beach. We thought the coast guard was confined to patrolling beaches but were about to discover that many of the landing craft used in the Pacific and on D-Day in Normandy were crewed by U.S. Coast Guard personnel. In fact, the coast guard, which was under the navy department in wartime, had the highest percentage of its personnel overseas of any of the services. Our mothers visualized our patrolling the New Jersey beaches. It was a snap to get them to sign.

After graduation, at which I expected no honors and received none, and after a week at the Ocean City shore house, we left on June 14 for boot camp at Manhattan Beach on Long Island. I loved boot camp even though it was a very hot summer in Brooklyn. The worst experience I had was doing garbage duty at the mess hall during a hundred-degree heat wave. We used steam hoses to clean the galley and loaded huge garbage cans on trucks then rode the trucks to the dump where we had to dump each can on an immense pile of fermenting garbage. It was one of the very few occasions in my life when I nearly passed out and had to be given smelling salts.

Boot camp was physically very tough and demanding, but the food was great and plentiful compared with home meals restricted by rationing (too many meals of Spam or codfish balls). I gained almost twenty pounds in six weeks and was better conditioned than I had ever been. Friendships were formed quickly and easily. I was able to meet all the physical demands put on us. I began really to like myself.

Only five weeks into training, the first atomic bomb was dropped. We knew then that the war was about to end, although nobody really fully understood the implications of what had just happened. I remember some commentator worrying about the risk that the bomb would set off a chain reaction that might destroy the world. Today one worries that even though he was scientifically wrong, he might yet prove to be prophetic.

Within days I would be forced to make an honest-to-goodness adult decision and begin another leg of the journey to independence.

Dad holding me, 1928

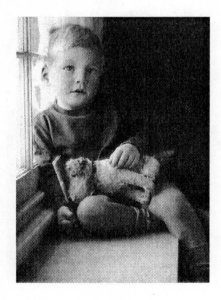

Two years old

Ahla Miller holding me, age seven

With my sister, Mary Anne, 1934

With Mom and Dad, Ocean City, 1931

My grandparents' house, where we lived from 1932 to 1943

Camp Ocean Wave, Avalon, N.J., 1938

Tenderfoot Scout, 1939

Uncle Bill, Nana Thompson and her sister, Aunt Edith Jenkins, 1942

Age fifteen

Lower Merion High School

Lower Merion soccer, 1944

Lower Merion yearbook picture, 1945

U.S. Coast Guard, Santa Rosa Island, 1946

With Rinky Pollock, 1945

Dottie Biddle, 1946

CHAPTER TWO

Gaining Independence: Coast Guard and College

A Year in the United States Coast Guard

Shortly after the atomic bomb was dropped on Hiroshima and when we knew the war was about to end, I was summoned to the base commandant's office. I went trembling, thinking that I had been accused of some wrongdoing. After greeting me and asking a few questions, he told me that I was one of a handful who had been chosen, based on excellent grades received on the tests given to all recruits, to attend a preparatory school for the Coast Guard Academy in New London, Connecticut. Once again I was being confronted with evidence that I was smarter than I thought I was.

I thought of this offer as going back to high school, while he, who was an academy graduate, thought it was a great honor. The thought of being separated from my new buddies was upsetting, particularly now that we were about to leave boot camp for some interesting duty. I told him I wasn't sure I wanted to do this, but he continued to browbeat me until I folded.

By mid-August the Japanese had surrendered and I was in Groton, Connecticut, across the Thames River from the Coast Guard Academy, studying algebra and trigonometry. At the same time my friends in Company 29 were leaving for duty in the Pacific, specifically to man troop transports to bring the boys home. They visited many ports, including Shanghai, Okinawa, and Tokyo while I was reading English literature. Ugh! And all the while I knew I did not want to go to the academy.

By Christmas of 1945, I was sure that studying in Groton was not what I wanted to do under any circumstances. Several friends and I applied for a transfer to sea duty. But before doing so, I had to face my mother's objections. She was very comfortable with my being a couple of hours away and able to get home on liberty at least one weekend a month. Why, she wondered out loud in dramatic fashion, would I want to expose myself to some "hazardous duty" in some far away place? Dad was supportive, but uncharacteristically quiet. Finally, I simply told her that while I loved her, I was going to do it despite her frequent pleading letters and phone calls.

I dwell on this experience because it was an important step toward independence, particularly from Mother, who was quite possessive of both my sister and me. The coast guard was also not pleased with the six of us who had asked for transfer. We were sent to Boston and stationed on Constitution Wharf to await assignment on a North Atlantic Patrol Frigate which, while no longer needed for convoy duty, was used to locate and destroy icebergs that were a peril to the heavy transatlantic traffic of returning troops and materials.

We waited for the better part of a month, but there were no openings on the ships that came in. I spent time cruising Boston, including Scollay Square, infamous for its dives swarming with sailors and dominated by the Old Howard, a marvelous burlesque theater. (Scollay Square has long since been demolished and replaced by a very sterile government center.)

There was a dance hall in Newton called the Totem Pole that featured the big bands. It was there that I met a lovely woman who was a sophomore at Wellesley College. I was very smitten by her and we had a rapid series of dates via the Framingham Local. She was, of course, a redhead, as were all the women to whom I have been most attracted. Her name was Barbara Casely. It was a nice but short romance that ended when I received orders to report to New Orleans via a troop train. (During the summer of 2001 Warren and I had dinner with Barbara on Nantucket. She was widowed by then but was still an attractive woman, even with her red hair having turned gray!)

The troop train stopped in New York and Philadelphia. In New York, a car was tacked on to our troop car that was occupied by the troupe of the Barnum and Bailey Circus on their way to winter headquarters in Sarasota, Florida. I found a good-looking bareback rider and a group that had a bottle of whiskey! We had a gigantic party of circus people, sailors, and soldiers. We arrived in Philadelphia a bit snookered and I had lipstick smeared across my face (or so I was told later by my parents who were at the station to greet me for the ten-minute layover). Dad loved it, but Mother was a bit chagrined.

We got to New Orleans just in time for the first postwar Mardi Gras. I never kissed so many girls in one night, or even over several years. The noise, the celebratory atmosphere, and the sheer wildness were incredible. There was a fancy ball being held in the Roosevelt Hotel that was crashed by dozens of sailors and soldiers.

Finally, after a two-week wait, I was assigned to an air-sea rescue station that guarded Pensacola Harbor. We had a sixty-three-foot crash boat, a thirty-eight-foot picket boat, and a twenty-six-foot, capsize-proof, self-bailing lifeboat. We lived in a typical coast guard lifeboat station on a lonely and lovely beach on Santa Rosa Island.

We patrolled Pensacola Harbor, maintained the navigation buoys and markers, and performed rescue services for the Pensacola Naval Air Station. I thought it was great fun. We had very few serious incidents, such as disorder on some foreign ships, and one rescue of a downed flier. In the meantime we had some lovely beaches to explore, fish to catch, and sunbathing to do. Tough war!

A couple of my buddies were older men who had seen service in the Pacific. They were seasoned sailors and on the wild side. As a kind of initiation for the kid among them, they managed to get me quite drunk (and then sick) on cheap wine. It was many years before I could contemplate red wine again.

In April of 1946, our commanding officer (who actually was a chief petty officer) called me in to say that he had recommended me for promotion to seaman first class. I was the only seaman selected by him for promotion. He hoped that I would strike for Coxswain which was the next step up. I did, but I was soon to be discharged.

That year in the service was an important time for me. I grew up. It may be trite to say that I went in the service a boy and came out a man, but it is true. Although I cannot compare my easy time with friends who actually risked their lives for extended periods, the result was probably the same: we all grew up in a hurry.

Penn

I was discharged in late May of 1946. By then I knew that the University of Pennsylvania was ahead of me. While in the coast guard, I had applied, with Dad's help, to Penn. The dean of admissions was an old friend and classmate of Dad's. That was enough to overcome my miserable high-school record. I never took any exams for entrance nor did other returning veterans.

The summer of 1946 was spent earning money. Ike Kershaw and I printed business cards and advertised ourselves as available for simonizing, painting, and odd jobs. We were in demand and nearly fully employed, earning about a dollar an hour—considered good money at the time. Also, because we were veterans, we were entitled to unemployment checks as long as we were not on a payroll. We called it the 52-20 club, because it was $20 per week for a maximum of fifty-two weeks. We would pick up our checks on Fridays and head to the seashore for the weekend to spend some of it, cruising the boardwalk, looking for dates, and eating in cheap restaurants.

Meeting Ed Igler

I accepted an invitation to attend preschool soccer practice in late August. Many returning veterans had played at Penn or somewhere else before the war, and had much more experience than I had. I was, therefore, not very optimistic, but made the freshman team and played fullback. But the most important result of freshman soccer was meeting my lifelong good friend, Ed Igler. Ed had played soccer at Friends Select School and then spent three years in the Pacific as a radioman on a navy LST. That he befriended me was a major influence on my college years. His father was the Baptist chaplain in the university's Christian association. Consequently, Ed had grown up living near and on the campus and knew "the ropes."

I commuted to Penn in my freshman and sophomore years. At the time, Penn was composed of about 50 percent commuters. As with all colleges, the campus was bulging with returning veterans. Keep in mind that at the peak there were twelve million people in uniform and several million of those now wanted a college education as provided for by the GI Bill. We were given full tuition plus $50 per month, later raised to $75, for living expenses. Translate that to over $800 per month in today's dollars. It was plenty initially, but became less adequate as a result of inflation within a couple of years.

As a freshman in the Wharton School, I was a good but not outstanding student. There were too many diversions from sports and other activities, including fraternity rushing in the late fall. Ed Igler knew what fraternities were all about. We went through rushing together, and it was he who guided me toward Beta Theta Pi. The custom was to give a man a key to the house as a signal that the brothers had unanimously decided they wanted him as a member. I was "keyed" by Sigma Alpha Epsilon and Beta Theta Pi. Once Ed decided on Beta, I followed. I had a great sense of inclusion as I got to know the brothers and my fellow pledges. It was a wonderful group of men, many of whom had started at Penn before the war and were twenty-one or twenty-three years old. I had just turned nineteen.

Campus Life Centered in the Beta House

Beta was a huge part of my college years. My pledge class of about twenty men, most with war experience, was to give me many lifelong friendships.

In 1946 there was still an air of formality about college life. It was brought back to campus and preserved by veterans who had been there before the war. We were required to wear coats and ties to lunch and dinner in the Beta House. The only exception was made for varsity letter sweaters. Each meal was preceded by a grace that blessed both the food and the fraternity, sung standing with the right arm outstretched over the table.

Professors always wore coats and ties, and students were addressed as "mister" or "miss." The "preppy" look, as it later became disdainfully known, was "in." The men's daily uniform was khaki pants, white button-down shirts rolled up to the elbows and penny loafers or white buck or saddle shoes. The very short haircuts we had become accustomed to in the military were continued as the civilian fashion. Varsity sweaters were worn proudly. On weekends, sport coats, regimental striped ties, and khaki slacks were the dress for dates and parties.

One of the hallmarks of those early postwar college years was the maturity of the men students. While they were fun loving and could be devilish, any mischief was humorous and responsible, not destructive. They knew how to deal with and treat women, and how to hold their liquor.

Parties were dominated by singing. The Beta House was particularly known for its good voices. Every year while I was at Penn, the Betas won the interfraternity songfest. We had several fraternity brothers who played the piano by ear and were always willing to lead us through lunchtime practice sessions, as well as spend hours at the keyboard during parties.

The biggest parties of the year were the formal pledge dance to welcome new pledges, and our infamous shipwreck party. For the latter, we removed all the furniture from the dining room and brought in sand for the floor, fish nets, buoys, and a broken-down rowboat. The men wore tattered sailor outfits and the women wore bathing suits and sarongs.

Fraternity initiations were in the spring. Paddling, very *hard* paddling, was the norm. Hazing began after the Christmas holidays and ended in March. It was fun and harmless. Each pledge class had a pledge master who was the primary disciplinarian. I was pledge master my junior year, a job that was quite out of character for me. I was never able to be as tough and mean as other pledge masters. Initiation, the same every year, was designed to be psychologically traumatic, but physically fairly benign. It succeeded superbly in forming a great bond among us. Having been sworn to secrecy, that's all I can say about it.

We were confident that we were the best fraternity on campus. That conceited conclusion was supported by the fact that a committee of faculty members chose Beta from among thirty-seven fraternities as winner of two successive Sphinx Awards "for outstanding service to the university and excellence in scholarship."

The fraternity house was very large, comfortable, and centrally located. Five stories high, it had a balcony that looked down on the student pedestrians below, and was particularly known by the women as a daunting place to walk under the leering men who stood above.

There was a large living room on the second floor, as well as a cardroom, library, and two-table billiard room. The house slept thirty people. I lived there my junior year, rooming with my soccer-playing buddy Jack Burkholder, who was the sloppiest roommate possible. Though a terrific guy and good friend, Burk seldom washed his bedding, and by the end of the year, it was a dark gray color.

Several times a week, some guy would get bored with studying and stand at the bottom of the stairwell and scream, "Movie muster!" It always got a response from a few men who would clomp downstairs and go out on Woodland Avenue to hop a trolley and ride downtown.

The Beta House was directly across the street from Logan Hall, the home of the Wharton School. During hours when one had no classes, the house was convenient for studying or, more likely, for a game of bridge, cribbage, or pool.

Dates and Loves

I dated many different women, most of whom were Penn students. In my freshman year, I fell in love with Peggy Liebfried, a quite beautiful woman who was in the School of Nursing. Much to the chagrin of Ed Igler, I gave her my pledge pin to wear.

The romance did not last very long, perhaps six months, but it was the first time I had a "steady." Most of what are now called relationships were in those days confined to dating a couple of times a week and heavy petting in a car or a living room. This romance fit that pattern.

Peggy was also the last steady that I had until late in my junior year when I became enamored with a girl who was still in Lower Merion High School named Beverly Miller. She was about to graduate and go on to West Chester State Teachers College, now West Chester University. Bev was a stocky athletic woman with a rather round face. While a lovely person, she was far from being intellectually inclined and was studying to become a physical-education teacher. The Millers were a very nice, solid, all-American family. Her father was a physical-education teacher and coach in one of the local junior high schools.

The romance intensified that summer when my pal Dutch Buckley and I traveled to Maine and Canada after finishing summer jobs. Dutch had a 1939 LaSalle that went like the wind; he had it up to 120 mph on the brand-new Maine Turnpike, even with an aluminum canoe on top! (We put a tear in the canoe on a river run in Canada and returned with the canoe whistling loudly to us all the way home.)

Bev's family had a cottage on one of the Belgrade Lakes where her father was a camp counselor. We spent several days there, fishing and romancing. I continued to date her most of my senior year. We were "pinned," meaning that I had pledged my love by giving her my fraternity pin to wear. Suddenly, for no reason I could specify, I grew tired of the relationship and stopped seeing her or calling her with no warning or explanation. It was cruel of me, but I never saw her again until about a year later when she purposely bumped into me and thrust my fraternity pin at me without a word.

All during those years, I had a continuing interest in Dottie Biddle. Dottie was, and still is, a very pretty redhead, good athlete, and very good company. At one point, I thought I was in love with her, although my interest in her was never reciprocated. And then Warren came along. But Dottie and I have been good friends, and she has visited us both in Florida and New Hampshire.

Several years ago, Scott Carlson, Kathy Miller's husband, asked me how many women I dated in college. My quick estimate was thirty or forty. He was amazed. Yet that is the trouble with the social life of the young people today. They must have a "relationship" or nothing. Dating is not part of the maturing process the way it was for us. I think they are missing something very important: a wide variety of contacts with the opposite sex that are fun and but not serious.

Mom and Dad: Still Important to Me

As they had been all through earlier school years, my parents were an important part of my life during college years. Dad was teaching economics four mornings a week at eight o'clock, and many Wharton undergrads knew him. People still come up to me on alumni day and want to reminisce about classes with Dad. They entertained groups of my friends on Sunday nights, continuing the Miller Sunday-night tradition that began when Dad was in graduate school. Dad would make a large pitcher of martinis, and we young people would mix easily with my parents' friends. Supper was usually a huge pot of mulligan stew or some casserole that Mom had thrown together. It wasn't unusual to have fifteen to twenty people. My parents were known to my friends as Mom and Pop, and were always welcomed and often invited to our fraternity parties.

Activities, Work, and Honors

Schoolwork and activities kept me very busy during my junior and senior years— soccer in the fall, interfraternity sports, Kite and Key Society, *The Record* (Penn's yearbook of which I was sports editor), and various jobs during vacations. Sorting mail at Christmas; helping at florist shops at Valentine's Day, Easter, and Mother's Day; and doing summer jobs—all supplemented my $75 per month allowance from the GI Bill.

My GI benefits lasted only three years because of my short service. To help make ends meet during my senior year, I served as a senior advisor in a freshman dorm to earn my room rent, waited on tables at the Kappa Alpha Theta sorority house in return for lunches, and washed breakfast dishes at my fraternity to earn dinners. Even with all that, I had to borrow the $600 for my senior-year tuition.

Summer jobs included work in a nut-and-bolt factory owned by a friend's father, running an accounting machine at the Philadelphia Savings Fund Society, and doing a marketing survey for John J. Phelan and Sons, makers of famous Felin's hot dogs and sausages.

Summer weekends were spent in Ocean City, where Ed Igler and I found cheap accommodations in a garage behind a house on Central Avenue. We had many beach-party dates, drank a lot of beer (I did, but not Ed who has always been a teetotaler), and were part of a crowd of college kids who swarmed over the place on weekends.

Some weekends we hitchhiked to the shore because car ownership among our friends was rare. I think there were only three men in our fraternity who owned cars and we exploited them mercilessly. On weekends we could occasionally borrow the family car, but that was limited by the fact that two-car families were almost unknown. My close friend, Frank Hughes, owned a 1935 Ford Phaeton convertible nicknamed "Mamie." Frank and Mamie commuted to Penn from nearby Merion and often picked me up on the way during my first two years of college.

Autumns were filled with soccer. While I certainly was no star, I greatly increased my competence under the tutelage of Coach Charlie Scott, a man of outstanding character who had compassion for his players. I played on the freshman team and the junior varsity then played regularly on the varsity during my junior and senior years. I developed a strong left foot and was assigned to the left halfback position. Very strong friendships were cemented with several teammates, including Jack Burkholder, Pat Welsh, and of course, Ed Igler.

Those years were fun-filled and carefree. Nevertheless, I succeeded academically far beyond anything I had thought possible. I took naturally to economics and finance and became obsessively interested in those subjects. During my junior and senior years, I had all As in my major courses and was on the dean's list every semester. As a junior, I received the Steuer Award, given to a junior who is judged by the faculty of the Wharton School to have outstanding characteristics of scholarship, leadership, and personality. As a senior, I was chosen by the faculty for the honor of being the CEO for Wharton Day at Gimbels, a day during which Wharton students ran the store with their executives watching.

I was also elected to the Friars Senior Society, one of three senior honor societies. Every Tuesday was Hat Day, when all the members of honor societies wore their society's special hats signifying their membership. Dad had told me when I entered Penn that he had not earned a hat as an undergraduate but that I should consider them marks of distinction. The implication was that he would be very proud if I were to be invited into a senior honor society. He was.

Getting Ready for the Real World

Senior year was excessively busy. As graduation approached, there was a thesis to write, a yearbook to get to the press, and exams to take. There were also interviews through the university's placement service. My credentials were in demand. First, I was interviewed by the head of the placement service, Craig Sweeten. Craig had known me as a soccer player, having been one himself some years earlier. Craig was extremely smooth. He thought I interviewed well but that I should always say "yes," not "yeah," and "no," not "nope" or "unh-unh." He arranged several interviews for me with top companies, but another possibility came to my attention through the faculty of the finance department of Wharton.

The Federal Reserve Bank of Philadelphia had a training program for people interested in banking and central banking. For two years a person went through every department at the Fed, while taking two years of graduate school simultaneously at the bank's expense. It sounded too good to be true. It was, however, a tough competition among applicants from many different schools for only three slots. With the faculty's endorsement, my interviews went well, and by the end of April I got a letter accepting me. I would start in late June and register for a master's program in economics and monetary theory in Penn's Graduate School of Arts and Sciences.

A new kind of life was about to begin that would include the finding of my lifelong best friend and lover, my wife.

CHAPTER THREE

Work, Love, and Marriage

Off to the Real World: Federal Reserve and Graduate School

Following graduation, three friends, Ed Igler, Charlie Hough, Merle Hague, and I went to Maine for a week of fishing on Long Pond, part of the Belgrade chain of lakes. Merle had that rare possession, a car! We split the gas and tolls, but the cheapskate tried to charge us for depreciation. We refused.

We rented a cottage and a couple of small outboard powered boats. We fished with bait, which was all we knew to do, until an older couple at the same camp introduced us to fly-fishing. It was an immediate hit with me and was the beginning of a lifelong hobby. We caught hundreds (no exaggeration) of small-mouth bass and white perch and so greatly enjoyed the place that I returned many times in the following years, including once with my wife and three children.

Driving home, we heard the news on the car radio that the North Koreans had invaded South Korea. President Truman reacted immediately, and we entered another war only five years after the end of the big one. Would we have to go back in the service? I had served only eleven months, one month shy of the one-year requirement for draft ineligibility. To avoid the possibility that I might be drafted into the army I joined the naval reserve. For the next eighteen months I went to the Philadelphia Navy Yard for classes every Monday night. Finally, it became obvious that the draft was no longer a threat, although the war continued for over two years.

Starting at the Federal Reserve, I met my fellow trainees, John Boyer from the University of Virginia and Jimmy Roberts from Princeton. We became close friends quickly. (About twelve years later, John Boyer joined Drexel & Co.) I found that my Wharton education gave me a head start, particularly having had accounting and finance. They registered for Wharton's MBA program while I went for an MA to avoid duplicating my undergraduate experience. Our pay was $200 per month plus tuition.

In the trainee class ahead of us were Morrie Dorrance and Bill Eagleson, both of whom became good friends and went on to become CEOs of Philadelphia banks. The class behind me included another Penn graduate, Tom Kenny, who, along with me, eventually became another defector from banking to Wall Street, becoming a prosperous real estate specialist. Tom's father was with the U.S. Postal Service and was helpful in getting us night work at the main Philadelphia postoffice sorting Christmas mail for what then was an attractive hourly rate of one dollar. It was a welcome supplement to the meager pay we received at the Fed but it sure made a long and tiring day.

In truth, the work at the Fed was fairly dull and uninteresting. It was the graduate school that made the program tolerable. The classes were variously 2:00-4:00 PM, 4:00-6:00 PM, and occasionally 7:00-9:00 PM. The courses were both good and challenging, particularly a course in central banking given by Karl Bopp, the executive vice president of the Philadelphia Fed and an accomplished academic, and two courses given by Simon Kuznets, who not long after left Penn for Harvard and was a winner of the Nobel Prize in economics. I had an inkling of how good he was because Dad had taken his courses almost ten years before.

His lectures, particularly on the history of economic development, were spellbinding. The courses were difficult, and he was a very rigorous grader. Ironically, his two courses were the only Bs I received in graduate school. I earned As in all the others. At the beginning of the courses, he handed out an extensive reading list and a list of one hundred superbly difificult questions that required essay answers. What a study guide! Several hours of reading and research were necessary to answer any one question well. We split the questions among the ten or so students in the class and then met in study groups to discuss the answers. It was so extremely effective that I have often wondered why other courses and professors don't do the same.

I learned a tremendous amount in graduate school. I passed the oral examination for my degree easily and had only to write my thesis, which was on the merits of the U.S. Treasury issuing inflation-protected bonds, a notion that came to fruition about forty-five years later. Alas, my thesis writing would be interrupted and, as it turned out, never accomplished because my mind turned to love.

A Woman Enters the Scene!

While I was a lunchtime waiter at the Kappa Alpha Theta sorority house during my senior year, I had noticed an attractive woman with gorgeous shoulder-length auburn hair. Her name was Warren Shafer. I later came to know her slightly when she dated Dave Coulson, a fraternity brother and football star who was a year behind me.

In November of 1950, I had a date with Helen Hogg, an old friend, after a football game. I was then an alumnus and would go back to campus for special events. We ended up at a dance party at the Psi Upsilon fraternity house. Warren was there with a friend and fellow soccer player Charlie Hough. I could not stop looking at her. She danced and moved smoothly and gracefully. The more I looked at her, the more I became magnetically and obsessively attracted.

As Helen and I danced, I said to her, "I think I'm going to marry that sorority sister of yours."

My version is that she replied emphatically, "That's ridiculous; you haven't even dated her." Helen's version is that she said, "What makes you think she would have you?" Regardless, at the end of that evening, I knew I was going to get to know Warren Shafer.

Fraternity brothers usually follow a "hands off" code with women who are dating another brother. Dave Coulson was a respected friend, so I harbored my desire if only for the next few weeks.

Over the Christmas holidays of 1950, I received an invitation to a cocktail party at Gail Tinney's house on January 2, in Merion. Gail was a sorority sister of Warren's. My parents had also been invited as friends of both Gail and her parents. It was Mom and Dad's twenty-eighth wedding anniversary.

The day of the party, I was working at the Fed when I impulsively decided to make a connection with Warren. Dave Coulson, after all, had not seemed serious about a relationship with Warren, and anyway, he was home in Johnstown, Pennsylvania, for the holidays. From the bank, I courageously called Warren at her home. I knew where she lived because I had had an accidental date with her sister, Flip, about six weeks before when her midshipman friend showed up late after the Penn-Navy football game.

She said it sounded like fun and accepted the invitation. She would come into the city on the Reading Railroad. I would meet her at the station, and we would take another train out to Merion. I was there ten minutes early to meet her, but when the train arrived, she wasn't on it. My heart sank. When I called her home, her mother told me she had missed the train and was on the next one a half-hour later. She arrived, and we were off on our first date, going by train to the party and then to dinner with my parents at the Tavern (where I had been a busboy during high school) to celebrate their twenty-eighth anniversary. For years afterward, we would go to the Tavern to celebrate promotions and raises or just be romantic. That night, we delivered my parents to their house, and then I drove Warren to her home in Willow Grove, about forty-five minutes away.

It was as if I had been hit by a truck. I fell immediately in love with an intensity I had never felt before. This woman had it all. Not only was she beautiful and well built but also she had a brain. A Phi Beta Kappa and an economics major with an academic record above mine, she and I had intellectual interests in common. We also had similar family backgrounds—we had enjoyed a good childhood, our families had been affected by the Great Depression, and we both had happily married parents. We even found that we had met years before at a birthday party for her cousin Mary Eaton, whose parents were friends of my family.

We both had been active undergraduates, shared a love for Penn, and had a parent who was an alumnus (Warren's mother was class of 1925). That she was a

Theta at Penn, the sorority we men referred to as "the women you want to marry," and which my sister had just joined, made it all the better.

Both of us necessarily had worked summers to help with college. Warren had been granted a four-year scholarship to Penn by the local chapter of the Veterans of Foreign Wars in Roxborough. She had been salutatorian of her class at Roxborough High School. (When Warren read this, she demonstrated her addiction to complete honesty. She says that she wasn't actually salutatorian. That honor went to a girl who was in the commercial course. Warren was second highest in the college preparatory course.)

We complemented each other well. I am impulsive, she is deliberate. I am noisy and gregarious, she is quiet and reserved. I am an open book, she is very private. And neither one of us is very emotional. I doubt that these characteristics were consciously analyzed at the time, but my instinctive reactions were that we would each be a more complete person if we were together.

I am just as entirely smitten by her now fifty-four years later.

A Fast Proposal

After three more dates and a few kisses, I asked her to marry me. She was in her senior year and had just passed her twenty-first birthday. She looked at me in amazement and said that I couldn't possibly know after only three weeks and three dates. But I did know, and that whole winter and spring, I worked obsessively to convince her that she should marry me. She had a few more dates with other men, but in a couple of weeks, she was devoting full time to me. By the end of April, she still had not admitted that she loved me. I was a nervous wreck.

While Warren had had only one serious boyfriend about three years before, she was a very popular date. As I came on the scene, she was dating two other friends of mine—John Hackney and, as we have seen, Charlie Hough—in addition to Dave Coulson. Each of them was a very attractive, wholesome, popular guy. While I certainly did not sweep her off her feet as she had done to me, I was much more aggressive and persistent than the others who pursued her.

That spring her senior economics seminar professor, Irving Kravis, recommended that she apply for a summer internship at the United Nations in Geneva, Switzerland. Two American graduating seniors were to be selected by the state department, and he thought Warren had a good shot at it. Irv Kravis knew me because I had also had him for senior seminar. He was following our romance with interest and a smile, as he did our careers for many years following graduation.

She Leaves for the Summer but Not Before Saying Yes

In late April, the selections were made, and she was one of the two winners. In the meantime, she had also been hired as a security analyst by Wellington Management

Company, the largest mutual-fund management company. She was to begin work after graduation. This in itself was an honor in those days when professional women in the investment business were almost unknown.

My chronology is uncertain here, but I think it was shortly before winning the internship that one evening, after saying good night, she called to me from behind the front screen door of her family's house and said, "I love you."

That was the code for "Yes, I will marry you."

My elation was indescribable and has never since been matched under any circumstances. I sang in the car, driving home, and woke up my sister to tell her the exciting news. We celebrated and woke up our parents for an early-morning conversation. By the way, Mary Anne was dating Parry Scott at the time. Scotty had been a football star at Lower Merion a year behind me and had transferred from Colgate University to Penn to be near her. Scotty would become my brother-in-law in November 1951.

It remained for me to ask her father for her hand in marriage. But before that, her mother acknowledged that she approved. One evening, as she climbed the stairs in their tiny house, she turned and looked at me as she said, "Paul, I'm glad it's you." All her dad said, after my formal request for Warren's hand, was "That's fine."

Not long after this, she got the good news that she would be spending the summer in Europe. As proud as I was of her, the prospect of a summer without her was not pleasant. Europe, in those prejet days, seemed much farther away than it does now.

Warren did not want to announce our engagement until after she returned from Europe, when she could have a party to tell her friends. The secret was kept for the entire summer with only our families knowing about us.

She was off to Europe on a student-laden ship only days before Penn's commencement, which her mother attended so that she could tell Warren about it. Her mother, sister, and I went to New York to see the ship and say our good-byes. My heart was in my throat the whole time. I have never felt as lonely as I did for the next eight weeks. We both wrote daily letters, and I eagerly awaited the mail. Telephone calls were very expensive and rare. I think we talked by phone only once.

Getting to Know My Future In-Laws

That summer I spent many evenings with her family, getting to know them better. Her mother, Ella Warren (Eaton) Shafer, was one of three children, plus a half sister, from an old and proud family that had been fairly wealthy but had fallen on economic hard times. She was the beneficiary of a modest trust established by her grandfather. It provided a small income that was enough, together with her husband's modest salary, to allow them to live comfortably.

Tiny, as she was nicknamed, was a Penn graduate—class of 1925. She had majored in architecture, but her degree was in fine arts. She was denied a chance for an architectural degree because as a woman she was not allowed to take a required life-drawing class.

She was a tall large-boned woman, very intelligent, with a mischievously humorous and very personable manner. She loved naughty jokes and had her own repertoire, including bawdy songs. She and I had a very good relationship, had many a laugh together, and I always found her great company.

Warren's dad, Willard McIntyre Shafer, called "Willy" by his wife, had been reared as an only child in the very small town of Milford on the New Jersey side of the Delaware River north of New Hope. His formal education was limited, and his best talents were seen in his woodworking shop in the basement. He was a very nice guy but could be a dreadful bore, particularly after a couple of drinks. He was obviously deeply in love with his wife, and she with him, although she would occasionally show quiet frustration over something he said or did. More often than not, she was simply tolerant.

Willy Shafer worked as sales manager for a welding supply firm, having been employed in a family laundry business during the Depression. He, Tiny, and their two girls had been forced by the Depression to double up with grandparents just as the Miller family did. By the time I came on the scene, they lived in a very small cottagelike house in Willow Grove, Pennsylvania. I estimate that the entire first floor was only about thirty by twenty-five feet. The living room, made smaller by the space taken by the stairs at one end, was made to feel even more cramped by a grand piano and TV set. The upstairs had three small bedrooms and a single bath. To this tiny space, they also added a dog. What breed? A Great Dane! Fortunately, they had a backyard that let them stretch a bit in summer.

Warren's younger sister by two and a half years, Florence Esler Shafer, nicknamed Flip, was at home that summer as well. Flip is a delightful woman, built exactly like Warren, with a voice that is eerily similar.

The Shafer family and I had a good time together during those achingly lonely weeks of Warren's absence. Her homecoming was greeted by all of us with a huge sigh of relief.

Engaged Finally!

After Warren arrived home in late August, she arranged to announce our engagement at a tea for her friends on Columbus Day. The idea was to show them slides of her European trip but at the beginning was a surprise. It was a slide of me in Maine holding up a fish but with a photo of her substituted for the fish. The audience was indeed surprised and our engagement was then announced in the Philadelphia newspapers. We planned to marry the following June, but there was much to do first.

I was still in the Fed's training program and finishing graduate school. Warren was establishing herself with Wellington. And we had no money—literally none. I had spent $260 on an engagement ring and was flat broke, with no permanent job. I was giving half of my $200 per month pay to my parents for room and board. Other expenses took another $50. Warren was also paying for room and board, so from our combined income of $400 per month. we had less than $100 to save for a honeymoon and starting a household.

The one thing we did have was the most important: self-confidence. Not for a minute did our poverty concern us. We knew that we each had a solid set of tools. We both had been very successful undergraduates, both academically and socially, and had high confidence in our brains and personalities. But looking back I can now see how pleasantly naïve we were about the world we were entering.

In the months following our engagement, we met for lunch once or twice a week (Warren had discovered that she could buy lunch for only forty cents at the Colonnade Cafeteria). I was visiting Willow Grove with regularity, and that, together with continuing studies and a job, took a toll on my master's thesis. Fortunately, the Fed's program was not very demanding, and I could study several hours a week in the bank's library.

In the late fall, Mary Anne, who was only nineteen, and Scotty announced that they wanted to marry at the first opportunity. He had been drafted into the army and was in Georgia, at Fort Boenning. Our family was delighted at the prospect of having Scotty in the family. When he was able to schedule a short leave at Thanksgiving, a wedding was quickly planned and executed. I was an usher and Warren a bridesmaid as we set them on a happy marital course that has never been in doubt.

The Fed Wants Me to Stay

During the spring I had many interviews with Philadelphia banks. The Fed's trainees were very much in demand. Topping all the offers I received was one from the Federal Reserve Bank itself. They wanted me to join the research staff for the munificent sum of $4,300 per year. This was higher than the commercial banks were offering but below what industry was paying. My friend Ed Igler was making $5,200 at IBM, which was then a young and fast growing company. But I was committed to finance and jumped at the Fed's offer.

The Wedding and Honeymoon

We were married on June 14, 1952. There was the normal whirl of parties and showers before the wedding. Warren designed her own wedding dress, and her next-door neighbor, Perry Wunn, did most of the sewing.

The Shafer family did not attend any church at the time, so we decided to have the ceremony at the Church of St. Asaph, which had been such an important part of my family's life. Fraternity brothers, old friends, and Scotty, my new brother-in-law, would be my six ushers. Dad would be my best man.

A large wedding would have been a financial burden neither of our families could afford. However, a rich middle-distance relative of Warren's, Aunt Em Curtis, generously gave us a wedding gift of a magnificent reception at her mansion in Bala, almost next door to St. Asaph's.

Warren's sister, Flip, would be her maid of honor, and five of her sorority sisters, including my sister, Mary Anne, would be her bridesmaids.

If nothing else, we were a handsome wedding party. Here is a list of the participants:

Best Man: Paul F. Miller
Maid of Honor: Florence E. Shafer (Soars)

Ushers	Bridesmaids
William T. Andrews	Arden Bennett (Poole)
R. Brooke Friel	Helen Hogg (Gindell)
Frank W. Hughes	Joan Howarth (Igler)
Edwin R. Igler	Marilyn Richter (Jones)
Isaac Kershaw III	Mary Anne Miller (Scott)
Raymond P. Scott, Jr.	
John S. Wynn Jr.	

Of all the things that happened that day, starting with a pickup game of basketball in our driveway for the ushers, three impressions stand out. First is how utterly beautiful Warren was. Second is the feeling of relaxation and total relief I felt as we exited the church—she really was mine! Third was the conviction that I hold to this day, that our reception was the best party I have ever known. It was dominated by singing, both college songs and Broadway-show tunes, and dancing. We both remember one song in particular, the song that we adopted as "our song." We still sing it on special occasions. It was "You're Just in Love," made famous by Ethel Merman in *Call Me Madam*.

I hear music and there's no one there,
I smell blossoms and the trees are bare,
All day long I seem to walk on air,
I wonder why, I wonder why.
I keep walking in my sleep at night,
And what's more I've lost my appetite.
Stars that used to twinkle in the skies,
Now twinkle in my eyes, I wonder why.

(then the counterpoint)

You don't need analyzin',
It is not so surprisin',
That you feel very strange but nice
Your heart goes pitter patter,
I know just what's the matter,
Because I've been there once or twice.
Put your head on my shoulder,
You need someone who's older,
A rubdown with a velvet glove.
There is nothing you can take
To relieve that pleasant ache.
You're not sick, you're just in love!

The party lasted for four hours. We were very nervous about what pranks my friends might spring on us, and decided to sneak out through the garage where a chauffeur was waiting to drive us a short distance to pick up the Shafers' car that we borrowed for our honeymoon. But somehow our secret departure plans became known and the crowd descended on us in the garage. We had overestimated their penchant for mischief and made our safe getaway.

Our honeymoon was limited by our pocketbook, but it was wonderful. Our wedding night was spent at the Warwick Hotel in Philadelphia, reputedly the best in town. We left the car, a 1948 Packard, at the hotel entrance for the doorman to park. Thirty minutes later, as we were stripped to our underwear and sipping champagne, the phone rang. Our first thought was that our mischievous friends had found us. But no, it was the front desk telling me that I had failed to leave the keys in the car! I dressed again and with a red face handed the keys to a bellboy who came to the room.

A postscript is needed here. On our fiftieth wedding anniversary, we went back to the Warwick and asked for the same room, 1309. The hotel greeted us and gave us free drinks and a free breakfast. Our assistant, Betsy Taylor, had told them that I had the hotel bill from 1952 showing not only the charges but also the room number. But there was no thirteenth floor. In a renovation they had simply eliminated the thirteenth floor because so many superstitious people wouldn't accept a room there. (They should have known how lucky it had been for us!) So we were in 1409. When I went to the cashier to pay the bill the next morning it was for $12.39, the same charge we had fifty years prior!

The next day we drove the old Packard to Split Rock Lodge in the Poconos where we had our own small cabin for a week. It was a very hot day and cars were not air-conditioned. Warren was dressed in a dark blue suit that was very inappropriate for the unseasonably hot weather. On the way I was embarrassed when she shed her top and was in her slip and bra in the front seat as we passed the drivers of eighteen-wheelers whom I imagined to be obsessed with her!

The low point of the week, although retrospectively it was the humorous high point, was my upsetting a sailboat on Lake Harmony. It resulted in the near loss of my camera and the destruction of all our honeymoon pictures.

At the end of the week, we returned to a $75 per month apartment over a dry-cleaning store that we had rented and worked to furnish in the preceding weeks. After the honeymoon expenses, our only assets were $5 left in the bank and a month prepaid rent.

Beta Theta Pi house decorated for Navy game poster contest, 1948

Penn varsity soccer, 1949

Junior at Penn, 1949

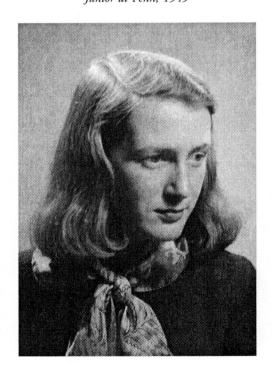

Warren as a junior at Penn, 1950

At the departure of Warren's ship to Europe, May 1951

Warren dancing with Dad

Leaving St. Asaph's, June 14, 1952

L. to R., Mary Anne Miller Scott, Marilyn Rector (Jones),
Flip Shafer (Soars), Warren, Arden Bennett (Poole),
Joan Howarth (Igler), Helen Hogg (Artigue, Gindele)

L. to R., Bill Andrews, Frank Hughes, Brooke Friel, Dad, Parry Scott,
Johnny Wynn, Ed Igler, (kneeling) Ike Kershaw

CHAPTER FOUR

Off to a Good Start

It Wasn't Much but We Called It Home

Our apartment was the second floor over the Arcadia Cleaners at 22 Union Avenue in Bala. It was directly across the street from the Bala School where my mother had spent some of her elementary school years. It was just around the corner from a twin house where I had lived for my first two years, down the street two blocks from the Egyptian Theater where I had been an usher during high school, and a quarter of a mile from the church where we were married. As it turned out, it was also just a short walk from where the first office of Miller, Anderson & Sherrerd would be located seventeen years in the future.

The apartment was always permeated with the odors from the dry cleaners below. The steam locomotives were still running on the Pennsylvania Railroad tracks a hundred yards away. They had to pass under a bridge over Union Avenue that precluded the smoke from freely rising. The result was that soot covered our little deck and not only came in through open windows but also under the windows when they were closed.

With all its drawbacks, we loved it. We had bought the cheapest furniture possible, covered the floors with woven paper rugs, and made bookcases from boards separated by bricks. We had a radio and a 45-rpm record player. A TV set was not to come until almost five years later.

On the plus side, the living room and bedroom were spacious, with large windows. There was a separate dining room and a small kitchen. The one bathroom had an old-fashioned claw-footed bathtub. No shower. We thought it was a palace.

It was only a five-minute walk to either the Bala or Cynwyd stations of the Pennsylvania Railroad's Norristown Local and then only a fifteen-minute ride to Center City. We made friends with fellow commuters, and the trip became a social affair, chatting about the day's news or doing the puzzles in the paper. If we had to travel somewhere by car, we would borrow my parents' 1948 Chevy, an inconvenience to both borrowers and lenders.

In the evenings, we shopped at the local Acme, located within steps of the train station. Our weekly food budget was ten dollars, which we stretched by having dinners such as Spam, hot dogs, or scrapple with mashed potatoes and Franco-American gravy. I mention these specifics to draw a contrast to the yuppies of today with their organic diets and bottled water. Without mooching on our families once or twice a week, we could never have made it on ten bucks.

Our obsessive short-term goal was to save to buy a used car, and eventually, a house, although the latter seemed a distant dream. Warren kept our budget in cash, with the money stowed in separate compartments of a small box for specific uses. We each took small weekly allowances for day-to-day needs.

Retrospectively, I can see how driven we were to become financially comfortable. Both of us had seen the Great Depression up close, and seen our parents struggle. We didn't want that for ourselves.

We thought of ourselves as "on the way" and never had any doubts about that. While many friends had a head start from inheritances or parental gifts and owned cars and starter homes, we never considered ourselves poor or deprived.

It took two years for us to save enough for a down payment on a used car. Scotty, my brother-in-law, sold us a black 1948 Mercury coupe. The previous owner had put a Mack Truck bulldog on the hood as an ornament that gave the car a kind of distinction. There was a Texaco gas station across from the front door of the apartment. Joe, the owner, gave us permission to park there.

What a feeling of freedom that car gave us, although we discovered on its first long trip, to Algonquin Park in Ontario, that it had a chronic overheating problem that we weren't able to cure.

Bored With Banking

Only four months into my job at the Federal Reserve, I grew very restless. I found economic research tedious and far from the real business world I began to crave. As time passed, I became convinced that I would not stay at the Fed. I talked with Dad and he suggested that I see Don Bishop, the senior partner of Bishop & Hedberg, an investment-counseling firm. Don had built an excellent reputation for running the money of wealthy Philadelphians while he was an investment officer at the Provident Trust Co., an institution with strong Quaker roots.

Although I talked to IBM and several banks that all wanted to hire me, I found something very appealing about a small firm in the investment business. In my talk with the head of IBM's local office, he asked me how much money I hoped I would be making ten years ahead. I knew he wanted an ambitious answer so I screwed up my courage, took a deep breath, and told him that $10,000 would be fine. In fact, in 1962, ten years later, I made $70,000, a number I remember because it was only $10,000 less than the $80,000 we paid for our Gladwyne house in that year.

Looking back, I think I was fascinated by the work Warren was doing at Wellington Fund. She was the first woman security analyst in Philadelphia. She would talk about her work and her fellow workers and how they were trying to relate economic developments to the security markets. I had been a long-time observer of financial markets through Dad, whose moods swung with the Dow-Jones Average. I had also been intrigued by course work at Wharton with Professor Julius Grodinsky who was the author of a highly regarded book called *The Ebb and Flow of Investment Values.*

I talked in depth to Bob Hedberg, Don Bishop's young partner. A big, husky former football player, Bob was a Wharton graduate about five years my senior, very bright and articulate. He was willing to spend time tutoring me in the art of security analysis.

Hooked on Investing

I started work with Bishop & Hedberg in November of 1952 at the same salary I had received at the Fed. The year ahead was filled with the ecstasy of learning and being part of a small business. I joined the Financial Analysts' Society of Philadelphia and attended their semimonthly meetings featuring corporate CEOs and respected senior economists and analysts. Warren was also a member, as were her associates, John Birmingham, Tom Pisano, Ed Crysler, and Ed Mennis, all of whom I came to know. A few years later Wellington hired Clay Anderson who would eventually become a close associate and partner of mine.

Bob Hedberg and I spent time analyzing company after company. Our tools were manuals such as Moody's and Standard and Poor's, statistical services that compiled a myriad of financial ratios such as Studley, Shupert & Co. (that we nicknamed Slightly Stupid &Co.), and reports from H. C. Wainwright & Co. that were based on company visits. Wainwright was one of only two Wall Street firms producing something of value for professional investors. The other was Smith, Barney & Co.

The Great Depression and World War II had left serious scars on investors. They were still very much in evidence in 1952. The business cycle dominated the thinking of economists and investors. Inflation was widely accepted as a postwar phenomenon that would fade as pent-up demands from the war were satisfied. A sense of economic stability being the norm, rather than the exception, would be built only gradually over the following fifteen years.

Bonds were considered appropriate investments to provide both income and safety of principal. The Federal Reserve had unpegged interest rates in 1951 as an understanding grew that with pegged rates, the Fed was becoming an engine of inflation. After an initial shocking jump, rates had settled in the 2 to 3 percent area. In late 1953, ten-year Treasury bonds yielded 2.7 percent, one-year rates were 1.7 percent, and AAA corporate bonds yielded about 3.1 percent. There was no concern that rates would rise meaningfully from those levels.

When we analyzed a company, we put it through a "depression test" to arrive at what we termed "sound value." The test was designed to estimate what would happen to a company's earnings and financial condition in the event of what today would be an unimaginable 10 to 15 percent decline in gross national product, a magnitude that was seen in the 1930s but never since then. We factored in what downside protection might be provided by a dividend after testing its safety, and by a firm's net asset values. We judged a stock to be acceptable if it was no more than 20 percent above sound value and very attractive at 20 percent below sound value.

Brokers and investment advisory firms were overwhelmingly dealing with individual investors rather than institutions. Pension funds were not yet an important factor, and mutual funds were just beginning to proliferate. Investment management was heavily concentrated in bank-trust departments and insurance companies. There were very few independent investment advisory firms competing with the larger institutions. Scudder, Stevens & Clark; Loomis Sayles; and Lionel D. Edie & Co. were providing old-fashioned investment advisory services, but discretionary investment management was almost unknown. Clients approved all actions either in personal meetings or by letters.

All of Bishop & Hedberg's clients were wealthy individuals. For the less wealthy, the firm had Rittenhouse Fund, a mutual fund that had only a few million dollars.

I studied a famous book, *Security Analysis*, by Benjamin Graham, who was known then as an extremely successful investor who sought stocks offering a large margin of safety. He is known now also as the mentor of Warren Buffett. It was by reading Graham that I first became imbued with the "value style" of investing.

While I certainly never rivaled Buffett, I devoured Ben Graham's work and all else I could find about investing. I found Julius Grodinsky's teaching about patterns of growth, maturity, and decay of industries to be applicable and useful. I loved analyzing industries and companies and felt that I had found my calling. Warren and I were doing similar work, and we learned from each other. Our offices were only three blocks apart, so we often met for lunch at the Colonnade Cafeteria where we could each eat for less than a dollar.

That year with Bob Hedberg was extraordinary training. We worked on many industries and dozens of companies. I became a stock-market addict, although we had no money of our own to invest. But the firm of Bishop & Hedberg was not prosperous enough to accommodate two ambitious young men. The assets being managed were not growing sufficiently and Don Bishop's personal clients were most of the business. Bob Hedberg and I wondered aloud to each other about the firm's future.

In the late fall of 1953 I had a chance chat with Schuyler Lippincott, who was a regular rider with us on the Norristown Local. Schuyler was an odd sort of duck—a face with a hawklike homeliness and an obsequious manner. A descendant of Joseph Wharton, the founding benefactor of the Wharton School, he was with Drexel & Co., an old-line, blue-blood Philadelphia investment firm. Drexel was located in the same office building as Bishop & Hedberg, so we usually walked the three blocks to and from the Pennsylvania Railroad's Suburban Station in Philadelphia together. Somehow he got the drift that I might be thinking of a change and suggested I talk with Drexel about joining their investment advisory department.

Drexel & Co.

After a long talk with Don Bishop and Bob Hedberg, I made an appointment to meet Bob Lee, a Drexel partner who ran the advisory business. Bob was an extremely intense person who loved challenging discussions. We had one centering on the economics of the oil industry. I had recently finished a hand-written analysis of Phillips Petroleum that I gave to him. He must have been impressed because an offer was almost immediately forthcoming for $5,200 annually.

In 1953, Drexel & Co. had about one hundred employees and eight active partners, two of whom were in New York. Two additional partners, Tom Gates and Gates Lloyd, were on leave in positions with the Eisenhower administration—one as Secretary of the Navy and one with the Central Intelligence Agency. Tom Gates, who went on to become Secretary of Defense, was the son of Thomas S. Gates, who also had been a Drexel partner and who was reputed to be the financial savior of the University of Pennsylvania during the Great Depression.

The firm traced its lineage back to 1838. Its founder was Francis Martin Drexel. In the late nineteenth century, his son, Francis Anthony Drexel, and J. P. Morgan became partners and for the years leading up to the Banking Act of 1934 the two firms, Drexel & Co. in Philadelphia and J. P. Morgan and Co. in New York, were partnerships in common, doing both a banking and investment-banking business. After the Banking Act was passed, which prohibited banking and investment-banking from being combined in one firm, Drexel chose to be a private bank, as did J. P. Morgan, but the two firms separated. In 1937 some partners from each firm left to start Morgan Stanley and Co. In 1940, Drexel chose to revert to an investment bank.

Drexel's partners were socially prominent Philadelphians, boarding school and Ivy League educated, aristocratic, and Brooks Brotherish in dress, and with a couple of notable exceptions, were clearly not the products of pure meritocracy.

One of the exceptions was the firm's senior partner, Edward Hopkinson Jr. "Hoppy," as he was called by his friends, was a direct descendant of Francis Hopkinson, a signer of the Declaration of Independence. He was a graduate of Penn and Penn Law, and had played a major role in Philadelphia's postwar revitalization, which was still going on in 1953.

Hoppy was a huge man, six foot three inches, with a magnificent full head of white hair and an alert but jowly face that jiggled as he talked. He walked with long, purposeful strides as if he knew exactly where and why he was going. He was a trustee of Penn and on the boards of several corporations. Hoppy was widely respected outside the firm and worshipped from within. He had the final say on everything and anything if he wanted it, which he often did not.

The firm's day-to-day activities were managed by Edward Starr Jr. The investment advisory activities were run by two partners, Morris Lloyd and Bob Lee. Bob was the other exception to my cynical comment about meritocracy. He was very smart, well-informed on investment matters, and was the source of most of the investment ideas passed on to clients. Unfortunately, he suffered a stroke about a year after I joined the firm and was not the same during the additional year he survived.

Drexel was a member firm of the New York Stock Exchange that required all employees dealing with the public to pass an examination. While I could handle the investment-related parts of the exam, I needed training in the mechanics of the brokerage and investment-banking parts of the business. That meant spending several boringly necessary months in the back office processing brokerage trades and investment-banking transactions. Then I spent a similar period in what was known as the statistical department. It was there that statistics were gathered to make company comparisons for underwriting purposes or for the investment-advisory department.

There was no original, judgmental research done by anyone. The advisory department subscribed to services such as Moody's, Standard and Poor's, and Argus Research, but that was it with the exception of quarterly visits of Harland Hoisington, a Princeton-based investment counselor who was used as a consultant. We would all gather in the conference room to hear his commentary on the markets and a few individual stocks. I thought he was inarticulate, amateurish, and of no value. However, we were in a strong bull market at the time and it was easy for anyone recommending stocks to look smart.

The firm was contentedly going nowhere. As a regional firm in an increasingly national market, it had become extremely difficult to compete for the larger and more profitable corporate underwriting. Drexel's brokerage business was tiny and was overwhelmingly coming from investment-advisory clients and a few closely connected endowments and pension funds such as the University of Pennsylvania, Philadelphia Electric Co., and the Pennsylvania Railroad.

The advisory business was stagnant at best and was run with no serious research to support its recommendations. It was truly an *advisory* business. There were no discretionary accounts; we made recommendations by letter or in meetings that were usually accepted. The accounts were reviewed every six months in weekly meetings of the entire department. In keeping with the general practice of investment advisors, no performance figures were kept. The performance race didn't begin until the late 1950s and early 1960s.

The brightest star in the firm was a New York partner, Walter Steele, who had pioneered the business of advising municipalities and states and the underwriting of tax-exempt revenue bonds, notably turnpike issues backed by toll revenues. This was the firm's most profitable, fastest-growing business in the late 1940s and through the 1950s.

Within a few months of beginning to actually work in the advisory department, I was immersed in being Bob Lee's assistant on a large number of accounts. I began to present common-stock ideas to the weekly meetings of the department, complete with backup numbers, projections of earnings, and possible future valuations. Nobody had ever done this before. The two I remember best were McGraw-Hill Publishing and Coca-Cola, both solid growth stories at cheap prices. These did well and I began to accumulate a bit of a reputation.

A Talent Vacuum?

It was increasingly obvious that I had walked into a talent vacuum. I did not necessarily feel more intelligent than those around me. Rather, my education and federal-reserve background put me at a different level of thinking. There was nobody in the firm who knew how the national income accounts were compiled and how to interpret them. There was nobody who had any deep understanding of the Federal Reserve and monetary policies. Interest rates were beginning to move around a bit after having been unpegged by the Federal Reserve in 1951. While at the Fed I had attended the congressional hearings on the unpegging and was well acquainted with the issues that would influence the money and bond markets. I began to write memos on economic and financial developments for internal use.

Gradually, I took primary charge of accounts, particularly after Bob Lee's death. I knew that my approach was different from that of the other members of the department. They were primarily concerned with investment "quality," a conventional approach at the time, stemming from the damage wrought by the Depression. I was much less worried about quality and more concerned with valuation. This was the product of my training under Bob Hedberg. I also had much less patience when it appeared that ideas were not working.

Not long after I joined the advisory department I became Hoppy's assistant on the Philadelphia Electric Pension Fund, the firm's largest advisory client. We made presentations to their full board of directors on a quarterly basis. I watched with admiration how Hoppy handled the group and believe I learned significantly from his example. Before long he was letting me make observations about the economic environment and turning to me to provide the arguments for the investment changes we were suggesting to our clients. That Hoppy trusted me enough for the task was a real breakthrough and morale booster for me.

Teaching: a Valuable Experience

Fairly early in my Drexel days, I was asked by the finance department at Wharton to do some part-time teaching. They actually came to me through Hoppy, who was a trustee of the university. With his and the firm's blessing, I began to teach Finance 1:

Money and Banking four mornings a week from 8:00 to 9:00 AM and arrive at work about 9:20. At the time the extra $200 per month came in very handy. I taught for four years before my business life became too busy to continue.

Teaching was an extremely helpful experience. I am convinced that having to stand before a class and be an articulate teacher strengthened my abilities to explain and persuade, as well as preparing me for speaking clearly without nervousness to much larger audiences.

I was still enrolled in graduate school and toyed with the idea of going for a doctorate. I had never written my master's thesis because I had been too concerned with courting Warren and then starting a household. But I could have gone on for a doctorate without stopping for a master's degree. To hedge my bets, I took a couple of additional courses at night and talked Dad into taking one with me two afternoons a week. As my responsibilities at the firm increased, I gave up the idea entirely. I never did write the master's thesis, and did not get a master's degree although I completed all the course work and then some and easily passed the oral examination.

My Social Blockade Worries

In the fall of 1955, the firm announced that Edward Starr III, the son of the managing partner, would be admitted as a general partner. I was stunned. Ted Starr was a very decent guy, a couple of years older than I, with no apparently special attributes other than his father's position in the firm. Had I joined a firm that, in addition to being conscious of social standing, was also riddled with nepotism? My dad had wondered out loud about this possibility when I had first joined Drexel two years before.

That Christmas, my concerns were relegated to the background when I was rewarded with a large raise, and in addition to a generous firmwide bonus, was handed a "latrine bonus," so-called because a check was handed to you in private so that others could not see it happening. The total was an amount well in excess of my expectations. In total I was paid over $8,000 in 1955. That's about $80,000 in today's dollars, very decent pay at that time for someone only three years into a career. Obviously, they liked me and my work.

Warren was also doing nicely, so after each raise or bonus, we celebrated our good fortune the way we would continue to for some years in the future: by having two martinis and a lobster dinner at the Tavern, the restaurant I had bussed in a decade earlier.

Time for a Child and a House

With increased financial security and a faster growing pot of savings, we began to consider having children and finding a house. But over a year and a half of trying, Warren had not become pregnant.

We had been in our little apartment for over three years. Warren's interest in building a nest had intensified, with a corresponding decline in her enthusiasm for business. Warren asked Thaddeus Montgomery, the same doctor that delivered me and my sister, whether quitting work might help her quest for a pregnancy. He said that it might help by putting her in a more relaxed mindset. She decided to quit working in February of 1956, effective on April 13. One day in mid-March, she went from her office to the doctor's office to confirm our suspicions that she was pregnant. She was, with the baby due in early December. We were overjoyed.

In late 1955, we contracted to build a house in Devon, Pennsylvania. It was to be completed by early fall so that we could move in well before the baby was born.

Jack Bogle, Our Brilliant Friend

In the early summer of 1956, we were invited by an associate of Warren's at Wellington, Jack Bogle, to spend two weeks in the Bogles' summer home in Bayhead, New Jersey. We had become good friends of Jack's during the previous five years. Warren and Jack started at Wellington at about the same time. He was a Princeton graduate and had written his senior thesis on mutual funds. The thesis had attracted the attention of Walter Morgan, the mutual-fund pioneer who founded Wellington.

I have often said of Jack Bogle that he has the highest native intelligence level of anyone I know. His intelligence is matched by his intense, competitive drive and a sizeable ego. He will come back into this story several times.

Jack and his two brothers, Buddy and David, had lost their parents some years earlier and had inherited a marvelous shingled house a half block from the beach. On the weekends, the three brothers arrived and we had parties well laced with booze and music. *My Fair Lady* had opened on Broadway a few months before, and we were captivated by the music, which we played endlessly.

Meeting Jay Sherrerd

Warren was just becoming obviously pregnant and was a bit restrained in her activities, but the boys were quite active, even playing pickup basketball games at a local playground. It was in one of these games that I met Jay Sherrerd, the brother of Jack Bogle's girlfriend, Eve Sherrerd. Jack had known Jay at Princeton where Jack had been a year ahead of Jay. While I did not have a chance to talk with Jay in any detail about what he was doing, I did discover that he had recently received an MBA from Wharton. A few months later Jay would join me at Drexel and we would begin a lifelong business partnership.

Some Stunning News

Early that summer I asked the firm if I could attend a financial analysts' seminar in Beloit, Wisconsin, in late August. It would be a weeklong intellectually challenging mixture of academics and practitioners. There would be a hundred attendees from across the country, including a number of friends from other firms and institutions.

On the Friday before the Sunday I was to depart for Beloit, Ed Starr asked me to join him in the conference room. He closed the door, and with a serious look on his face, sat down across from me. I thought I was to be scolded or fired and tried to recall something I had done to deserve a dressing down or worse.

As he spoke he gave me the most unexpected news I could imagine and a whole new world began to unfold.

CHAPTER FIVE

Making It

The Surprise Invitation

"The firm," said Ed Starr, with a look of seriousness bordering on solemnity, "has decided to invite you to become a partner as of October 1."

My eyes must have bulged. I clearly remember a feeling of lightheadedness accompanying what was the immense surprise. My face became flushed, and I was literally breathless.

"Before accepting this offer, there are a few things you should know.

"Drexel & Co. is a partnership so that each partner has an unlimited liability for the actions not only of himself but also every other partner. You will share in the profits, but you will also share in the losses. The firm has never lost money, but that possibility always exists.

"You will be expected to invest capital in the firm. We do not expect much capital from you initially, but it should become your major financial investment, and you should try to build it over time.

"There will be several other people also joining the firm." He continued to name them: George Bell, John Remer, Schuyler Lippincott, and Jim Couffer. I knew all of them except Couffer, who was coming from the outside to help grow the municipal-bond business.

"The others don't know yet and will be told in two weeks. We wanted to make sure you knew before going to the Beloit seminar. You need not give us an answer immediately. It's a big step, and you may want to talk it over with your wife."

Somehow, I gathered enough presence to assure him that I accepted the offer on the spot, and that I was flattered and pleased. But he should know that my capital was extremely limited. Most of it was committed to the new house.

The capital wasn't an issue, he told me. "Go have an interesting week."

I left the office early and ran to the train station and home where Warren and I whooped it up in our little apartment before going to The Tavern for martinis and lobster. And of course, we had to tell our families. Dad was a bit overcome by the news. He had felt, as I had, that a partnership was a long shot at best.

When the announcement was made public several weeks later, it was very big news, particularly in Philadelphia. It was Drexel's first effort to inject youth into what was considered a rich but terribly conservative firm. Congratulatory letters flooded my desk. Someone dug up the fact that I was the youngest partner (I would be twenty-nine in three weeks) admitted as a Drexel partner in the firm's 118-year history. I quickly became regarded as Drexel's "bright young star." One press account labeled me the Philadelphia financial community's "boy wonder." (Did they know I lived in a $75 per month apartment over the dry cleaners?)

I had no idea what the partnership would mean financially, but Warren and I examined our finances and made some estimates of what completing and furnishing the new house might cost. We concluded that my initial capital could be no larger than $3,500, by far the smallest of the five new partners. But I was told that my compensation would be only partially related to capital. As it turned out it was very weakly related, and in all the years I was a partner, the firm always made sure that my total compensation exceeded my expectations.

The year that followed was not one of Drexel's best. The Indiana Turnpike reported disappointing revenues for the month of September. Turnpike financing was a huge business for the firm, led by Walter Steele, a New York partner. We made markets in most turnpike issues and had several million dollars of inventory that suffered significantly. In October 1956, my first month as a partner, we lost over $100,000. In 1957 my share of the profits was $12,000, only about a third higher than my prepartnership income. It was, however, a high income for a twenty-nine-year-old in those years, about equivalent to $120,000 to $140,000 in 2003 dollars.

I Find My Lifelong Business Partner

My contemporary partners were terribly nice people with excellent social connections, but there was no outstanding talent among them. My Wharton education and graduate studies gave me a huge advantage and head start, although I had much to learn about the underwriting and deal-making parts of the business. It was clear to me that we needed some top-notch young people

In September, before I was given the partnership news, the investment advisory department had decided to add an additional account manager. I mentioned this to Jack Bogle, who suggested I talk to Jay Sherrerd, who was to become his brother-in-law and whom I had met at Bayhead the previous summer. Jay, a Wharton MBA, was working in the trust department of Philadelphia National Bank. He was the son of Bill Sherrerd, a partner of Butcher & Sherrerd, a well-regarded Philadelphia investment-banking and brokerage firm.

We offered Jay a salary of $4,200, which he told us was $100 less than his salary at the bank. With some humor, we matched the bank's compensation and he joined us. He was Drexel's first hire of an MBA. Jay would become a partner three years later and would remain my partner through my entire career. In retirement, we have adjacent offices, just as we have had since 1956.

First Child

They were heady days for us, particularly late 1956 and through 1957—a new partnership, our first child, and a new house, all in the span of four months. Actually, we had hoped to be in the house several months before the baby was due to arrive in early December, but the builder was operating on a financial shoestring and the delays were very frustrating.

Warren had decided on natural childbirth. We attended classes at Jefferson Hospital to prepare us both. I was to be present at the birth—a relatively new idea at the time.

Warren called me at the office at noon on December 5 and told me that my mother would be driving her in town to the doctor's office. She was not quite sure, but something seemed to be happening. It was, and we were off to Jefferson Hospital.

Thaddeus Montgomery, our family friend, was the attending physician. He had a gentle, soothing manner, but was extremely strict in his procedures. Warren was magnificent, except that she kept throwing off the sheet covering her in the labor room and the various doctors kept carefully replacing it. Finally, my usually modest wife tore off the sheet and said to the attending intern, "Look, if you don't mind, I certainly don't!" But when Dr. Montgomery came in and calmly put the sheet over her, she was meekly silent.

Ella Warren (Winky) Miller was born with no complications at 12:06 AM on December 6, 1956. Nothing had prepared me for the emotional, thrilling, and happy experience of tearfully hearing the initial wail of one's first born.

Back to our little apartment we went with our baby girl. When she was born she had one eye glued shut and I playfully suggested we call her "Winky." The name didn't stick right away, and we actually called her "Mugs" or "Muggins" most of the time during her first year. She was very round-faced and not the typical Gerber Baby Food model!

The house at 220 Forest Hills Circle in Devon was ready for us in late January. It was a three-bedroom, two-and-a-half bath split-level on a hill in a woodsy setting. It was white stucco with black shutters and very attractive. We thought it was a palace. Over the previous months, Warren had worked on the furnishings and decorating although our budget was limited. All available cash had been either spent on completing the house or invested in my capital account at Drexel. Even though our income had risen, so had our expenses, and for a while we were living hand-to-mouth.

I look back in some amazement to realize that by the age of twenty-nine, three of the five most defining moments in my life had already occurred: the marriage to my life-long lover and best friend, the birth of our first child, and my selection as a Drexel partner. The other two would be the founding of Miller, Anderson and Sherrerd in 1969, and my election as Chairman of the Trustees of Penn in 1978.

Two More Children in Quick Succession

The difficulty we had starting Warren's first pregnancy led us to try for a second without much wait. *Bam!* No problem. By June of 1957, only seven months after Winky's arrival, Warren was pregnant again. The baby was due in late March or early April.

April sounded good. The winter would be past and daffodils on the way. Wrong! On March 24 we were smashed by a record-breaking blizzard. Over thirty inches of wet, heavy snow fell in our neighborhood. Electricity went out in the middle of the storm, so we had no heat and a baby only fifteen months old. It was impossible to drive anywhere. Fortunately, one part of our street had not lost power and we were kindly invited to stay with a family at the top of the hill. But we lived in dread that Warren would start labor and we would be delivering the baby there.

Fortunately, Katharine (Kathy) Shafer Miller decided to wait until April 5 to make her debut as a beautiful redhead. Again, Warren opted for natural childbirth and I was again in attendance. The emotional impact was as great as the first time. Paul Bowers, Thad Montgomery's younger partner, handled the delivery competently and with some humor to relax us.

That summer, we rented an apartment with my parents on the beach in Ocean City, New Jersey, for the month of July. With two in diapers, we were kept hopping.

By May of the following year, Warren was pregnant again. The baby was due in February and Paul F. (Buzz) Miller III arrived about on time, with me as an observer again. By that time, I think I had the experience to have assisted in the delivery. Needless to say, we were thrilled to have a son.

For a short time, there were now three in diapers. We decided that three was enough under any circumstances and made a conscious decision to have no more.

Home life was hectic but joyous. I was not yet in the heavy traveling mode that came two years later, so I took over most of the dinner feeding, bathing, and bedtime reading.

The next several years are a bit of a blur to me now. Between the excitement of creating a new business for Drexel & Co. and three young children, life was a bit crazy.

Warren Wants a Bigger House

With three children growing up fast, Warren prodded me to think about a bigger house. We looked up and down the Main Line for something we considered in our price range. Warren knew just what she wanted, she thought. We found nothing after looking for several months. Then one day she called me at the office. It was March of 1962. She said she had looked at a house that afternoon that had none of what she wanted, but was a handsome place in a great location.

I caught an early train to look at the house at 115 Maple Hill Road in Gladwyne. The street was private, and the house sat on three acres of lovely land. As we drove into the driveway, I fell in love with it just as she had. With a bit of bargaining, we paid $80,000, a price about equivalent to my income that year.

In 1973, we put on an addition, and a couple of years after that, we were able to buy the adjoining two-acre field. We have been in that house ever since and love it as much now as we did then. Whenever we are away and then return to it, one of us invariably remarks how very comfortable we are there. It will always be home to us.

Lucky Timing

I see now that my timing in entering the investment business was part of my good fortune. From the 1929 stock-market crash through the Depression, war, and postwar years, no young people went to Wall Street. Consequently, the competition was old, and fresh talent was rare. Although the stock market, after an early postwar stumble, had been performing well, there was no boom atmosphere to attract youth. Thus, a twenty-nine-year-old with a good education in economics and finance and a willingness to work hard could easily be a standout.

In addition to taking on several more large investment-advisory clients, such as the Pennsylvania Railroad Pension Fund and Delaware Power and Light Pension Fund, I was asked to do some research on the paper industry. The objective was to solidify the firm's investment-banking relationships with two paper companies, Scott Paper and The Mead Corporation. Bob Lee had been a director of Mead and when he died Bud Dempsey, who had come to Drexel as a partner after retiring from Merck and Co., took his place. I visited all the mills of both companies and became well acquainted with the managements and the economics of the industry. When Bud Dempsey reached retirement age in 1963, I was elected as his replacement on the board of Mead. This was the first of my several corporate directorships which I discuss later.

Birth of a Research Department

As noted earlier I had begun to periodically write papers for internal use on the outlook for the economy and the financial markets. These found their way into wider circulation through other partners and clients. Soon I had an interested readership outside the firm, particularly among the local banks and insurance companies.

In the course of 1957, I had conversations within the firm about the possibility of starting a research department that would do serious, in-depth research, not only to serve our investment advisory department but also to provide to institutions in return for brokerage commissions. Difficult as it may be to believe from the vantage point of 2003, this was a new concept for the brokerage business in general. In 1957, institutions gave their brokerage to firms largely on the basis of personal relationships or as reciprocal business favors, not for research help. As I have said earlier, only two firms, Smith Barney and H. C. Wainwright, were doing any professional quality research.

Institutions, particularly mutual funds, were beginning to be performance conscious, led by Gerald Tsai at Fidelity Fund in Boston. The earlier postwar bull market had lifted all boats, so investors had not yet begun to distinguish among asset managers on the basis of performance. That was about to change in a huge way and the market for good research would mushroom.

I regularized my economic analyses and continued to cover the paper industry, which was regarded as a growth industry. Corrugated shipping containers were replacing wooden crates, publishing was enjoying a postwar and post-Depression resurgence, and sanitary papers were invading the home market.

Jay began coverage of steel and insurance, and we made our first research hire, Bob Plumb, a Wharton MBA and ex-navy pilot, to cover nonferrous metals. Jay did a thorough job of creating a solid understanding of the insurance business and furthering an appreciation of the industry's ability to garner return on stockholder equity from the investment of premium flows. Bob became so expert at understanding nonferrous metal fundamentals and pricing that he was ultimately hired away from us by American Smelting and Refining.

We began to peddle our work in New York, Boston, Chicago, Minneapolis, and San Francisco. We were a bit shaky at first. Neither we nor our clients were accustomed to this new kind of relationship, whereby we were not selling specific securities as much as a continuing research service.

Drexel was well-known, but regarded as a regional firm. Some clients expected news and analyses of only Philadelphia area companies. Others wanted as much inside information as we could provide through partners' directorships. A prominent Boston mutual fund told me that Goldman Sachs had a couple dozen directorships among its partners, and provided monthly income statements to him on several of the companies.

Inside information was a tool of the trade. If you had it you could sell it. But we didn't have it to any meaningful degree. The Texas Gulf Sulphur case, which gave rise to the laws and rules governing inside information, did not occur until 1963-64. A senior officer of Texas Gulf Sulphur knew of an important mineral find in Ontario that could not be publicized until mineral rights were concluded. In the interim he bought stock for himself and tipped off some other people close to him. They profited handsomely. He and the others were prosecuted as criminals.

A chill settled on Wall Street. It and subsequent cases have resulted in extremely tight set of rules governing the use of "inside information" for personal gain or the gain of others to whom such information is given. Until then, the markets sought inside information, and it was traded widely in Wall Street. I benefited in a small way from a tip from an insider when Hoppy came back from a board meeting of the Finance Company of Pennsylvania, a closed-end investment company trading at a 25 percent discount from net asset value. He told us that the board had decided to have the company become open-ended, which meant that the price would rise to net asset value. We had the news several days before the public announcement and I bought all the stock I could afford. I realized a profit of about $1,500—very big for me at that time!

In a humorous and less profitable instance, we received information that the next issue of *Time* magazine would be running an article about a small mining company in New Mexico. The company, whose name I have forgotten, had discovered a huge cave full of bat guano—a potential fortune in fertilizer. The fifty-cent stock had already risen to a dollar when several of us jumped on board. Indeed, the article *was* in the next issue of *Time*, and the market reacted by sending the stock down to eighty cents. The moral of the story: if you hear so-called inside information, somebody else has probably heard it first.

My First Investment of Our Money

I must mention my very first purchase in the stock market, very early in my Drexel career. National City Bank, the ancestor of today's Citicorp, had a rights offering to stockholders. Stockholders could buy additional stock in amounts proportionate to their existing holdings at a discount to the current market price. Therefore the rights had value and traded on the stock exchange for the three weeks until the offer expired.

For reasons I cannot remember, the stock weakened and the rights, that had been selling at about a dollar, declined to ten cents. I gathered my nerve, figured I could gamble about $300, and bought the rights. That night when I told Warren what I had done, she was uncharacteristically furious. What was I doing jeopardizing our hard-earned savings? Fortunately, the rights went back to seventy cents and I pocketed a $1,800 profit. Warren said that would be the last time she would ever question my investment judgment. And it was. But we both have wondered what would have happened if I had lost the $300!

Rapid Growth of Research-Generated Commissions

Gradually, our little research department gained credibility. Commission income from stock transactions, which was less than a million dollars per year when we started, was becoming a major part of Drexel's revenue and profit. By 1960 we had a staff of five or six and were planning to expand further. Mutual funds were having a major growth spurt. Endowments, which had been overly conservative for too many years, were turning more confident as people began to understand that the U.S. economy was experiencing a new kind of stability. Depression fears had all but disappeared.

Volume on the New York Stock Exchange was rising rapidly, and we were gaining share of it. In 1956, daily volume was in a range of 1.2 to 3.9 million shares. By 1961 the volume ranged from 2.2 million shares to a high of 7.1 million shares. (Contrast this with today's volume that regularly runs 1.5-2.0 *billion* shares on the New York Stock Exchange and another 2.0 billion shares on NASDAQ (formerly called the Over-theCounter market, NASDAQ is an acronym for National Association of Security Dealers Automated Quotations.))

As our reputation gained ground, I began to be invited to make speeches at annual conventions of the National Federation of Financial Analysts, conferences sponsored by the National Industrial Conference Board, and local analysts' societies. These appearances further advanced our stature.

Jay and I Venture Abroad

In April 1960, Jay Sherrerd and I made our first trip abroad to London and Edinburgh, followed soon thereafter by trips to Paris and Geneva. It was the beginning of the development of an extensive business with foreign institutions. From that time on, we traveled to Europe at least annually and sometimes semiannually—mostly to London, Edinburgh, Paris, and Geneva—but also to Rome, Zurich, Basel, Munich, Perth, Lisbon, Amsterdam, Rotterdam, and Brussels.

At Ed Starr's suggestion, we had prepared for our trip by visiting Perry Hall, the senior partner of Morgan Stanley, who agreed to give us letters of introduction to see the major investment firms in London and Edinburgh. He was very curious about what we were selling. He couldn't believe that we would actually recommend specific stocks in writing. It would be many years before Morgan Stanley entered the institutional-research business. They were entirely committed to investment banking and had a long list of loyal blue-chip corporate clients. They did not view us as competition.

Through the Drexel/Morgan connections, we were to be hosted by Lord William Harcourt, the senior partner of Morgan Grenfell. Bill, as we eventually called him, proved to be very helpful in facilitating our visits to other London firms and assigned his son-in-law, Crispin Gascoigne, to be our guide and chief entertainer.

That first trip is one I will always remember. I had never been to Europe. Jay had been there once following his graduation from college. It was also my first trip by jet. When we arrived in London, a combination of jet lag, nervousness, and perhaps one too many drinks in the hotel the night before left me with a terrible hangover on our first morning. In addition to not feeling well, the Morgan Grenfell offices, where we were to see Lord Harcourt, had no central heating and were pervaded with a dankness and dampness remindful of a scene from Dickens. I was shivering in front of the "electric fire" when Lord Harcourt entered, looked at my pale face, and told me to go back to bed. What a beginning for our first foreign venture!

Jay and I each had specific stocks to talk about. We had learned that was the best approach rather than trying to sell them a research service. After four days of trying, we had not received any orders. Then on our last night, Richard Baker-Wilbraham, of Helbert-Wagg and Co., called us in the hotel to invite us for cocktails at his apartment and give us an order for ten thousand shares of Wellington Management Company, which had its initial public offering not long before our trip.

We were elated at our first order, modest as it was. When we returned home, Ed Starr remarked with humor that it seemed like a lot of wheel spinning for a small brokerage order. I set my jaw with determination and told him to "just wait and see." Indeed, it was the start of an excellent flow of business and many good friendships, particularly in London and Edinburgh.

Several years later, feeling the need for a European resident to guide us in marketing, we found Gian Carlo Cicogna—a cosmopolitan, sophisticated son of an Italian count—to head the European effort. Gian Carlo spoke four languages fluently, knew all the large potential clients, was charming to a fault, and was more than occasionally a real pain in the rear end. But he certainly knew his way around the financial centers of Europe and gave us a huge head start toward expanding our business there. He also was great at picking restaurants and hotels! His father had an ownership interest in a small private bank in Geneva and was particularly well connected in the Vatican. You should have seen Jay and me, secular Protestants to the core, trying to sell our research to the head of the Society for the Propagation of the Faith!

Before long, we were hosting "Drexel Forums" (conferences) in Paris and Geneva. They were very popular, and attendance, at the peak, was more than one hundred people from all over Europe and Britain at each forum.

Interestingly, there were very few firms competing for research-based brokerage business abroad. The most serious competition was from a new firm called Donaldson, Lufkin, and Jenrette, founded by three Harvard Business School classmates. We would often bump into one or more of the three of them while making the rounds in Britain and on the continent. Competition was friendly, and we had high mutual respect. As I write this, Bill Donaldson is the chairman of the Securities and Exchange Commission (SEC), having been variously the president of the New York Stock Exchange, the first dean of Yale's School of Management, and the CEO of Aetna. Our paths crossed many times over the years, and he will be back in this story again.

Clay Anderson Comes Onboard

In 1962 we hired a man who had been gently pushed out of Wellington Fund's research staff named Clay J. Anderson Jr., the son of one of my older colleagues at the Federal Reserve whom I admired and enjoyed very much. Clay Jr. had impressed me on several occasions. Warren and Clay had had adjacent desks at Wellington. She had great respect for his mind and market savvy. Jack Bogle was quite upset that the research people at Wellington had forced him to leave. Clay, first and foremost, was an original thinker. But there was no question he was an iconoclast and certainly not a person who would easily adjust to the kind of time-disciplined research-production line that Wellington had become.

Clay would add a tremendously important dimension to our research. He was always looking for the really big opportunity to make really big profits. He had a thorough knowledge of history in general and financial history in particular, which gave him a special kind of perspective.

The bear market of 1962 had two selling climaxes. The first, in May, was sparked by President Kennedy's tough stance against the steel industry's attempt to raise prices. The stock market had been in a speculative phase marked by a hot new issue market and a craze for compound annual growth rates. Compound annual growth became talked about as if it were a kind of organically inevitable mechanism that would send earnings and stocks, particularly stocks of small growth companies, higher and higher. So the steel price standoff was more of an excuse for the bear-market correction of speculative overvaluations than its cause.

The second selling climax came in October, precipitated by the Cuban Missile Crisis. When the Soviet ships carrying missiles for Cuban deployment turned around rather than face the American blockade, the stock market soared. I remember Hoppy standing near my desk, reading the news ticker, and then suddenly saying, "The Russians have turned around!" The feeling of relief in the atmosphere was palpable.

Coming off the bottom of the bear market, Clay presented both a historically supported argument and an economic rationale for why the stock market leadership would undergo a complete change. After past market breaks, the industries that had led the market during the bull phase were replaced by different industries as the market recovered. This we clearly illustrated in a series of scatter diagrams, plotting the previous market returns by industry on the vertical scale and the succeeding market on the horizontal scale. In each set of markets we could also document how and why the structure of economic growth had changed, and how those changes related to the changes in stock market leadership.

Using the thinking derived from this approach we correctly identified the industry leaders of the coming bull market, and directed our research effort toward those areas. At the time there were very few strategic approaches to portfolio construction. We were successful pioneers and our reputation soared.

In addition, Clay was quietly looking at the effects that the introduction of jet aircraft would have on the economics of airlines. The conclusions were that not only would demand skyrocket because of the increased speed and comfort but also costs per seat mile would drop significantly. Drexel became the authority on airlines as their earnings and stock prices doubled and redoubled in the space of a few years. They eventually became the Internet craze of their time.

My Low Price/Earnings Ratio Paper

In 1962, I wrote a research paper that drew attention. It was a study of the thirty Dow-Jones Industrial Stocks from 1937 through 1961. I calculated the price-earnings ratios of all thirty stocks at each year-end, ranked them from lowest to highest, and then tracked the performance in the following year. I found that the ten lowest P/Es substantially outperformed the middle ten and highest ten. Because the lowest ten P/Es are usually the dregs of the moment in the minds of investors, the study surprised many people, especially those who were committed to investing in recognized growth stocks. (For more on this, see the chapter called "On Investing.")

Subsequently, when computers came on the scene, we expanded the study to a much larger group, with the same results. Many academic studies have followed, most of which support my findings. But of all the work I have ever done and of all the papers I have published, that rather simple initial paper remains my signature work.

An Amusing Episode (in Hindsight)

While not amusing at the time, as I look back in the context of the recent outcry against companies bringing pressure on analysts to modify research conclusions, I can see that there is really nothing new in Wall Street. Here is what happened.

One of our analysts, Jerry Lakarnafeaux, wrote a report on General Foods, one of the bluest of the blue chips. His conclusion was that the company's apparent growth acceleration was due to nothing more than a decline in the price of coffee beans. The beans were a major raw material for the production of Maxwell House Coffee and Sanka, General Foods' major brands. Jerry had stated that the stock was overpriced relative to the company's slow growth rate.

Tom Gates, the former Drexel partner who had been Secretary of Defense under Eisenhower and was now chairman of J. P. Morgan, called me a few days after the report was published. The CEO of General Foods, he said, had just called him and was hopping mad. He told Tom that he should do something about his former firm putting out such trash about a quality company like General Foods. Tom called me and I listened as he ranted over the phone, asking me to retract the report. I told him that the evidence that we were right was overwhelming. We had used great care to make sure the conclusions were sound. I would not have the report retracted or rewritten. To his credit, Tom listened, and then muttered that at least he could tell General Foods, a major customer of his bank, that he had made a good faith effort. But, he admitted, it sounded as if we got it right.

Bill Baugh, Our Obsessive Analyst

I had known Bill Baugh for many years. He was a Penn graduate and son of a Penn Professor of English. His brother Dan was a fraternity brother of mine. Jay also knew him from their days at the Episcopal Academy. Bill was working to provide research to a retail sales staff at a local brokerage firm when he came to see me. I think it was 1963. He wanted a job as an analyst. Bill did not have the perfect set of credentials, but he was bright and he sure had enthusiasm. We hired him and he went to work on technology stocks.

Bill was a terrific in-depth analyst who did not know when to stop on his learning curve. He never seemed to know enough about a company and would obsess too often on small issues. He was the kind of guy who would protect against every eventuality in his personal life except the one that would hit him. Despite his shortcomings, he knew his companies well and came up with several big winning ideas. The biggest was Sony Corp., which was then a relatively unknown Japanese company that had the best color-TV technology. Bill was also very early in understanding the potential of cable TV and transistors.

Bill became an important player in my story some years later.

Fast Growth

Demand for Drexel's research services exploded. We began to hold "Drexel Forums" in various cities in both the U.S and abroad. In New York, Chicago, and San Francisco these were attended by hundreds of clients. We also individually traveled all over the map to visit clients in their offices and give luncheons and dinners where we spoke while clients ate. I was on the road at least ten days out of every month. I was also called upon to make numerous speeches, including keynote presentations, at several national conventions.

In a typical week, I arrived at the office at seven thirty and left at about five thirty. I made it a point to be home for our family dinner. When the children were young, I bathed them and read to them. When there were special school events, I did my best to build my schedule around them.

About every third week was set aside for travel. We usually traveled in pairs. Leaving on Sunday afternoon, we would spend entire weeks in some cities like New York and Boston. Typical schedules were two or three days in Chicago, Atlanta, Milwaukee, Minneapolis, San Francisco, and Los Angeles, trying as best we could to squeeze two cities into a week. The mornings were spent visiting at least two institutions, followed by lunch with three or four lesser clients, then two afternoon calls. Dinner was with still another group, although we tried to leave some dinners open to enjoy ourselves. It was hectic and tiring and Fridays came none too soon.

Commission income was growing rapidly. Our reputation increased to such a degree that when the *Institutional Investor* magazine polled their readership and asked what firms they would like to own if they went public, Drexel and Donaldson Lufkin and Jenrette were at the top of the list. The price-to-earnings multiple they were willing to pay was a lofty twenty even though there were no public financial statements. Knowing what I knew about the business, I told myself that I would never pay twenty time earnings for us!

The Harriman Ripley Merger

As noted earlier, I became a director of The Mead Corporation, a major forest products company, in 1963. In 1964, Drexel & Co. and Harriman Ripley, an old-line New York investment-banking firm, comanaged a $25 million bond issue for Mead. I had sole responsibility as the partner in charge of that financing. (In those days it was common for a company's investment banker to be on the board of directors. Now it is correctly viewed as a conflict of interest. Also, investment-banking relationships used to have a permanence to them that has long since disappeared.) It was my first such experience. Hal Berry, president of Harriman Ripley, worked with me. We got to know each other well.

A year or so later, Hal called me to invite me to lunch in New York. He said that he had been impressed by me and had looked at the quality research product we were producing. Did I, he asked, think there would be any interest among my associates in discussing the possibility of combining our two firms? He pointed out that we complemented each other. Drexel was strong in research and institutional brokerage while Harriman Ripley was a major underwriting firm. True, it had withered a bit, but the two firms together would reinvigorate the investment-banking business. Also, Harriman had a strong Chicago office that would give our research-generated brokerage a stronger presence in the Midwest. (Drexel had already opened an office in San Francisco.)

Drexel Harriman Ripley

It was an intriguing idea and I took it back to my partners for discussion. Drexel had faded as a first-line corporate underwriter and there was a strong desire among the investment-banking types to get back on the national scene with clients like Deere, Boeing, and Firestone—all clients of Harriman Ripley. We began negotiations.

The merger was effective in late 1965. Hoppy, who was approaching eighty at the time, said it was up to us. He was indifferent. Sadly, he was dead within a year, felled by a massive stroke as he returned from a Westinghouse board meeting. He was one of my heroes.

Drexel was much the more profitable firm, and came out of the merger with the larger share of stock ownership in what would be called Drexel Harriman Ripley, Incorporated. Our partnership days were over. Instead of being a partner I was now an executive vice president. Hal Berry would be chairman, and Bert Coleman, a capable, wealthy Philadelphian who had come to the firm only a few years earlier, would be president and CEO. That was all fine with me. I had no desire to run the organization. As long as my large contribution to the firm's profits was well recognized in my total compensation and I was left alone to manage the research effort, I would be happy.

As always happens, the corporate form tends to breed hierarchical structures. Vice presidents and assistant vice presidents proliferate. Jealousies arise. Infighting becomes part of the game. Drexel Harriman Ripley was no different. But not at the beginning.

A Strong Start

There was a long honeymoon as we successfully exploited our new geographical and investment-banking strengths. Offices were opened in Boston, Atlanta, Houston, San Francisco, and Paris. Aided by good markets between 1966 and 1969, our brokerage business exploded. Our Drexel Forums were sellouts. Analysts had difficulty handling both their research responsibilities and the demands on their time from the sales force.

Up until the merger, our research orientation, as opposed to block-trading expertise, meant that we were often compensated with so-called give-ups, whereby the firm executing the order simply sent a specified dollar portion of their commission to us rather than giving us the transaction. Remember that commissions were fixed by the New York Stock Exchange and were many times the percentage they are today. As I recall, they could run as high as 1.5 percent of the dollar value of a transaction. That compares with about 0.1 percent or less today.

As our business grew after the merger, we increasingly enjoyed block business, whereby a client might give us fifty thousand shares to either buy or sell, allowing us to seek institutions on the other side of the transaction, thus producing two commissions rather than one. Our commission revenue, which had been less than $500,000 when we started our research effort ten years before, was now $15 million or more—a lot of money in 1967.

But I Am Spread Too Thin

I found myself burdened with work I really did not enjoy—the management of a large group of people and coordinating their research activities along with the heavy demands of marketing. My travel schedule was more extensive than before. Additionally, I was asked to make too many speeches and presentations to groups of institutional brokerage customers, as well as being involved with cementing relationships with investment-banking clients. I had become the primary person in charge of our relationships with Scott Paper Co. and Rohm and Haas Co. in addition to being the point man with Mead. I had also maintained primary responsibility for several large investment-advisory clients, particularly the pension funds of both Philadelphia Electric and Penn Central.

My extracurricular activities included being a trustee of Penn, elected in 1966 and serving on the trustees' executive committee, a director of Mead, and a director of the Reliance Insurance Company, a large property insurance company in Philadelphia. I had also become Chairman of the Trustees of the Philadelphia Award, and president of the Financial Analysts of Philadelphia—the latter just in time to host the annual convention in Philadelphia.

I was spread too thin, with far too little time to think about substantive investment matters. I was feeling "put upon," simply overloaded, and doing many things I would rather not have been doing. I remember working in the vegetable garden one weekend in May and concluding that I wanted a simpler life.

Enter Jack Bogle

Jack Bogle and I had been playing golf together for about five years. Every Saturday morning, I picked him up at about 7:30 AM, and we walked the Merion Golf Club's West Course, carrying our own bags. We finished eighteen holes in just about two hours, which was as much time as we thought we wanted to be away from our families after our very busy weeks, and in my case, often being away for much of the week.

I thought Jack's life was simpler and more pleasant. He was doing things he really enjoyed. I went to talk with him to see if there was something we might do together that we might not do separately. He enthusiastically agreed that we should talk seriously. He had been concerned about the future of Wellington Management Company. Walter Morgan, Wellington's founder was still active, but had effectively turned management over to Jack.

Jack was particularly worried about Wellington's lack of a good growth-oriented fund. John Neff, who was in the process of becoming a legendary investor, had joined Wellington in 1962 to manage the Warwick Fund (it later became the Windsor Fund), but was a value-oriented investor. Jack had had some preliminary discussions with a Boston firm, Thorndike, Paine Doran and Lewis, about a possible combination. The Thorndike firm managed the Ivest Fund, a growth fund that had compiled an admirable record and was clearly going somewhere and would nicely complement Wellington's value orientation. They were a smart group of Harvard Business School types who had big ambitions. But how would I fit in?

And a Proposal

Jack and I spent a couple of days in Boston, having discussions about structuring a combination firm that would build a traditional money-management business in addition to mutual funds. The hierarchical questions were temporarily settled by all of us agreeing to the title of managing director. Jack and I would be based in Philadelphia. It looked as if my compensation would be roughly the same as at Drexel but my business life would be considerably less complicated. This was probably a naïve hope, but I latched on to it.

After further refining the concept, I decided to break the news to Drexel that I would be leaving. I thought my decision was final.

A Counterproposal

The firm's reaction was swift and decisive. After telling me to wait a few days, they came to me with a proposal. They would create a new class-C stock that would be credited with ten times the retained earnings that the ordinary stock received. In other words, its book value would grow ten times as fast. There were two other parts to the proposal. First, I could have any title I chose, although I would not be CEO because the research effort needed me to manage it. Second, they would lend me $100,000 to be invested in securities of my choice, with any profit accruing to me but none of the losses. Such an offer would be unacceptable today, but at that time it was stunningly attractive. With a family to think about, I had no choice but to take it. I would become president of Drexel Harriman Ripley in the fall.

Jack Bogle was crushed. I was too, having had a small taste of possibly going back to research and portfolio management—my two primary loves. Jack went ahead with the merger and was actually fired by his new partners a few years later. His firing gave birth to his new creation, the Vanguard Group, which has become a mutual-fund giant. Jack has become a giant also, a real leader in an industry that desperately needs the kind of integrity he has brought to it.

I have maintained a very strong friendship with Jack. His brother-in-law and my partner, Jay Sherrerd, has always maintained that Jack and I would not have been good partners because we are both strong Type A personalities that would eventually clash. He may be right.

Back to the Grind

I was able to tackle my responsibilities at the firm with renewed vigor. For the next three years, I worked harder than I have ever worked before or since. It was from 7:30 AM to 6:30 PM on most days, with briefcases full of homework. Travel, speeches, meetings, and directorships all on top of doing enough research to make presentations of substance and direct the whole effort. Jay was an immense help and took over much of the day-to-day management responsibilities in the research department while I became ever more involved with other activities as a member of the executive committee, particularly planning for the future.

Sara Carter Vogel

I had a very efficient secretary, really a full-fledged assistant, who had been with me since 1960. Sara Carter was in her midthirties, attractive, well educated, and at her peak, she was the best I have ever seen at taking shorthand and typing. In addition to having an assistant, I had a good friend. In 1965 Sara married Bill Vogel, who would soon thereafter become a common-pleas court judge in Montgomery County, Pennsylvania.

Sara, or Sally as I called her, actually ran me and my business affairs for the next thirty-nine years. She knew everything about me, my schedule, clients, other employees, and how to separate the wheat from the chaff before it reached me. I could not have navigated those busy years without her. In her forties, she was afflicted with rheumatoid arthritis but continued to work despite the pain. She retired in 1999, but we continue to talk regularly as very good friends.

Problems and Planning

The exponential increase in trading activity on Wall Street led to a severe problem that began to arise in late 1966 and continued for the next several years. Predictably, perhaps, the mechanisms for the receipt and delivery of securities became terribly overloaded as trading volume soared to fifteen to twenty million shares per day, about triple the level of only a few years before.

Huge delays in deliveries among firms caused backups in the settlements. When a firm's clients sold securities, the client was paid upon delivery, but then the firm involved had to collect from the firm whose client had bought the security. There was a clearinghouse that could take care of some of this load but not all. Computer systems were, for the most part, still in the punch-card era. The sheer volume of shares being traded strained the back offices of all firms and "fails"; that is, failures to deliver securities in time for specified settlement dates skyrocketed.

Rising fails took their toll on profits. When a firm failed to deliver yet had to pay the customer who had delivered to it, the delay had to be financed with working capital that, in turn, had to be bolstered by bank borrowings. Interest costs went through the roof, and we had the ironic combination of soaring business and declining profits. We had faith that time and technology would cure the problem, but in the meantime, most of Wall Street was on the ropes. Although back offices went to twenty-four-hour operations, it took almost two years to straighten things out.

Planning for the Prospect of Negotiated Commissions

By the midsixties, the SEC was talking with the New York Stock Exchange about moving from fixed commissions to negotiated commissions. They maintained that the "give up" system, whereby a firm would give up part of its commission on large orders to other firms at the direction of the customer, was prima facie evidence that commission rates were too high. Wall Street fought back for a while, but it was clear that sooner rather than later, negotiated commissions would happen.

Our executive committee began to discuss the implications of negotiated commissions, particularly whether their advent would necessitate a basic change in our business model of relying on research-generated commissions. I was appointed to study the issue and present some conclusions by mid-1969. It meant surveying our customers about their intentions, estimating what the new level of commissions might be, projecting what growth in trading volume we might expect, and examining the whole structure of the future growth of institutional-asset management.

I needed help, so I enlisted the efforts of Riggs Parker, a lawyer who had joined us from Drinker, Biddle and Reath, our firm's counsel. Riggs was a smart, sensible guy who had a good way of connecting the dots. I also hired Frank Burger, a young man with a management consulting firm, to put the data together.

We worked for about a year. The basic issue, after cutting through the noise, was whether institutional money management and the research-generated business would be growing at a fast-enough rates at least to offset the lower commission rates over the coming decade.

If not, what should we do? Devote increased resources to building the corporate investment banking business? Begin a major push into retail brokerage where the pressure on commissions would probably not be as severe?

For me, the time spent on the study was a big subtraction from my research efforts in a period when calls on my time to meet with clients and give speeches were unabated. All the while, moreover, the fails problem continued to plague us and significantly impaired profitability. It seemed clear to some of us that we were not doing as well as some competitors in meeting the challenge of fails. There was no critical crash effort to analyze and solve the problems.

We presented our conclusions to the executive committee in May 1969. In essence, our recommendations were to stay the course, have faith in the growth of assets under professional money managers and growing trading volume, and expect the market share of mutual funds and large money managers to expand at the expense of traditional institutions such as banks and insurance companies. Yes, negotiated commissions would hurt profitability for a while, but the longer term would be okay. While an expanded effort in investment banking was a worthwhile strategy, there was no need to enter the retail-brokerage business.

The business that looked most attractive was discretionary institutional-money management, and we made a strong recommendation to begin such a business. It would be quite different from our traditional nondiscretionary investment-advisory business and would provide another outlet for our research work. It would, however, put us in competition with some of our brokerage clients.

After intense discussion, the executive committee accepted our recommendations. The marketing and research people breathed a sigh of relief.

The Apple Cart Is Upset!

I planned to take the month of July to spend at Rockywold Camp on Squam Lake where we had been going for the past three years. I was very tired and ready for a vacation.

During the third week of July, Gene Cheston, who headed the firm's marketing activities and was a good friend, called me. His news was shocking. The executive committee, acting in my absence, had decided to reject the recommendations they had accepted only several weeks before.

I was speechless. How could they possibly do this, particularly with no further discussions with me, the person who had made the recommendations? I don't understand it to this day. I was furious. When we arrived home a week later, I angrily told Bert Coleman that I was leaving. I was insulted at the way they made the decision and felt that I could never work with them again. Jay Sherrerd and Clay Anderson, my two closest associates in the firm, were also appalled, as was Gene Cheston.

Cooler heads tried to calm me down. Riggs Parker made a special effort to convince me that leaving would be counterproductive for all concerned. Wouldn't I, he pleaded, spend the next several months helping the firm emerge from the continuing fails problem that was eating up our profits?

Very reluctantly and without any enthusiasm, I said I would stay and try to help. That was in early August. But I continued to stew about the future. I hated the job I had accepted, and even knowing it was temporary did not help.

CHAPTER SIX

Miller, Anderson & Sherrerd

The Birth of a New Firm

One day in early September of 1969, after being frustrated over some issue I cannot now remember, I stormed into Jay's office and said simply, "I can't take it anymore. I'm leaving. Do you want to go with me?"

Jay's response was immediate. "You bet. Let's do it!"

Within an hour, we decided that Clay Anderson should join us in whatever we decided to do. Down the hallway, we went to ask him. He also made the decision to leave on the spot. The three of us decided we needed some additional research talent and tapped Bill Baugh to go with us.

We needed other help as well. Jay, Clay, and I were very attached to our assistants, Sally Vogel, Fritzie Flack, and Karen Mahoney. When we told them what we were doing and asked them to join us, they each said yes immediately.

Fritzie had an afterthought, and asked, "You are going to pay us, aren't you?" Then she added, "Just don't leave me here!" Sally, Fritzie, and Karen were willing to trust in our ultimate success even though we would start with zero business on the books. For that, I have always been extremely grateful.

We had no real idea of what we would do, where we would do it, or how we would do it. Initially, there was no business plan and only a vague concept that we verbalized as "wanting to manage money, not people."

Jay and I remembered the great line from Robert Frost's poem: "Two roads diverged in a wood and I,/ I took the one less traveled by;/ And that has made all the difference." We took it as our private motto.

We certainly didn't know that we had just given birth to Miller, Anderson & Sherrerd, a highly successful business to which we would devote the balance of our careers.

We had to tell the firm the news that four of us, the four who were the real backbone of the research department and who had been primarily responsible for its reputation, were leaving.

I also had to tell my dad. He was so proud of his son being the president of Drexel that I was unsure just how he would react. We had lunch at the Racquet Club, and over a drink in the bar, I told him the whole story and how determined we were to start a new firm.

His comment was, very simply, "You sure have balls, kid!"

It was very big news, appearing in all the major newspapers as soon as a press release was written. We worked to make the parting sound as amicable as possible. It was in the interest of both parties to do so. For the most part, people in the firm wished us well, but the relations between me and certain executive-committee members were very strained. When Hal Berry called me to rant and rave, I told him to go to hell, and hung up. We were told that it would be best if we left as soon as possible, preferably within two weeks.

I would be forty-two in three weeks, Jay was thirty-nine, and Clay was forty-four. We tabulated our capital. Amazingly, we each had $200,000 cash capital available.

Flirting with Capital Research

Could we do it alone? Or should we seek a partner, another firm that would give us a jumpstart with an established record, computer systems, and other infrastructure? If the latter, who?

We all had huge respect for a Los Angeles firm called Capital Research and Management, a mutual-fund management company that was planning to enter the pension and endowment asset-management business. Jon Lovelace, the son of the founder of the firm, had become a good friend of mine. We were both members of a small group of investment people who went away together twice a year to talk about investment and economic issues. When Jon heard we were leaving Drexel, he enthusiastically invited us to come see his firm about our either being the East Coast branch of Capital Research or their owning a piece of the new firm.

We were very impressed with what we saw. Their record was superb—not flashy, but extremely solid. It was a record that was very saleable and would give us a head start in garnering assets.

The Decision to Go It Alone: Feeling Free

On the plane back to Philadelphia, we gathered around a table in the first-class cabin to talk about what we had heard and seen. We were very tempted, but it lacked an important ingredient: the independence that comes only with 100 percent ownership. Bill Baugh was the one who finally verbalized what we all had been thinking: let's go it alone! By the time the plane landed, the decision had been made to start our own business.

I had an immense feeling of relief—a sense of being free from all the demands and obligations that had grown around me, almost like prison walls, over the previous few years. What I had been trying to accomplish in my flirtation with Jack Bogle's firm three years earlier was now going to be done in a way that was much more in harmony with my temperament.

It was mid-September; we had to vacate our offices in two weeks and had no place to go. In addition to finding some physical space, we also had to name the firm. Because I was the best known of the four of us, it was assumed that my name would come first. Jay and Clay drew straws to see who would be second. We had an agreement with Bill Baugh that he would not be a name partner.

At my direction, Jay, Clay, and I took equal shares of two-sevenths, and Bill received a one-seventh share. I certainly could have taken a larger share but decided that our relationship would be much healthier if we were equal. I believe that decision paid for itself many times over.

We Could Run the Money, But Who Would Run Us?

One question bothered us. Who would do all those things like accounting, payroll, taxes, and dealing with lawyers and regulators? These were tasks we not only did not like but also we were lousy at doing. I had a solution. I would talk to Warren about it.

That night I asked Warren if she would be interested in going back to work. Her job would be to run us, meaning doing all the things we would be too busy to do and did not enjoy doing but needed to be done

Warren's answer was a brief "Would I ever!" And she did for the next fifteen years. Our children were the perfect age for her to take on this job. Buzz was nine, Kathy was eleven, and Winky was almost thirteen. They were in school all day, and Warren vowed that she would always be home to meet them after school. She came to the office after nine and left at three.

A Few Other Possibilities, But . . .

I had several interesting phone calls during the short interim before we announced the founding of the new firm. One was from Dick Dillworth, who asked if I might be interested in joining him at Rockefeller Brothers. Another was from Bill Donaldson of Donaldson Lufkin and Jenrette. Out of courtesy, I went to see Bill in New York. He wanted me to join his firm and would even provide a car and driver for commuting from Philadelphia. I couldn't conceive of anything that I would enjoy less. However, Bill and I have always been friends, and it was he who was responsible for my becoming a trustee of the Ford Foundation thirteen years later.

Open for Business with a Unique Business Strategy

On October 15, 1969, we officially opened for business. Formal announcements that listed the names of the partners were run in all the major papers, including the various regional editions of the *Wall Street Journal*.

Our business strategy was unique. We knew that if we had more than fourteen accounts, we would have to go through the red tape of registering with the SEC. We made known that we would limit ourselves to fourteen clients and would require a minimum initial account size of $20 million.

And a Primitive Office

We set up shop in a relatively new poor-quality building in Bala-Cynwyd. The furniture was all rented. Our office on the first floor had been designed as retail space, so there was a large display window that we kept covered with a venetian blind. We contracted for nine hundred square feet in a new building across the street that would be available in a few months.

A Pioneer Boutique

We were immediately labeled an "investment boutique." The firm was a pioneer. Only one other similar firm was beginning at the time: Jennison Associates in New York.

After we left Drexel, the press hounded us for the "real story" of our departure. In interviews, we always maintained that the parting had been amicable, but we were sure that other players might say otherwise. Amazingly, they did not, presumably because it was in everyone's self-interest not to have the facts widely known. Popular opinion was that we would take several prime Drexel accounts with us. We steadfastly denied that we would do so and never did.

Later, we found out that most people thought we were starting up with several accounts already signed up. Far from it!

Some Great Publicity

Institutional Investor magazine, a relatively new publication, had become the most popular publication among investment pros. It was a clever combination of meaty, interesting articles on investing and a gossip medium. Because I had been a featured speaker at several of their annual conferences, I knew the publisher, Gil Kaplan. Gil sent a reporter to see us, and we held our breath.

The result, when it finally was published in January, was a stunning piece of good publicity for us. We were the feature article, with a bust of me on the front cover. The article was flattering, had ample quotes from all of us, referred to our excellent research reputation, and wondered what I had seen in the future of asset management that had prompted the move.

We, of course, used copies of the article quite effectively in our marketing.

Initial Marketing

We began to develop a full set of marketing materials:

- We said we were a firm that would devote intensive attention to client portfolios.
- We emphasized our valuation consciousness.
- We stressed our approach of designing portfolios to take advantage of shifting patterns of economic growth.
- We said that there was little evidence that large research departments enabled institutions to achieve superior performance. We would use Wall Street research as a library and not as a source of recommendations.
- We pointed to the record of the Drexel Equity Fund as evidence of our abilities. (Clay had been the fund's portfolio manager.)
- We gave fee discounts to nonprofit organizations.

We made dozens of phone calls and wrote many letters. We did not expect fast results. We were prepared to wait a complete year without any compensation to ourselves.

Our First (and Last) Capital Contribution

Our employees were four in number; we had added Grace Taylor, a lady who seemed to know what the primitive computers of the time were all about, to keep track of clients' accounts. We had a payroll to meet and rent to pay, so each of the three of us put up $75,000 and Bill half that amount. Thus, our initial capital was $262,500. Actually, only $70,000 of that total was put up in cash, and the balance remained uncalled. We reckoned that was about three months' expenses. In the entire history of the firm, there was never another penny of cash capital contributed by any of us.

The Big Break

The first breakthrough came in early November. George Stewart, treasurer of Johns Hopkins University, said he wanted to meet with us. We had called regularly on George and his predecessor for several years, giving them our research conclusions, answering their queries, and giving our thoughts on portfolio strategy.

The university's investment committee was unhappy with their current investment advisors, who had been only advising the committee, not running the money on a discretionary basis. After meeting with George, we met with several individual committee members and then the committee as a whole. Because both Jay and I were active with universities (I had become a trustee of Penn three years earlier), they seemed comfortable talking to us as peers rather than a couple of young guys trying to sell something. We made our pitch and waited. Soon thereafter, George called to tell us that we would be hired to manage $50 million of endowment as of the beginning of 1970.

You can imagine the whoops that went up. Our first account would be the endowment of a high-prestige university! A fee of about $200,000!

Did we really know what we were doing? We thought so, but in the first week of managing the Hopkins money, we had several trading errors. I remember that Jay and I both sold the same holding of Atlantic Refining. Fortunately, the stock went down after the sale, and the broker covered at a profit.

Year One: In the Black

I remember the elation I felt even while doing such simple chores as collating marketing material. We did this by each of us walking around a table and picking up pages in order and stapling them together. Everybody was enthusiastic about doing the smallest tasks. Our optimism was high, and Jay and I joked about wading waist high in thousand-dollar bills by year-end.

By the end of April, we had four additional accounts: Colgate University and the pension funds of Smith Kline and French, Sun Oil, and J. C. Penney. By then, we were well in the black ink before partners' compensation. More accounts followed over the next two years, including Texas Instruments, Cooper Union, and Wesleyan University. We ended our first year with a solid profit, well ahead of our plan, and with our fourteen-account limit more than half absorbed.

Reaching Escape Velocity

The investment-management business enjoys great economics. Fees charged are calculated as a percent of asset. For smaller accounts, our fee was 0.5 percent. The fee was scaled down for size, so for a $100 million account, the fee might be about 0.3 percent or $300,000. Costs rise in a very lumpy fashion as a firm sporadically adds people to meet the time and talent needs. In-between these lumpy-cost increases, a very high proportion of increased fees flow through to the bottom line.

Over the next three years, we added clients rapidly, including the Carnegie Corporation of New York, the Carnegie Institution of Washington, the German Marshall Fund, Williams College, the Baptist Ministers and Missionaries Pension Fund, and the Philadelphia Orchestra Endowment.

We also instituted a performance-based fee for a few accounts that wanted it, and in 1971 we outperformed sufficiently to earn extra money. My share, over $500,000, was beyond anything I had imagined. It proved to be a temporary high point, but by

1973 our profits were rising rapidly, and my share of the partnership's income was more than three times the income I had been earning at Drexel Harriman Ripley.

We had reached what we humorously called escape velocity, a term from the space program referring to the speed necessary to leave the gravity of the earth and enter orbit. The firm's name had become well-known, and we had gained an excellent reputation; we were receiving excellent press in *Institutional Investor*, *Pension News*, and other publications. Inquiries were coming to us from many potential clients.

I continued to be invited to speak at meetings of various analysts' societies and conventions, the National Industrial Conference Board, and *Institutional Investor's* conferences in, among other places, London, Toronto, Los Angeles, San Francisco, New York, and of course, Philadelphia. I labored over these talks and believe they did our firm a service in two ways. First, they were good marketing in getting our name out there. Second, making a talk focuses the mind. It forces you to think through the meaning and consequences of a particular economic and financial environment in a disciplined way to reach rational conclusions.

ERISA

The Employees Retirement Income Security Act was passed in 1974. In effect, it made every investment manager a fiduciary. It also required that managers who managed pension funds be registered with the SEC. We had reached our fourteen-account limit and knew that we had the clout to go considerably beyond that limit. We had no choice but to register and free ourselves for another wave of expansion.

Two New Partners

With a full stable of clients and looking to further expansion, we needed help. Each of us was by now (1973) carrying a full load of research, portfolio management, and client-relations responsibilities. We began to search for top talent that would also be compatible with the other partners. Several friends on the sell side of the business suggested that we get to know Morris Williams, a vice president and portfolio manager at the Mellon Bank in Pittsburgh.

After Jay paid an initial visit to him in Pittsburgh, we invited Morris to Bala-Cynwyd to talk and look at the Philadelphia area to see if he might consider a move. All of us were very taken with him. He was a Duke graduate, married, with two young daughters, and seemed to have both the abilities we were seeking and a value system that fit well. We hired him with the understanding that there would be a period of up to two years before we might accept him into the partnership. We did not wait that long, and Morris became a partner in 1975.

Meanwhile, a former colleague, a man I hired at Drexel & Co. in 1964, Tom Beach, approached us with a fervent desire to join us. Tom, a very bright guy, had graduated from Michigan and the Harvard Business School. After our departure, he and Ernest Widman had set up shop as a research boutique with only moderate success. With Morris now with us, we saw no immediate need, particularly for an equity-oriented person. However, Tom was able to convince us that we should begin to build a fixed-income management business. He would train himself to take on that responsibility. We finally capitulated.

We ended the 1970s with six partners, a dozen employees, and about a billion dollars under management.

The 1970s: Not an Auspicious Starting Time

It is a great wonder in retrospect, and especially looking at that period in the context of subsequent changes in investment structures and attitudes, that we had such a good start.

Beginning in the last half of the 1960s, inflation rates began to rise, approaching 6 percent by 1970. Actually, the inflation rate rose every year from 1962 to 1970. President Nixon tried to put price controls on in an ill-conceived move that had no permanent effect. The economy went into recession in 1972-73, but in 1973-74, inflation took off again, rising to 11 percent in 1974 after the OPEC oil cartel showed its muscle.

Afraid of the negative effects of soaring oil prices, monetary authorities around the world, including the Federal Reserve, did not tighten the financial markets and effectively validated the OPEC move to raise oil prices.

Long-term bond yields rose sharply, with the thirty-year U.S. Treasury bond yield climbing steadily to reach over 8 percent by early 1978. It was an era of a "stop and go" economy that was called stagflation, a combination of high inflation and unsatisfactory economic growth. It was a tough time for both stocks and bonds. By late 1979, both the Treasury one-year and thirty-year bonds were yielding over 10 percent. The inflation rate that year was over 11 percent and would rise to 13.5 percent in 1980.

Our primary business was managing common-stock portfolios. Consider that over the ten-year period from 1968 to 1978, U.S. Treasury bills outperformed common stocks. Then add the characteristics of the bull market of 1971-1973. It was a bubble, but the bubble was limited to a handful of blue-chip growth companies that became known as the nifty fifty. The advocates of these growth stocks called them "one decision" stocks, stocks you simply put in your safe and forgot about. No need, said this approach's advocates, to analyze the economy or forecast interest rates; these stocks would weather everything, and one need not worry.

Investors with any sense of market history and who placed trust in fair valuation as a prerequisite for investment were appalled at the prices to which these stocks soared. To make matters worse, the rest of the market looked fairly priced, even cheap. That's where we had our clients' money invested. This fairly priced segment of the market did not just sit there; it did something. It went down while the nifty fifty continued to rise! It was the most frustrating market of my career.

Finally, in 1973 the bear market set in, and everything went down. It was the worst bear market since the 1930s. Amazingly, we lost no clients during the two years when the nifty fifty were carrying the market averages higher and higher while our portfolios declined. But in December 1974, at the bottom of the bear market, Wesleyan University had had enough. They took all the funds being managed by both us and other managers and placed them with a manager who had been entirely in Treasury bills. Unfortunately for Wesleyan, that manager stayed in that defensive position as the market recovered.

A full five years later, we were the rare firm that could say that we had lost only one account during our entire history. We could also say that we had zero turnover among our partners and staff.

I believe we were able to keep the business intact and grow it because we had established very strong relationships with clients and communicated with them regularly, not just at periodic meetings. They knew what we were thinking and thought we were rational even if wrong!

Fixed-income Management: A New Business

Coming out of the bear market of 1972-1974, we had decent performance. And while we didn't regain all of our performance shortfall that had occurred during the market's nifty-fifty days right away, both we and our clients were satisfied.

However, while prior to the bear market most clients were focused almost entirely on equities, the interest in fixed-income as a managed part of portfolios was increasing..

There were strong reasons for this. First, bond yields, which had provided very poor returns after inflation during the 1960s and early 1970s, had risen to the point where real returns not only began to look possible but also might be competitive with equities. Second, the bear market had inflicted enough pain that pension funds and endowments saw fixed-income as a way to dampen volatility.

There were very few firms specializing in fixed-income management. In fact, it was not even widely acknowledged as a necessary skill before the 1970s.

We had been managing the fixed-income portions of several balanced accounts and had compiled quite a respectable record. This led us to see fixed-income management as an opportunity, but we lacked both the time and the skills to pursue it. Tom Beach was making some attempt at it, but his first love was the equity market. We kept our eyes open for someone who might fit.

In 1978, Tom said that he had heard a man from Goldman Sachs—an economist who specialized in money markets, bond markets, and analyzing interest-rate moves— speak at a conference. Coincidentally, I had recently read something this man had written. Still very young, he had not yet been considered in Goldman Sachs's latest round of making new partners.

The man's name was Richard Worley. Rich was soft-spoken, very analytical, obviously bright and well educated, and very pleasant. We did a courting dance for a couple of weeks and hired him to help us build a fixed-income portfolio-management business. If he did well, we told him, there was a partnership waiting in two years.

Hiring Rich Worley was the most important single decision we made to further the firm's growth. Over the next fifteen years, he would build one of the two top fixed-income businesses in the country. Miller, Anderson & Sherrerd, which was all-equity management in 1978, would become very heavily weighted toward fixed-income management by the early 1990s.

When Rich came onboard in September 1978, we were managing almost a billion dollars. We had twenty-one clients and twenty-two people.

Paul Volcker was named chairman of the Federal Reserve in 1979. He was determined to put an end to the virulent inflation of the 1960s and '70s. He began to do so almost immediately, and bond prices plummeted (interest rates skyrocketed).

Inflation psychology is a hard thing to kill, and it took considerable time. Inflation, as noted earlier, peaked at 13.5 percent in 1980, the first year of Volcker's term. One-year Treasury yields peaked in March of 1980 at 15.8 percent, subsided, and then spiked again to16.7 percent in August of 1981. The long-term thirty-year Treasury reached a peak yield of 14.7 percent in September 1981 and stayed well into the double digits for four more years. Even after yields subsided, they remained in the historically high range of 7 to 9 percent through 1993.[1]

All the while, the inflation rate was dropping significantly to as low as 1.9 percent in 1986. Thus, the inflation-adjusted return from bonds was extremely attractive. In retrospect, one can easily see why fixed-income management came into its own during this period.

Under Rich Worley's leadership, the firm became an authority on mortgage-backed securities, beginning with the AAA-rated mortgage-backed securities of Government National Mortgage Association, known as Ginnie Mae, where the mortgages are federally guaranteed. These securities were not well understood by many traditional fixed-income investors and therefore provided yield premiums well above what their quality and liquidity should have indicated. They were a cornerstone of our portfolios, and when

---

[1]   I am sorry for the need to insert here a note for the many nonfinancial types reading this. First, understand that as bond yields rise, bond prices decline. For example, if a bond pays a 6 percent coupon, $60 per $1,000, to yield 6 percent, then if interest rates rise, say, to 8 percent, the bond must go down in price to the point where the 6 percent coupon is providing the higher yield.

Second, U.S. Treasury bonds are not only the best credit quality in the world but also are extremely liquid. They can be converted to cash in twenty-four hours. They are the standard against which all other fixed-income securities are measured. Thus, when we speak of Treasury yields of 15 percent, we are also saying that many borrowers were paying 20 percent or even more.

rates finally dipped from their peaks, we scored a fantastic annual return of over 50 percent for our clients. The fixed-income client list grew rapidly.

Tom Bennett became a partner in early 1984 to help Rich run the mushrooming fixed-income business. Tom had been in the pension-management department at DuPont in Wilmington. Quiet and efficient, a big horse of a man, with good humor and a loud laugh, Tom was a key addition.

The Knob Family

At Drexel & Co., the head trader was a man named Ed Knob. A really nice guy, Ed had served in the marine corps during the war. If he had had the benefits of a college education, he could have been a world beater. Eddie and I had become good friends, and I missed his market expertise.

After about eighteen months of trying to handle our brokerage orders ourselves, it became obvious that we needed professional help. Ed had moved to Laird and Co. in Wilmington and was happy there but was interested in coming with us. He made a big difference in our capabilities. He joined us in the spring of 1971. One look at how the business was expanding led Eddie to say we needed still more help, and Ed suggested his daughter Mary Ann, nicknamed "Pinky." She had just graduated from Gettysburg College. Equally as bright as her dad, Pinky allowed us to expand comfortably, particularly in the fixed-income area.

When Ed died in 1996, both Jay and I spoke at his memorial service, and the U. S. Marine Corps Honor Guard was in attendance.

As this is being written, Pinky is still working in her thirty-third year with the firm and its successor. And her son, who had a summer job in the mailroom, will be going to Penn. Eddie would be very proud.

Equities Did Well Too

Another key person was added to the partnership in 1981 after a year's tryout. Dave Atkinson had been a partner of Tom Beach in an unsuccessful attempt to create a management company to manage the endowment of the University of Pennsylvania. He then had joined Morgan Stanley in research.

Dave, a Cornell graduate with an MBA from Wharton, is a very good investor. He is devoted to finding money-making ideas. He is a man of few words, but when he speaks them, they rush at you in whole paragraphs at lightning speed. Wry humored, caustic at times, and always very blunt, even undiplomatic, Dave is never in doubt, although not always correct. He was a big addition to our group.

As a firm, we correctly identified the overwhelming investment consideration of the 1980s. It was disinflation. Businesses that had either been hurt severely by inflation or companies that were perceived as not having earnings that were sufficiently responsive to high inflation—like food processors, retailers, and stable service businesses—appeared attractive to anyone who was convinced that the juice was really being squeezed out of inflation. Between Dave and Morris Williams, whose temperament has always seemed to lead him to steady moderate growth, we selected stocks very well.

In 1987, on my sixtieth birthday, the stock market took a terrifying dive of over 20 percent in a single day. We had been cautious most of the year, feeling that stock prices had moved up too far, relative to an increase in interest rates that had been occurring. But nobody saw the big break coming.

In the middle of the day, the office surprised me with a birthday party, complete with cake and champagne. As we were uncorking the bottle, Eddie Knob stuck his head in the door and yelled, "We're down more than five hundred points!" We looked at one another, shrugged our shoulders, and drank a toast to our clients.

What might have been a soft continuing correction was severely aggravated by something called portfolio insurance, a stupid concept at best. A firm in California had studied past markets and had determined that if an investor had sold a proportion of his holdings after a specified percentage decline in prices, then continued to do so as a market decline continued, then bought stocks back after specified percentage increases in prices, he could both stabilize returns and garner most of the benefits of the upward long-term trend of prices. It was called portfolio insurance, a plan that "insured" a portfolio against major loss while enabling it to enjoy most of the gains. With a herd instinct, many investors, particularly pension funds, bought this "insurance."

When stock prices declined in September and October, they reached the trigger point for sales, sales at any price, of a major portion of insured portfolios. The rush to sell was the match that lit the fire, and it was followed by a more general panic.

A part of the crash was recovered in short order, but the stock market remained in a funk at substantially lower prices than before the event. Throughout 1988, we were able to find very attractive opportunities.

Our equity portfolios were poised to benefit from what turned out to be a continuation of a major bull market that had begun in 1982. They did. By the late 1980s, we had compiled excellent records in both equities and fixed-income. Assets under management rose rapidly to $5 billion in 1984, $10 billion in 1986, $15 billion in 1988, $20 billion in 1989, $25 billion in1992, and eventually grew to over $30 billion. We added many more partners during the '80s and early '90s so that we eventually had twenty-two by 1996.

Two of Our Founding Partners Die

By the mid-1970s, it had become clear to us—particularly to Jay, me, and Warren—that Clay Anderson was an alcoholic. We talked gently about it to him, and he promised to do something about it. He went to a "dry out" place for a short while, but it didn't last for very long, and he was soon back where he had been.

In 1979, Jay and I talked more forcefully to him and suggested that he cut back his firm interest. He did so, but eventually, we mutually decided he should become a limited partner. Jay and I believe he was disappointed in his own ability to master the swiftly changing markets of the 1970s and lost his confidence. In any event, he was really a noncontributor after the early '70s. It was a shame. In his prime, Clay had been the best investor and one of the more interesting people I have known.

Sadly, in 1982 Clay developed pancreatic cancer. By the time he knew it, he was already dying. Lasting only a few weeks, Clay died in December of 1982. He was fifty-six.

In November 1980, Bill Baugh knocked on my office doorframe (we seldom closed our doors) and said he must talk to me right away. I was very busy at that moment, and knowing Bill's tendency to think everything was urgent, I told him that a few minutes later would be more convenient. No, he said that it couldn't wait.

"I'm going to die" was his opening sentence. We all knew Bill was a hypochondriac. I used to tease him by saying that his epitaph would read, "I told you I was sick."

But this was not hypochondria. Bill had advanced melanoma, the result of having a growth on his back that was removed about eighteen months prior, accompanied by a pathological report that misdiagnosed it as a blue nevis, not melanoma. He turned to extreme dieting and anything else that he could turn to but to no avail. Bill died in April 1981 at the age of fifty-one.

Bill had been a sporadic but significant contributor to our equity results. He was an expert on technologies and correctly spotted the beginnings of the electronic revolution, the emergence of Japan as an economic and tech powerhouse, and the future potential of cable television. He was among the first owners of an Apple computer. He would have been in his element in the 1990s.

Redistributing the Partnership

For the first decade or so of the firm's existence, Jay and I effectively made the decisions on the distribution of interests in the firm. We were always predisposed toward having a true partnership and not holding on to control forever. When new partners came along, we tended to be generous in allotting interests.

In the mid-1980s, at a meeting of the partners, Jay and I told the younger ones that if they grew the firm, they would get the bulk of the benefits. We would reduce our percentage interests.

We did that; and in a very short time, with rapid growth, we equalized our shares among six partners: Jay and me, Morris Williams, Tom Beach, Rich Worley, and Dave Atkinson.

Permanence of Interest and Liquidity: Ongoing Concerns

As the firm grew, our personal incomes grew enormously. But there was no way to capitalize on the value of the firm. Also, as a general partnership, there was no way to have a permanent interest. When a partner died, for example, his interest in the firm was bought by the other partners at book value, a number well below the actual going-concern value.

Our solution was to create permanent limited-partnership interests for the six people who had grown and nurtured the firm to where it was. These interests were, in effect, founders' stock. We also continued as general partners, with our general partnership representing our ongoing contribution.

We were willing to sell a part of this permanent interest but not control. But who would be interested in a minority interest in a privately held business?

At the time, 1985, the Japanese were riding high. The Tokyo stock market was skyrocketing. The Japanese were purchasing businesses and real estate around the globe and paying top dollar for Rockefeller Center, Pebble Beach Golf Club, various Hawaiian resorts, and many other trophy properties.

We had an unusual Japanese connection. In the sixties, Warren and I had volunteered to be a host family for the International House, located on the Penn campus. Among those we had hosted was a twenty-five-year-old Japanese man attending the Wharton School's graduate program on a Fulbright Fellowship. His name was Koji Hirao.

At the time, Koji was employed by the Long-Term Credit Bank of Japan, a type of bank formed after World War II to lend long-term capital during the reconstruction. By the 1980s, the bank was long past fulfilling its original purpose and had become a lender to capital projects around the world in addition to Japan.

Koji rose fast in the bank's management, became a director by 1985, and was running the New York office. When he visited us for a weekend in 1986, I mentioned that we might sell a minority interest. He pleaded for his bank to be considered as a possible buyer.

Long-Term Credit Bank of Japan Becomes Limited Partner

We went to New York and negotiated with his associates. It was clear that they wanted an interest in us as a way to learn the money-management business. Their concept was to have a jointly owned affiliate that would manage dollar assets of Japanese pension funds and insurance companies, and might also eventually manage Japanese assets of American companies. The Tokyo market was high and speculatively priced, and we warned them that American companies would probably have little interest, but that did not cool their interest.

We negotiated a price of $70 million for one-third of the limited permanent interest in Miller, Anderson & Sherrerd, and agreed to create the LTCB-MAS Trust Co. as a jointly owned company that would be controlled by them. The $70 million was considerably above what we might have received anywhere else and valued the entire firm at over $300 million.

My share of this sale of minority interest was close to $12 million before taxes. For the first time in my life, I actually had a sizable pot of real cash! I jokingly said at the time that I knew I was rich, but now I had some real money. Jay and I were both able to transfer enough of our interest to Penn and Princeton before the sale to create endowed professorships.

Continued Growth

By the late 1980s, we had over one hundred employees and over $10 billion in assets. Our mutual-fund series, the MAS Pooled Trust Fund, had been started in 1983 and was attracting assets of smaller and medium-size accounts, and both the fixed-income and equity businesses were booming.

We added considerably to the partnership Ken Dunn, Jim Kichline, Bob Hagin, Dan Forrestal, Ellen Harvey, Gary Schlarbaum, Scott Richard, Robert Marcin, Steve Esser, and Steve Kreider among others. By the time of the sale to Morgan Stanley, there were twenty-two partners managing over $35 billion.

Need for Professional Management: Howard Whitmore and Marna Whittington

One addition of particular importance was Marna Whittington. Marna was and is a real star. Having been treasurer and director of finance for the state of Delaware under Governor Pete DuPont, she joined Penn as a vice president in the earl 1980s. Both Rich Worley and I had watched her with admiration as she reorganized Penn's financial operations, controlled expenses, managed people very well, and gained the total confidence of Penn's trustees.

A tall and strikingly beautiful woman, Marna is a very fast learner and a keen observer of people. She eventually became the executive vice president of Penn and was in charge of all nonacademic operations.

Rich and I both told Marna that if she were ever to consider leaving Penn, we wanted the first shot at her. Several years after that, she did decide to see what other opportunities there were and talked to us.

Miller, Anderson & Sherrerd or MA&S, as it had become known by both employees and clients, had ample investment talent, but little operating talent. We also had no real management structure—a reality that was beginning to be a disadvantage in a partnership of twelve people by 1988.

Warren stopped working in 1985 and was replaced by at least four new people, including Howard Whitmore, a friend of Tom Beach's and the head operating person at the Harvard Business School. Howie proceeded to build an operating team, including a human resources department. We became progressively more bureaucratic—a penalty of size, I suppose—but I didn't really like it.

We needed more professionalism in management and planning, and Marna fit the bill perfectly. Tragically, Howard died of cancer in 1990. Marna joined us in 1992 and immediately started the development of a strategic plan that carried us up to the point of sale to Morgan Stanley.

My Sixty-fifth Year: Retirement

While I had considered retiring earlier, I had mentally resolved that it would be no later than year-end 1991. During my last three years, I took more time off and reduced my general-partnership interest each year. On December 31, 1991, we cut the knot, twenty-two years and three months after the firm's founding, although I continued to own a considerable slice of the business through my limited partnership.

Three years before my retirement, Jay and I agreed that we needed a managing partner. The firm had grown immensely, both in assets and complexity. Twelve partners made governance difficult. We never had designated a managing partner, and while Jay and I were often deferred to, the firm was run pretty much by consensus.

After long discussions and some disagreement, a consensus was reached (Jay and I always insisted that we should not have the partnership actually vote on issues) that Rich Worley should assume the role of managing partner.

Rich ran the firm ably, and in 1995, we began to think that the time had come to find an interested buyer. There were many opportunities we couldn't effectively pursue, particularly abroad. Also, many of the older partners were speaking of retirement. We did not simply want to sell the firm. Rather, we wanted a buyer who could expand the possibilities for our considerable pool of younger investment talent while, at the same time, enable those of us who had created most of the value to realize it in cash or a quality stock.

Sale to Morgan Stanley: The End of a Success Story

Over the course of three years, conversations were held with Chubb, a major insurance company; Goldman Sachs; and Swiss Bankcorp. None of them quite fit the bill. In 1995, we approached Morgan Stanley, arguably the top-quality firm in Wall Street at the time.

Dick Fisher, who was just then retiring as CEO of Morgan Stanley, was an admirer of MA&S. As the chairman of the investment committee of the Baptist Ministers and Missionaries Retirement Fund, he was a major client of ours. Dick had been on the committee in 1971 when they became a client, and had seen us in action ever since. And of course, Jay and I knew Morgan Stanley and its people well during our days at Drexel & Co. They seemed to be the right blend of integrity, culture, and breadth of business to meet our desires.

I was involved only peripherally in finding a buyer and negotiating a price. Rich Worley and Marna Whittington led the effort.

Long-Term Credit Bank was near death as a result of bad loans during the Japanese bubble and happily agreed to a sale. (Not long afterward, the bank went into terminal bankruptcy. There were accusations of mismanagement, several executives went to prison, and at least one committed suicide. Fortunately, our friend Koji had retired by then and was saved from the bank's inglorious end.)

The price negotiated for our firm, excluding certain provisions of earnout for continuing partners, was $350 million. Cash was paid for the limited-partnership interests and a mix of cash and stock for general-partnership interests.

Marna negotiated various protections for retired partners, including office space, use of computer systems, and health care.

The consummation of the transaction was both a sad and a happy day. Sad because we were parting with a creation we had loved and nurtured, and because we were placing our employees in a different environment with a different set of objectives. We hoped that they would enjoy the fruits of expanded opportunities, but we also knew they were at risk. It was a happy event because it was our years of work coming to financial fruition.

Unfortunately, Morgan Stanley merged with Dean Witter not long thereafter, and the firm's management shifted toward the Dean Witter side, which had much more of a traditional retail-brokerage bent. The culture we thought we had in Morgan Stanley was not what we got.

The Miller, Anderson & Sherrerd name disappeared after about three years, all but four of the partners have retired, the firm is run from New York, investment performance has been largely uninspiring, and many of our old clients have jumped ship. Yet the assets under management of Morgan Stanley Asset Management Co. have climbed well past $100 billion, and many employees have had opportunities opened to them that would not have been there in the old MA&S.

There are now four hundred employees, most of whom don't know who I am.

But Jay and I still have our adjacent offices, along with Morris Williams, Rich Worley and Tom Bennett. Jay and I will always think of ourselves as partners. In fact, we all share ideas on an informal basis and remain good friends.

That's the story of Miller, Anderson & Sherrerd—a wonderful twenty-six years for a pioneering firm but no more than a meteor across the sky of time.

Our first home over the dry cleaners, where we lived from 1952 to 1957

Our first house, Devon, Pa., 1957-1962

Our present house in Gladwyne, bought in 1962

Warren's parents, Tiny and Willy Shafer, circa 1958

Mom and Dad, circa 1955

Dad with Muskellunge, Thousand Islands, 1954

Toasting the end of the Campaign for Penn with Martin Meyerson, 1980

Miller, Anderson & Sherrerd partners, 1985. L. to R., me, Dave Atkinson, Rich Worley, Tom Beach, Jay Sherrerd, Morris Williams

Penn's Trustees, 1980

*With me are: Margy Meyerson, Sheldon Hackney, Lucy Hackney,
Martin Meyerson, Warren, 1981*

With Dave Packard, Hong-Kong, 1991

Receiving honorary degree, 1981. Flanking me are Sheldon Hackney,
Penn's President, and Don Carroll, Dean of the Wharton School

Tianamen Square, Bejing, 1989, on Ford Foundation trip

With Bill Milliken and Ed Spencer, in India with Ford Foundation, 1990

*With Buzz Miller and Bill and Sara Vogel at my retirement
from Rohm and Haas board, 1998*

Singing "our song", You're Just in Love, at Rohm and Haas retirement party, 1998

With Jack Bogle, Cabin Bluff, Georgia, 1979

Spike Beitzel and I, Colonial Williamsburg, 1997

Garden of the Gods Group, Bermuda, 1967, on my fortieth birthday. No, that's not my wife on my lap! (But she's standing in the background, third from the right)

The Garden of the Gods Group

In the mid-1960s, a brokerage client in Denver, Fred Meyer, invited Warren and me to the Garden of the Gods, a lovely resort in Colorado. We would be joined by a handful of other people whom Fred regarded as among the most interesting and provocative investors he knew.

It was the first of many such gatherings, held once or twice a year at resorts all around the United States and in places such as Bermuda, Jamaica, Puerto Rico, Mexico City, and Baja. We attended them faithfully for about twenty years and made many good friends, and went with several of them on nonbusiness trips.

Present at that first meeting, in addition to me and Fred Meyer, were Edus Warren, a partner of Spencer Trask; Bill Grant, who would become the president of Smith; Barney; Jon Lovelace, the son of the founder of Capital Research and Management and who would be the leading light of that excellent firm for many years; and Russ Morrison, the CEO of Standard and Poor's. Others would be included over the years, including John Neff of Wellington Management, Rory O'Neill of Travelers Insurance, and Richard Baker-Wilbraham from the prominent London merchant bank of Helbert Wagg.

The meeting format was for each of us to speak on a topic—sometimes assigned, often self-chosen—and then lead a discussion. We would work mornings for three days and then play golf or tennis each afternoon. Most of the time, the discussions were good and proved valuable to me, but we also wasted a lot of time listening to others air their political and ideological views. I did not like the latter, and as people in the group were promoted from being active investors or changed professions and as the topics became more general, my interest began to wane.

But it sure was fun while it lasted and was an important part of my business life.

CHAPTER SEVEN

My Other (Corporate) World

In 1963, my life outside my central business responsibilities began to expand. I was invited to become a director of the Mead Corporation. Over the following thirty-five years, I was to serve in nine additional directorships and trusteeships that collectively became a major part of my career.

The Mead Corporation

Drexel & Co. was the investment banker for Mead, a medium-sized paper company headquartered in Dayton, Ohio. Having led a company-saving financing during the Depression, Drexel had very strong historical ties to Mead.

When I joined Drexel in 1954, Bob Lee, the partner of Drexel who was my immediate boss, was a Mead director. Mr. Lee, as I called him at the time, was a first-rate thinker, and I am sure he was a valuable director. To have a company's investment-banking firm represented on the board of directors in those years was both accepted and common. That is no longer the case. But in the 1950s and through the late 1960s, the business world was rather unconscious about conflicts of interest and appearances of conflicts. It was a comfortable all-male community with a high degree of self-trust. That's difficult to imagine in the litigious atmosphere in which business is conducted today.

Bob Lee died young in 1957 and was replaced by another Drexel partner Bud Dempsey. Bud was a retired CEO of Merck who needed a "desk" at which to stay active. A nice guy with street smarts, Bud was good with people but had little financial knowledge or acumen. When he reached retirement age in 1963, I was the probable successor. But I was only thirty-five, about to become thirty-six. Not many corporate directors in that era were under fifty.

Mead had most of its board meetings in their New York office in the old New York Central Building immediately north of Grand Central Station. I was escorted down into the bowels of the station to a bar where the CEO issued the invitation. I was reminded that I was wanted as a director primarily because I was a partner in their investment-banking firm, but that they were pleased with what they had seen of me as a person!

I had begun my relationship with the company seven years earlier when I was given the job of cementing Mead's tie to Drexel by publishing an in-depth analyst's report on the company for institutional investors. Sound familiar? It should because it was exactly what investment-banking firms were criticized for—indeed, sued over— during the stock-market bubble of the late 1990s. Recommending stocks of clients because they are clients, not because you think the stock is attractive, has been part of the investment-banking business forever. Now, however, analysts must confirm that their recommendations are completely free of any cajoling on the part of the investment bankers in the firm.

To study Mead, I traveled to each of their major paper mills in Ohio, Georgia, and Alabama, read extensively about the chemistry of papermaking, the technology of paper machines, and the economics of paper markets. The industry was still in a healthy growth phase as paper replaced wood in shipping cartons, replaced glass in milk bottles, and as sanitary products such as towels and tissues exploded across the world.

Mead spent most of its strategic effort trying to free itself from the terrible market economics of the commodity aspects of the paper industry. In the late 1960s, the company went on an acquisition spree, buying paper merchants, container plants, specialty-paper companies, and even a foundry and rubber-gasket manufacturer. As was the case in my entire directorship career spanning several companies, most of these acquisitions were not successes and were either sold or liquidated over the following fifteen years.

The board had some members who were fascinating, particularly to a young man who was still learning his way around. Clarence "Clare" Francis was the recently retired CEO of General Foods and the man who really put that company and its famous brands of Jell-O and Maxwell House coffee on the map. He was a tall, gangly man with a constantly pleasant way about him. To watch the way he judiciously and diplomatically expressed his wise opinions, was an education. One of his favorite ways of expressing his willingness to take business risks was to say, "When you come to a par three hole over water, always take a new ball out of your bag."

Following the postwar boom, the paper industry was not and is not an attractive industry from the standpoint of profitability and earnings growth. Demand grows slowly, pretty much in line with or a bit less than GDP. Paper mills are expensive and large and add huge increments to industry capacity when they start up. Product pricing is extremely sensitive to small supply-and-demand changes. In tonnage terms, the industry is not very cyclical, but because the profitability of paper mills is highly dependent on continuous operations and high-capacity utilization, very competitive pricing is the norm when demand softens. When profits are good, the industry chieftains have been unable to resist building new capacity or reconditioning and adding tonnage to old capacity. I was a director of Mead for a record-setting thirty-five years and saw only three short periods of really solid financial results.

At various times over this period, we fought off or discouraged any potential acquirers of Mead through "poison pills," staggered directors' terms, and aggressive use of Ohio law. All of these defenses I favored until the 1990s when it became obvious to me that they were designed more for the benefit of management than the shareholders. I then began to argue against them.

As a partner of Drexel & Co., I personally oversaw two large debt financings, the kind of conflict of interest that was common then but became taboo by the late 1970s. When I left Drexel Harriman Ripley in 1969, I told Mead that they should feel free to ask me to resign as a director because I had been elected in the first place *because* I was their investment banker. I was asked to remain on the board and I think both they and I felt relieved to be able to solve the "conflict" problem so painlessly.

Much of what I say here may make it sound as if a Mead directorship was no plum. Actually, I maintain it was the best corporate board out of the half dozen I was on. It was a well-run company trapped in a lousy industry.

Jim McSwiney, a high-school graduate from Georgia, became CEO in about 1969. He had demonstrated his management abilities in a senior production position and had come to headquarters as a senior vice president. Somehow "Mac" had gained knowledge of corporate governance and formed a committee of the board in 1972 to study the role of directors and make recommendations on reorganization of the board. Bill Jones, who was married to a sister of the company's founder, George Mead, chaired the committee. He was also the entrepreneur who developed Sea Island, the wonderful resort on the coast of Georgia. And I must add, a marvelous man with a soothing, gentle voice that reminded me of the bedside manner of a good doctor.

This ad hoc committee, of which I was a member, made a number of recommendations that were ahead of their time.

First, that the board should be composed only of outsiders except for the CEO.

Second, that a nominating committee be established to deal with finding new board members and evaluating the CEO's performance.

Third, that a corporate-responsibility committee be formed to evaluate corporate performance in achieving a diverse workforce, meeting environmental responsibilities, and balancing employee/stockholder tradeoffs. The corporate-responsibility committee would be controlled by outside directors but would include in its membership three employees elected from the ranks by their peers, in certain functions or facilities on a revolving basis.

Fourth, that we form a corporate-strategy committee to evaluate strategic options such as major capital expenditures to expand certain businesses, acquisitions, and divestitures.

Each subsequent year the board would revisit the board's organization through the nominating committee. Many modifications were made over the years. But the initial foundation that was laid in 1972 remained in place. The chief operating officer (COO) was added to the board once we added one to the corporate hierarchy. (COOs were not common as titles in those years, and the CEO was usually both chairman and president.) Ultimately, the employee membership on the corporate-responsibility committee was eliminated as we found the employee members generally unable to make contributions on policy matters and too interested in operating minutiae.

All of this sounds commonplace today, but we were twenty years ahead of the crowd on many of the issues that came to the fore in the 1990s.

I chaired the finance committee for many years, and for the last decade of my tenure, I chaired the nominating committee. As chair of the nominating committee, I instituted an annual review, not only of the CEO but also of both the board's performance and the performance of individual members, the latter being done by me and the CEO. I also insisted that the board adopt a clear mission statement that I wrote, emphasizing its role as representative of shareholders in the quest for corporate value. While I never asked to be named "lead director," a term that has more recently become popular, I clearly functioned as such for the last decade of my involvement.

Mead faced many serious challenges over this thirty-five-year period. We had eight different CEOs, one of whom we fired, and fought off one hostile takeover in 1978. We built a major new business in information technology, Lexis/Nexus, a major player in legal and general information retrieval. Ultimately, we sold Lexis/Nexus for $1.5 billion when it became obvious that it needed huge amounts of development expense and management expertise and time. It was a good decision, as proved by future technological developments in information storage and retrieval.

Mead did a good job in terms of efficiency, and its efforts to produce higher value-added products such as school supplies were largely successful. However, the cyclical nature of product pricing never allowed the company or other companies in the industry to gain investment stature. Three years after I retired, in early 1998, Mead and Westvaco joined in a merger of equals, a move that we contemplated many years earlier but we couldn't awaken Westvaco's interest.

In the six years or so of my final tenure as a Mead director, the company was paranoid about a hostile takeover that might succeed in stripping the company of its assets. Many times we were shown how much more valuable the company might be to a liquidator. In fact, this is exactly what happened to Scott Paper Co., a company that was once a blue-chip growth stock that was torn apart and sold piece-by-piece for a total sum considerably in excess of its stock price.

I was like a broken record on the reasons the company should buy its own stock. My favorite point was this: if we thought the company was attractive and the stock was undervalued to a potential acquirer, then why wasn't it attractive to us? QED, we should buy our own stock in the open market. We did so, with great success for several years, but the allure of a major paper mill for sale in Maine was too much for the executives who had been raised on papermaking. I called for a direct comparison of the effect of repurchase of stock vs. purchase of the mill, but of course, the rosy profit projections for the mill won the day. Stock repurchase was abandoned to make the acquisition that turned out to be unprofitable for many years. It was a lesson to me on how a board, despite all its best intentions, can be unwilling to do something that is against the wishes of management or unconventional in the context of its industry.

But this is not a history of the Mead Corporation except insofar as it touched my life. And it did just that in several ways. It gave me a view of a real business and its problems that many professional investors never get. I learned immensely from all my board experiences, but Mead, I believe, had one of the best boards in the corporate world. It's just a shame that the paper industry was such a terrible place to be locked in with hard, immovable assets.

As a Mead director I was privileged to meet and rub shoulders with several interesting people. Charles "Boss" Kettering, who had invented the electric starter for automobiles and founder of the Sloane Kettering Institute, was a Dayton resident and friend of the Mead family. I met him several times and had dinner with him once when he was eighty-four years old. He was a tall man with an alertness and humor that was immediately appealing. He told me that as a younger man he had compiled a list of things he wanted to do before he died. They included learning to play the piano, flying a plane, traveling to exotic places, and making a parachute jump. He had done them all except the jump, which he was seriously contemplating!

Barbara Jordan became a Mead director after she retired from her congressional seat in the mid-1970s. Barbara had become a well-recognized TV hit during the Watergate hearings when she let loose in deep stentorian tones with wonderful questions and remarks. She was confined to a wheelchair and needed a companion when traveling. Although she never clearly stated what was wrong with her, we assumed it was muscular dystrophy.

A democrat and a liberal on many issues, Barbara was not an ideologist. Overtly supportive of building diversity in Mead, she was also very critical of the black male culture, saying that Supreme Court nominee Clarence Thomas, at the time involved in difficult Senate confirmation hearings, was an example of the problems of that culture. One night when we were interviewing a black man for a potential directorship, she asked him where he hoped to be in a decade. At the time, he was the CEO of a subsidiary of a larger company. He replied that he hoped to be a CEO of a major company but that he had doubts because there were so few blacks who seemed to make the grade, presumably because of racism. She lashed out at him, saying that he certainly would not get his wish with that attitude.

Barbara knew very little about corporate affairs and organization, but she had a common sense about her that quickly built our respect. Warren and I had many long conversations with her at our annual strategy sessions in Cabin Bluff, Georgia. We covered politics, race relations, and economics. At those same meetings, we sang in the evenings around a piano, and Barbara would lead us in singing black spirituals.

We were all shocked when Barbara was found dead in her swimming pool, evidently of a heart attack. She was a hero of mine.

The Reliance Story

In the mid-1960s, I joined the board of Reliance Insurance Company, a solid, well-run property and casualty insurance operation headquartered in Philadelphia. The CEO was Bill Roberts, a congenial man who had become a good friend. I had a good understanding of the financial economics of the insurance business, thanks to my partner, Jay Sherrerd, who had become a specialist in analyzing the industry. But I saw that Bill Roberts and I were alone among the board members in having such understanding.

In 1968, we found that somebody else appreciated the insurance industry.

Saul Steinberg, a thirty-year-old Wharton graduate, made a hostile bid for the company, offering to pay over $60 per share for Reliance, using the stock of his computer-leasing company, Leasco, as currency. At the time, Reliance stock was selling in the high 30s. We knew that Leasco stock was inflated and certainly not worth even half of its price. Steinberg knew it too and was obviously seeking an asset-rich company to put into Leasco and provide downside protection to his overvalued stock. But finding a defense against him was frustratingly difficult. We tried everything from asking the state insurance commissioner to intervene to finding another company to top Leasco's bid. In the end, Bill Roberts and I were successful only in exacting a higher price from Steinberg.

Saul Steinberg asked me to join the Leasco board. At first I refused, but finally did so after Bill Roberts pleaded with me to give him some help in trying to preserve the insurance business. The Leasco board was everything a board should not be. Cronies and relatives of Saul dominated the board. Conflicts of interest were overlooked. After hearing their nonchalant reaction to the Foreign Corrupt Practices Act that required U.S. companies to adhere to domestic laws in operating abroad on such things as bribery of officials, I looked for a reason to resign. In 1978, I got one. When I was elected Chairman of the Trustees of Penn, I told Saul that I would be too busy helping to run his alma mater to continue as a director.

Several years after I left the board, the stock of Leasco, by then called Reliance Group, became depressed and Saul took the company private. He then groomed it to become a public company again at a huge profit to him and his pals and family. From that point on it was all downhill as Saul milked the company for all it was worth, taking cash out in every way possible. It filed for bankruptcy in the late 1990s.

Rohm and Haas Co.

In 1967, while still at Drexel, I was invited to join the board of Rohm and Haas, a major and very successful well-respected specialty chemical company in Philadelphia. I would serve on that board for thirty years. The invitation was issued sometime after my favorite partner, Hoppy, died. Hoppy had been a director from the time of the first public offering of the stock in 1948. Prewar, the company had been partly owned by the Rohms in Germany and at the beginning of the war that stock was taken over by the Alien Property Custodian. When it was offered at auction in 1947, Drexel & Co. and Kidder, Peabody submitted the winning bid.

Rohm and Haas, when I first became a director, was still operating under the influence of the Haas family as represented by the founder's two sons, Otto, a PhD in chemistry, and John. They were superb human beings—gentle, considerate, thrifty, and inconspicuous almost to a fault. While the chairman of the board was a research scientist, management rested in Otto's hands as the CEO. It was obvious that he did not really enjoy it. To his immense credit, he saw the need to install professional management. He surveyed the senior management of the company and asked each member who they would pick as CEO other than themselves.

The winner by a large margin was a forty-five-year-old vice president who was not even on the management committee. His name was Vince Gregory, a Harvard MBA, World War II fighter pilot, full of boundless energy and ideas. Vince would be CEO for nineteen years.

At about the same time, I left Drexel Harriman Ripley to start Miller, Anderson & Sherrerd. I immediately went to Otto Haas to tell him that the director who represented his investment-banking firm was leaving that firm. He forcefully asked me to continue as a director. I think, as in the case of Mead, both he and I were relieved that I would no longer have any conflict of interest.

The transition to professional management was very interesting to observe. The company had a culture of almost old-world stiffness about it. I called it a "tight ass" culture at a strategy meeting some years later and drew guffaws in the room.

When I joined the Rohm and Haas board in 1967, it was a very formal, stilted affair. There were quarterly meetings at which the executives read scripted reports on their areas of responsibility. There were only two outside directors—a representative of Kidder Peabody and me. Our directors' fees were in an envelope at our seats— crisp new $100 bills. When I retired as a director in 1998, the annual director compensation was close to $100,000, about in line with fees of similar companies.

A couple of years after Vince Gregory took over, I convinced Mead and Vince that both Rohm and Haas and Mead would benefit from his becoming a Mead director. He was elected a director in 1976. Many of Mead's board innovations were thus carried back to Rohm and Haas. We established a committee to monitor the company's efforts to become more environmentally responsible and a committee to oversee other issues of corporate responsibility, especially employee safety. In both of these arenas, Rohm and Haas went from being a laggard to being a leader, even winning prestige awards for their environmental efforts.

Rohm and Haas was, like most companies, concerned about possible hostile takeovers, particularly during the 1980s when such activity was at its peak. However, we took comfort from what we jokingly called our "Prussian Shield," i.e., the effective control of the company by the Haas family. (Prussian was a reference to their German origins.)

Maintaining the takeover shield may have been costly because it prevented the company from making any sizable acquisitions for stock that would dilute the family holdings. But it may also have prevented us from making acquisition mistakes. Certainly the overall record of industrial acquisitions has demonstrated that most of them turn out to be disappointing. The company did make some small acquisition mistakes, but eventually was able to use cash to buy and then build a profitable business in specialty chemicals used by the electronics industry in producing semiconductors and circuit boards.

Vince was an excellent CEO once he got the hang of it. There were a few initial stumbles and problems, especially with employee health issues related to the production of certain chemicals. These were treated with the utmost ethical concern at a considerable cost. Also, the company had attempted an entry into synthetic fibers, competing with the dominant producer, DuPont. It didn't work and the business was finally liquidated. (Lesson: don't challenge a profitable company with a dominant market share unless you have a new proprietary technology that is clearly superior in either cost or quality.)

When Vince Gregory retired, he was succeeded by Larry Wilson, a man of great integrity and very solid training in all aspects of the company, but especially in finance. Larry appreciated the benefits of repurchasing stock, which the company did aggressively in the mid-1990s, retiring about 18 percent of the outstanding shares. Again, as in Mead's case, I strongly supported this strategy. We were the best acquisition candidate in the industry and we could acquire ourselves without paying any takeover premium. By then, family control had become less of an issue.

Not long after my retirement, Rohm and Haas acquired Morton, another specialty chemical company with good cash generation from its large salt business. At this writing I still cannot tell whether this has worked to the advantage of the stockholders.

There were several very interesting board members of Rohm and Haas, including John MacArthur, former dean of the Harvard Business School; Spike Beitzel, a retired vice president and director of IBM and a good friend; Sandy Moose, a very able woman in the management-consulting business; and Gil Omenn, dean of the University of Washington's School of Public Health. (Subsequently, Gil became head of the medical center of the University of Michigan.)

We worked well together as a board, handling succession issues and executive compensation in a very responsible manner, conducting a thorough and frank annual review of both the CEO and the board's effectiveness. Here, as at Mead, I originated a board mission statement. I felt very good about my contribution to the company.

The company compiled a solid but not dramatic record of earnings growth. While it was unable to divorce itself from the business cycle and a vulnerability to rising hydrocarbon prices, its cyclicality was usually more muted than for the chemical industry in general. The company was highly ethical and a good corporate citizen. I believe it served its investors quite well over my thirty years as a director.

Hewlett-Packard

In late 1983, I received a phone call from a major head-hunting firm asking whether I would be interested in a West Coast directorship. No other information was given. My first reaction was very negative. I told them I doubted it but would think about what circumstances might lead me to a different conclusion. At that time, Kathy Miller was just starting Stanford Law School, so regular trips to the West Coast might be interesting.

Warren and I talked about it, and we decided that I would say yes if the company was either a major firm or if it offered an opportunity to make a substantial amount of money from investing in it. When I told them this, they revealed that it was the Hewlett-Packard Co. The company, they said, was anxious to have an investment expert as a director because of the huge pool of pension and profit-sharing assets that had accumulated and were managed internally. A retiring director who was a senior partner in State Street, a Boston investment-management firm, had recommended me as one of several nationally known investment people to replace him.

I was invited to Palo Alto to meet with the CEO, John Young, who was the first person to follow Dave Packard in running the company. A few weeks later, John called with the invitation for me to become a director.

Before the next board meeting, I had a two-day orientation and was immediately immersed in the business of the finance committee—first as a member and then as chairman within the year.

Service on the board of Hewlett-Packard was a strong contrast to both Mead and Rohm and Haas. Dave Packard's and Bill Hewlett's imprints and shadows were in every nook and cranny of the company. Both men were still on the board, and Dave was chairman. The company they had founded in a Palo Alto garage almost a half-century earlier had grown into one of the most respected corporations in America. They and their foundations still had immense stockholdings. While they were not officially part of management, they were always the five-hundred-pound gorillas in the room. Dave, more than Bill, often spoke up to either squash some idea or inject a new one.

Dave Packard was a large man, about six feet four, with a voice to match his size. He walked with long and purposeful strides. It was clear that people loved and respected him, but there was also always an element of fear present that, while small, was quite palpable. His occasional barks and growls were enough to make any presenter to the board extremely careful and thorough. One had better have good answers to his questions.

Bill Hewlett was distinctly different from Dave. More interested in the technological and research side of the company, Bill was gentler, a very sweet man. Dave would often turn to Bill and ask for his opinion. Bill seemed to want Dave to lead the way.

Together, Bill and Dave (they were always referred to as a pair) had created a corporate culture called the HP Way. I cannot adequately describe the HP Way in these memoirs. Books have been written about it, including one by Dave in 1995 of which I have a personally signed copy. It's sufficient here to say that it started with a companywide recognition of the importance of profits because profits are a measure of the company's contribution to society. Dave also wrote and said that profits were also the financing blood of the company, and debt was to be avoided.

Importantly, the HP Way inculcated in the culture a high respect for individuals, job security based on performance, opportunity for personal satisfaction in an environment that fosters creativity and initiative, and a wide latitude of freedom in working toward established objectives and goals. It also emphasized good corporate citizenship. All doors were always open to receive ideas or complaints. Profit sharing was an important part of compensation.

The company was known for never having had a layoff. When recessions hit, the employees were asked to reduce their compensation by reducing their hours worked. Everyone took a pay cut, including the directors, although many also voluntarily refused to reduce their time on the job.

The HP Way was not just words, as is the case with many corporate statements of missions, objectives, and operating philosophies. There was a notable absence of top-down directives at HP. Objectives and strategies were determined at the division and department levels. One hammered out objectives with one's superior, but a wide degree of freedom was given in the formulation of strategies for reaching the objectives.

Beginning in the early 1980s, the HP Way was to become severely tested by business conditions, rapid technological change, the necessity to seek corporate-wide strategies, and economies of scale that were being inhibited by the autonomy of the many small divisions in the company.

The personal computer and the client-server based information technology it created for science and business were in their infancy when I joined the board in 1984. That year saw the introduction of the HP LaserJet printer that became the world's most popular desktop printer and the advent of HP's first inkjet printer. HP had a strong business in minicomputers, effectively having challenged Digital Equipment. The Internet had not yet become a household word. HP's sales were about $10 billion. When I retired from the board in 1998, sales were $47 billion.

I never gained the sense of satisfaction or participation from the HP directorship that I did from Mead or Rohm and Haas. There was an air of formality in board discussions, a lot of show and tell. No corporate strategy issues came to the board because there *was* no companywide strategy, only strategies of the individual businesses. Meetings were pretty well scripted. And Dave and Bill were always there.

As personal computers, printers, and printer supplies began to grow, manufacturing issues surfaced. Mass production of printers, PCs, and their components took over from the production cells that had characterized test and measurement instruments—

the original base of the company. Downsizing in many parts of the company became necessary, which was a very painful process for an organization that had never had any layoffs. They were made carefully, utilizing attrition as much as possible, and always making job counseling available to affected employees.

By the late 1980s and early '90s it was becoming obvious that the company's reaction times were suffering from some kind of hardening of the arteries. It was taking too long to make decisions, getting products from the labs to the market was taking much too much time, and earnings were very flat for a few years. Dave was not happy. He appointed a board committee, chaired by "T" Wilson, a former CEO of Boeing. I was a member of that committee.

The Wilson Committee met a number of times, interviewing a number of senior executives, including John Young, the CEO. What became clear from the meetings and some behind-the scenes work by T Wilson was: first, that the company's decision-making process was unnecessarily encumbered by too many committees; and second, that there was too little communication with Dave. A purging of committees followed and it was not very long after that when John Young announced his "retirement." What exactly went on between Dave and John, the board was never to discover, but it was rather obvious when John publicly supported Bill Clinton in the 1992 election that Dave, an ardent Republican, had about had it.

In fact, the company did speed up its reaction and idea-processing time, and a period of great prosperity followed, only partly the result of the Wilson Committee's work, and importantly because of the immense boom in printers and printing supplies that began concurrently.

Lew Platt became CEO, but only after the first choice, Dick Hackborn, the builder of the printer business, turned down the job. Again, many of us were not privy to all that might have gone on in this process, but Lew, who never dreamed he was in the running for the job, inherited a company that appeared to be doing very well. However, it was falling behind in matching the innovations and effective economics of Dell Computer on the one hand, and on the other, failing to recognize the immense power and business opportunity offered by the Internet.

At a 1993 board meeting in Geneva, Switzerland, after hearing about the roaring success of the inkjet printer business, I asked, "What's our encore?" After a short silence, indicating that I was throwing a wet blanket on the meeting, the reply was that there was plenty left in the imaging business but that management would prepare a presentation on new products in development at a future meeting. That meeting was about six months later, as I recall, and we were shown the potential of digital photography and a few ideas that were meant to sound exciting. Digital photography has, indeed, taken off, but as far as I know, the other ideas have come to naught.

So while there was still plenty of potential in imaging, it was well into the exploitation of inkjet before we, the board, understood that the profitability of that business was primarily in the consumable supplies of ink cartridges.

Jay Keysworth, a board member who had served as Reagan's White House science advisor, was particularly exercised about our missing the rapidly developing Internet. I asked Lew Platt if we could have a presentation on how the company was positioning itself for the growth of the Internet. When we finally got one, it was weak and unsatisfactory in the opinions of several of us. I have often thought that had HP been strategically-minded, it might have precluded the advent of Cisco Systems, a company that garnered an immense share of the market for Internet-related products.

At virtually every board meeting, the discussion of financial results included data on how fast prices for printers and PCs were eroding and how costs had to be taken out of the system. The company executed very well on reducing costs and good results continued as volume gains remained very healthy. Its share of the printer market got as high as 70 percent.

Several times in my last few years as a director we were asked to respond to questionnaires about board effectiveness and say what might be bothering us as directors. I thought I gave some thoughtful answers about what I saw as the necessity of beginning to establish some companywide strategies rather than just product and divisional strategies. But if there were ever any substantive discussions on this subject, I never heard them. Macro thinking about the industry in a strategic context was never obvious.

In fairness, I should point out that simply matching the immense growth of the industry was a substantial task in itself, let alone trying to strategize about the future. Also, the people were superb, excellent at what they did, and I always came away marveling at the way they managed their growth. I had a personal rule that every time the stock declined by at least 20 percent or more, I would buy more, and consequently ended my fourteen years on the board with a very healthy holding.

We had several very interesting trips as HP directors, including visits to South Korea, Hong Kong, Japan, Spain, and England. HP was and is a truly international company, in terms of locations of facilities, sales, and the composition of management. It also had the most diverse workforce of the companies I knew well in terms of race, ethnicity, and sex.

I retired in early 1998 and the company was still riding high. By 2000 the stock was selling for a very high valuation and I was also a bit uncomfortable about its future growth post the boom in printers. Therefore, I hedged half of my stockholding and substantially moderated an otherwise substantial loss as the stock-market bubble broke.

I was obviously not part of the controversial acquisition of Compaq in 2001. I did, however, sympathize with Walter Hewlett's opposition to the merger and expressed myself so publicly—the only ex-director to do so. I saw that the savings would be forthcoming from the merger because the company is so very good at executing, but I questioned publicly, and still question, the strategic contribution to the company's future.

I never met Carly Fiorina, HP's controversial CEO, but she strikes me as more of a cheerleader than a thoughtful strategist. (As this book was going to press, she was forced out as CEO.)

The First Pennsylvania Company

I first knew the Pennsylvania Company by the name of Pennsylvania Company for Insurances on Lives and the Granting of Annuities. That was the name carved in stone above the entrance at Fifteenth and Chestnut Streets. That banking floor was where my grandfather Thompson had walked in, sat on a bench, and quietly died in 1943.

I came to know it better as a partner of Drexel & Co. A former Drexel partner, William L. Day, was CEO of this banking company when I first came to Drexel. It was one of the four major banks in Philadelphia, and highly respected. It had both a good banking business and a trust business of some note. Not long after I joined Drexel, the Pennsylvania Company merged with the First National Bank of Philadelphia and became the First Pennsylvania Company, a holding company owning the First Pennsylvania Bank and Trust Company.

Bill Day, who was also the Chairman of the Trustees of Penn, was a lovely man—gentle, very conservative, and wholly of the Philadelphia establishment. He died unexpectedly in the early 1960s, and his successor was Bill Walker, the former CEO of the First National Bank. Bill was a gregarious man and had a great leadership talent. Bill and I got to know each other well through our common directorship of Reliance Insurance Co. Bill Roberts, the CEO of Reliance was a director of First Pennsy, as we called it. So was another friend of mine, Jim Ballengee, the CEO of Philadelphia Suburban Water Company.

The four of us, Roberts, Walker, Ballengee, and I, talked quite a bit about who should succeed Bill Walker, who was about to retire. There was a Philadelphia-establishment type, Jim Bodine, an able enough man who seemed to be the obvious favorite. But there was another man, John Bunting, who had joined the bank from the Federal Reserve Bank of Philadelphia. John was an economist by training, a very articulate guy, good public speaker, was always ready with a very quotable statement for the press, and had the image of the poor but smart boy making good.

John Bunting and I had met years before when we both had summer jobs at the Philadelphia Savings Fund Society running accounting machines. John's father was a teller at the Seventh and Walnut Street branch where we worked. He was a great friend to us and other young people at this branch, which was the original location of PSFS.

As seventeen-year-olds, John and I went to Ocean City on several summer weekends—strolling the boardwalk, picking up girls, and even setting up pins at the bowling alley for some extra money. At summer's end we said goodbye and never expected to have our paths cross again. The war and college intervened. When I joined the Federal Reserve bank, there was John Bunting, a research assistant in the research department. During my two years of training, John and I played ping-pong after lunch and renewed our friendship. When I was hired as a permanent employee of the Fed, our ties grew stronger.

John was short, dark, and handsome. His voice was deeper and more resonant than what you expected to emanate from his almost petite body. He was always sartorially splendid, although he walked with a bit of a slouch and was somewhat round-shouldered. Everyone thought he was very smart.

Roberts, Ballengee, and I (even though I was not a director) campaigned for John to be the next CEO of First Pennsy. Bill Walker was sympathetic but needed the added push and John was selected as CEO in about 1967.

Bunting took the banking field by storm. He used his speaking and writing abilities effectively and became the talk of the town, if not the entire banking industry. First Pennsylvania Company became an aggressive lender, and adventurous in its asset portfolio. It seemed to work. The bank did very well, and John became something of a business hero—at least in Philadelphia.

John had a way with words. Feature articles were written about him. The financial press designated him as a favorite. At one point he said that in a few years he did not want to be known as a banker, a reference to his acquisition-mindedness. A wag in the industry was quoted as saying, "What makes him think he is regarded as a banker now?"

In another article, it was reported that in answer to the question about where he had gone to college, John had replied, "I went to Temple-O." When asked what that meant, he said that whenever he told people who asked about his college that it was "Temple," they always said, "Oh." It was an obvious but humorous jab at the Ivy League establishment.

In 1974, John invited me to become a director of his company. As a personal long-time friend, I was intrigued and accepted.

At my first board meeting, John announced that the Federal Reserve bank examiners would like to report to the board about their recent examination. Into the room came a man I had worked with as a trainee at the Fed, who proceeded to tell the board that the asset quality of the bank was unacceptably low. I was shocked.

It was all downhill from there. I joined the audit committee and we puzzled over how we would monitor the loan quality and the other assets. We decided to seek a director, a so-called professional director, who would be specially paid and who would report directly to the audit committee. We found such a man in Jerry Hildebrand, who worked effectively to keep the board informed on asset quality. But things did not get better. John had decided to make some interest-rate bets in the bond portfolio and went into longer maturities at the wrong time. The resulting decline in asset values was too much for the Fed. One day I got a call from the president of the

Philadelphia Fed, a man I knew but not well, but who knew of me and my former connection with the Fed. He asked me to come to his office as soon as possible.

"The Board of Governors in Washington," he said, "are very concerned about the First Pennsylvania Company. The quality of assets has deteriorated further and they do not think that management is responding adequately. We think that John Bunting must go and we want you to lead the board to that conclusion. We are prepared to keep the discount window open and do everything we can to prevent a panic among the bank's customers. The Federal Deposit Insurance Corporation is prepared to work with you on management succession."

I was being asked to lead the board in dumping my friend! However, John was also trying my patience. On several recent instances, I felt that we were not getting straight answers. Our professional director had become increasingly frustrated.

After talking with the audit committee, I traveled to Washington to visit with the Federal Deposit Insurance Corporation. I convinced them that rather than seeking an executive from outside, it would be better for the time being to have an internal person succeed John, a person who was as little tainted by John's missteps as possible. We suggested George Butler, the COO, a decent, honest guy who never would have been CEO under different circumstances.

It remained for Roberts, Ballengee, and me to do the dirty deed, which we did, offering John about a million dollars to depart quietly without comment to the press. Our fear and the Fed's fear was that if he bad-mouthed us, it might start a run on the bank. John took the news badly and walked out. I have seen him only once in the intervening twenty-five years. He completely disappeared from the Philadelphia business scene.

The stock of First Pennsy had declined sharply, and stockholder suits were expected and came. With good legal advice, we were able to negotiate a "global settlement," avoiding any substantial harm to the company and any financial liability to the board.

Not long thereafter, Miller, Anderson & Sherrerd started its own mutual funds and the law at the time precluded me from continuing as a director. With a sigh of relief, I resigned from the board.

First Pennsy was a "beached whale" for several years, until the Philadelphia National Bank decided to buy it. PNB became CoreStates, then First Union, and at this writing, it is Wachovia.

All the major Philadelphia Banks are now extinct, having become parts of out-of-city and out-of-state holding companies. The local bankers, at one point very powerful people, are no longer a force in the community.

SPS Technologies

John Selby, the CEO of SPS Technologies, called me in 1985 to see whether I would join their board. I did not know John well, but I liked what I saw of him, which was as a fellow director of Berwind Corp. SPS was the old Standard Pressed Steel Company, a maker of specialty fasteners that had the highest-quality product line in the business. By virtue of this quality, they became a major supplier to the aerospace industry, worldwide, as well as a supplier to the automobile industry. The company was subject to the vicissitudes of the business cycle, as well as the vagaries of fluctuating commercial and defense aircraft spending.

SPS was a well-respected Philadelphia-area company and was still heavily influenced by the Hallowell family's stockholdings. The Hallowells were far from controlling numerically, however, and when I joined the board, Mario Gabelli's mutual funds had the largest block of stock, about 26 percent.

John Selby, a former Ingersoll-Rand executive, was a quite capable manager with a pretty good team, in a company whose profitability was constantly assailed by its powerful customers who unceasingly pushed for lower prices. When volumes were rising, all was rosy, but when they flattened or declined, the bottom line all but disappeared.

The board was only six in number and included Tom Hallowell, the patriarch of the founding family; the CEO and COO; and a Wharton professor of minor distinction.

About halfway through my ten-year tenure, in a period of general corporate angst over hostile takeovers, a large buyer of the stock appeared, the Ruttenberg family, noted for having disrupted several corporations by muscling their way onto boards. John Selby was quite paranoid about this and sought a standstill agreement with the Ruttenbergs that limited their holdings to 15 percent and gave them a board seat.

The Ruttenberg's family representative on the board was son Eric, a diminutive very well-educated young man with a deep voice that could be direct and cutting. But Eric knew his business—or rather, he had thoroughly studied and thoroughly knew SPS's business. He also knew the structure and economics of the fastener industry as well as or better than management. And while he indicated no desire to dismantle or sell the company, he had the clear objective of making it more valuable.

Management was panicked. They pointed to the Ruttenbergs' history of disruption and lack of success in increasing values. My own view was that much of what Eric had to say made sense. At one point, John Selby brought to the board an offer for the company from a competitor at a price well above the market that Eric Ruttenberg voted to refuse. This indicated to me that he was serious about increasing value by improving the company.

It began to be obvious that any major changes required a change in management. The company was in a down cycle, and the major steps needed to improve profitability were not going to be made by Selby and his team. John had done several good things, especially engineering some excellent small acquisitions, and had run the company well during the good times. He simply could not, however, undo some of the company's mistakes. Nor could he slash costs (fire people) to the extent necessary. Yielding to some pressure, he decided to retire.

The search for a new CEO was short. Eric knew a man with Watts Industries in Boston who was available—a man with considerable experience in operations as well as making and improving acquisitions. His name was Charles Grigg. We hired him and loaded him with options at a depressed price for the stock.

Charlie was the right guy at the right time. He sold the company's headquarters building—a much too large and fancy property—sold the company airplane, reduced headcount, got into the heart of the manufacturing operations to improve costs, and overall was a success, working in rapid motion.

The changing of management by a board is a very traumatic time for all involved, but that is especially so when the CEO is a personal friend who invited you on the board in the first instance. Yet one learns that managements can be immobilized, trapped by their own past errors, and that only a change can release the company and put it on a better course.

I asked to resign from the SPS board two years before I would have been required by age to do so. It was taking more of my time than I wanted to spend, particularly at those times when I wanted to be either in Florida or New Hampshire. As the stock recovered, I sold most of my holding at a good price, a price that was not to be realized again for three years when the company was sold to Precision Cast Parts. SPS is no more.

Berwind Corporation

My naiveté about wealth and wealthy families and my general disinterest in the social scene in Philadelphia left me unprepared for my first contact with the Berwind Corporation.

A well-known lawyer and partner of Dechert, Price, and Rhoads, Al Gilmer, had seen me in action doing a valuation of the Amchem Corp., a small specialty chemical company, in preparation for its sale to William H. Rorer, best known as the maker of Maalox. Al was the lawyer for the Berwind family and the Berwind Corp. At the time, I did not know the proud history of the Berwind family and the company, which had been a major coal producer in the 1920s but which had been decimated by both the Depression and the conversion to oil heating.

Charles Berwind and one of his sons, Graham, bought the remnants of the company from trusts at J. P. Morgan in 1963 for about $23 million. At the time, the company had a negative net worth but owned potentially valuable coal properties that were producing minimally.

Charlie gently guided Graham and gradually let him take over. For the most part, they got out of the coal-production business and leased their properties to other producers. The bituminous-coal business began to show decent growth as electric-generating capacity soared. Berwind's cash flow from coal land leases was diverted into acquisitions as the financial underpinnings of the company were strengthened.

Some acquisitions were good and some were terrible. The better ones included a Puerto Rican tugboat company, a producer of lead wheel weights, and several specialty machinery and equipment companies. The bad ones included portable parking garages, a Caribbean airline, and a cosmetics company.

Always in the background were the coal properties, generating cash. When the energy crisis of the 1970s developed, there was a rush by energy producers to exploit coal and the value of coal properties soared. Graham saw the opportunity to reduce the reliance on coal and gain some considerable cash in the process. Major coal properties were sold to Shell Oil for prices that looked unbelievably high only a few years later.

Graham was driven to succeed. He said to me at one time that he would like to see the family wealth restored sufficiently that they could once again be in Newport, which was a kind of symbol to him. He never, to my knowledge, actually pursued the Newport objective but he could have done so given the eventual success of the company.

When I first met Graham, he had a burr haircut and seemed very square. While I thought I came to know him well, he surprised me several times in both his business decisions and his personal lifestyle. His hair grew much longer, he divorced his first wife with whom he had three children, married again, and then strayed from her to be with a company employee.

The Berwind board of directors operated as a true board for many years and the directors owned stock in the company. As I recall, I invested about $30,000 in the early 1970s or earlier, and when Graham decided to confine stockholdings to family and family trusts, I sold my stock back to the company in the early 1980s for about $100,000—a figure that was very substantial to me at the time.

Eventually, the board of directors became an advisory board to the trustees of the family trusts that controlled the stock of Berwind and several of its subsidiary companies that were spun off as separate entities.

During the 1980s and 1990s the Berwind Group, as it was renamed, grew significantly and the value of the group came to exceed one billion dollars and probably a great deal more than that. Graham was an astute trader of companies, not in a short-term sense, because he truly bought and built for the long-term. But when a company appeared to reach a valuation pinnacle, he was willing to sell and buy something new.

By the 1990s, Berwind had established itself in the pharmaceutical market as a supplier of coloring agents and fillers for prescription and over-the-counter drugs. Attempts were made to add to this platform but with little real success. Nevertheless, this business grew on its own into a major property.

In the early 1990s, Berwind acquired a manufacturer of security equipment, including alarms and locking devices. This business also grew nicely and was finally sold to General Electric. All the while, other smaller businesses were being bought and sold or created, including a specialty lubricant company, an internal investment-banking arm that was not a success, a real-estate investment and management company that did succeed after a terrible start, and others.

I retired from the board at the age of seventy-three, even though Graham had told me that I could stay if I desired. I was ready for a change of scenery and left at year-end 2000.

I could write much more about Berwind and especially about Graham Berwind, but I feel it would be a breech of confidence to say much more about this very private company and this very private person.

Philadelphia Suburban

There were several other companies along the way that deserve some brief comment. One in particular, Philadelphia Suburban Water Company was an interesting case study. A well-financed water company with a good supply of quality water from both reservoirs and artesian wells, PSW was a regulated public utility with a solid, slow but consistent record of growth.

Jim Ballengee, an able and affable man who had started his career as a lawyer with Sears Roebuck, was hired to run the company sometime in the 1960s. I knew Jim because Drexel & Co. was the company's investment banker and had showed Jim a couple of possible acquisitions outside the water business. I also knew him as a fellow director of Reliance Insurance and Berwind and we eventually served together as directors of First Pennsylvania Company. He asked me to join his board in 1967.

Jim felt hemmed in by the water company and wanted to build a small conglomerate using PSW stock as currency. He bought a large heating and air-conditioning contractor, a painting contractor, and most importantly a company that rented oil-field equipment called unsurprisingly, National Oil Field Rental. It was located in Dallas. Oil Field Rental was purchased fortuitously in 1972 almost on the eve of the oil cartel's (OPEC) shocking the world with tightly controlled production and a major increase in the price of oil.

As long lines developed at gas stations all over the country, the drilling business took off. The board visited the Texas and Louisiana producing areas, which were so bustling with activity, they reminded me of large supply depots in time of war. Equipment, from drill pipe to drilling bits, was in huge demand and rentals of equipment soared, as did the profits of Oil Field Rental. It became the dominant part of PSC. In the meantime, feeling that the water business was dragging down the valuation of the whole company, we spun off the water company and changed the name of the remaining company to Enterra Corporation.

The problem was that we did not sell the oil-field rental business when it was booming. Actually, Graham Berwind, who was on the board, suggested that a sale might be a good move but Jim couldn't bring himself to recommend it. What could he do with the money to replace the profits of the equipment-rental business?

As the tight oil-supply situation began to ease in the early 1980s the rental business fell like a stone. We were left with a plethora of equipment that we had purchased in huge quantities during the boom. Because customers had been using rental gear only at the margin, rental revenues plummeted and the company went into the red.

In the meantime, a West Coast investment group had bought a major position in the stock and sought control of the board. Constant squabbling with them was no fun, and because I had no major financial interest in Enterra, I resigned. Subsequently, Enterra went into a lengthy recovery and Philadelphia Suburban Water has continued its slow consistent growth. Retrospectively, the PSC story is a good lesson in three ways. First, stick to what you know best. Second, don't let the stock market determine corporate strategy. And third, when a business looks too good to be true, it probably is. Sell it!

Gemini Fund

In 1966, Jay Sherrerd and I were in London on what had become our annual business visit. While there, we heard about closed-end dual funds, a new type of fund being sold in the British market. The idea was that the income and capital growth of a portfolio could be separated and sold to investors with different investment objectives. For example, if $100 million could be raised in two $50 million pieces by issuing income shares and capital shares, the income shares could receive all the income from the total portfolio and the capital shares would get all the growth in asset value. The income shares would have a finite life of, say, ten years. At the maturity of the income shares, the capital shares would be redeemable at net asset value.

Jay and I we were taken by the idea and returned home to talk to Jack Bogle, the head of Wellington Management Company. He was equally fascinated and we, Drexel & Co., started a process of registering such a fund with the Securities and Exchange Commission, thinking we had a jump on the rest of Wall Street

The fund was named Gemini Fund, after the Gemini Twins. I think we threw the SEC for a loop. They had never seen such an animal and took an extended period to look at it, talk to us and others about the concept, and generally delayed so long that several other investment firms went into registration with the commission with similar products. Finally, they approved all such funds simultaneously so that four funds were being underwritten at the same time.

Gemini would be managed by John Neff, who, while not yet as legendary as he was to become, was nevertheless, a highly respected investor as manager of the Windsor Fund. Jay and I would be directors of the fund along with Bogle and Neff. John still maintains it was the best board of directors that any fund ever had. Unfortunately, lawyers decided it was a poor idea to have investment bankers on the board, especially since we had our own open-end fund, Drexel Equity Fund, of which we were also directors. So the "best board there ever was" had a very short life of only about two years.

But Gemini proved to be a great success. John naturally emphasized dividend yield in his portfolio selections, so the income shares had a yield greater than twice the yield of the S&P 500. Also, John was a devotee of the idea that as dividend yields on his investment successes declined due to price appreciation, he would "recycle" back into higher-yielding stocks. It worked beautifully. As I recall, the yield right from the start was over 9 percent, and the income grew consistently at a rate well in excess of dividends generally. The capital shares were, in effect, a 50 percent margin account at the start, with the cost of the margin equal to the dividends sacrificed to the income shares.

As is often the case with closed-end funds, the capital shares sold at a modest discount to net asset value, but the income shares enjoyed a premium that grew and grew and grew. As the capital shares increased in asset value, they provided more and more income leverage to the income shares. I do not remember the exact numbers but I think the yield on the initial $10 issue price of the income shares reached about 20 percent, at which time the shares sold for $18. While the capital shares also did well, the best total return was enjoyed by the income shares. This was a surprise to those who thought that it would be more profitable to own the shares that would enjoy all the appreciation.

The other dual funds underperformed Gemini significantly because they tended to invest in lower-yielding growth stocks to emphasize the capital appreciation of the capital shares. The income shares were the real winners. Not only did they receive all the income but they also benefited from the growth of the income. Under John Neff's approach, the fund emphasized not only higher dividend yields, but as John sold his winners that had gone up in price and down in yield, he would also recycle the money back into higher-yielding stocks.

The income shares went to a huge premium, 80 percent or more over their ultimate redemption value. Purchasers were able to get a sufficiently high current yield that they were willing to experience a certain decline in the shares as they approached the redemption date.

I think that the dual fund is a good idea that might make a comeback. But none will have both the conceptual and investment strengths that the "best fund board ever" imparted to Gemini Fund.

What Did I Learn? What Did I Accomplish?

Looking back at all these corporate experiences, my first reaction is that I was always very happy to see the workings of corporate America from the outside, without ever really being part of it. That is, I was privileged to see how business decisions were made in corporate hierarchies without having to have my career or income depend on the final result.

Some might say that until you have the responsibilities of a chief executive officer of a major corporation, you cannot really understand the forces pulling at you. Perhaps, but I believe I gained considerable perspective on how people react to pressures and how do deal with those reactions. I have actively participated in the selection of about two dozen CEOs and in the firing of several. It was always the firings that took an emotional toll on me.

The selection of a new CEO is almost always followed by a period of adjustment, as the newcomer (even if he had been with the company for many years) becomes comfortable with the greater responsibilities. There is always a shakedown period during which they work to get the hang of it. My experience in watching this process many times has made me wonder how and why we can expect new presidents of the country or of universities to hit the ground running, especially as their every action is analyzed backward and forward by an aggressive press.

Over the thirty-four years that I was involved as a corporate director, I came to appreciate more and more the importance of corporate governance to the success of a business. In the early years, I had the view that the economics of the business were all that counted, and while I still believe that economics is plenty important, I think that the integrity of the people, the way a company organizes itself, and the culture it engenders are really paramount.

I looked at companies from a very different vantage point from that of other directors. I had the view of an investor, someone who needed to understand the economics of the company and its industry, someone that was interested in improving the lot of shareholders. On the few occasions when I compromised that view, or did not speak forcefully enough, I later had regrets.

One can tell a lot about a company by the way its CEO lives. Palatial mansions, expensive yachts or other signs of ostentation are warning signals. Also, large and fancy office buildings can be a sign that the company wants to show off solely for the gratification of management.

I like to see a company with entrepreneurial rather than bureaucratic attitudes, a management group that looks at its business as owners not managers, has involvement in its communities, spends modestly on trappings for itself, engages in philanthropy (but not with the CEO's personal favorite charities), and develops a board that is truly involved in a mission to serve the shareholders first and consider management as a means to an end.

In the late 1990s, the excesses that boards had tolerated in executive compensation and the carelessness they exhibited in overseeing corporate affairs came to light in scandalous fashion. I was ashamed of the business world. However, I can honestly say that the companies I served and the boards I was on were able to hold their heads high.

I can state very confidently that I truly represented shareholders. My retirement citation from Rohm and Haas describes me in wonderful calligraphy as "director, shareholder, and *proponent of shareholder interests.*" I doubt that many retiring directors of that company or others are described that way. This was not an apt description at the beginning of my directorship career when I was representing the company's investment banker. It took a while, I'm ashamed to say, before I gained not only the attitude of a shareholder but also the self-confidence and diplomacy to voice openly any opinions and concerns that are critical of or in disagreement with management. It is very difficult to take an opposing stance from a management team you regard as friends, and with whom you may have social relationships. Yet, bashfulness when you have something constructively critical to say serves nobody well.

Many if not most of the truly great directors I have seen in action were not CEOs of other companies. They have been financiers, scientists, university and foundation presidents (even professors), and management consultants. Yet CEOs typically prefer other CEOs as directors. They will, it is believed, better understand their problems. One piece of advice I would give any corporate director is not to let the CEO of another company be chairman of the compensation committee! They never have seen another CEO's pay that wasn't too low.

In 1997, I was sufficiently motivated by governance problems that were responsible for miserable shareholder returns at such companies as IBM and General Motors, to write an article for a publication called *Directors and Boards*. It urged companies to adopt mission statements for their boards that clearly acknowledge the primacy of responsibility for creating value for shareholders.

I had been amazed on several occasions by how little fellow directors knew about the returns to shareholders, especially relative to competitors. I had also become critical of boards looking at their responsibilities largely in legalistic terms. Consequently, I had urged mission statements on the boards of Hewlett-Packard, Rohm and Haas, and Mead. In each case a mission statement was adopted. The wording differed, and Hewlett-Packard's statement was not as strong as I wished, but essentially, the lead paragraph took the following form:

> *The mission of the board of directors of the (blank)—Company is to help produce long-term value for its shareholders. The board believes that the company should rank in the top quartile of peer companies in producing shareholder total return as measured over five and ten-year periods.*

I worked with managements through board committees to reach agreement on how returns are to be measured, and choosing time periods appropriate for the nature of the business. Companies with long capital-investment cycles, for example, had to be measured over sufficiently long periods to capture the results of large investments. Choosing peer companies is not simply a matter of listing competitors. Companies with similar economic characteristics—such as capital intensity, cyclicality, markets served, or research dependence—might also be considered peers.

If performance is not satisfactory, does the board understand why? Do management and the board understand what the better performers are doing that their company is not? Is the company on a course to rectify the situation? And finally, of course, is management or the board the problem?

Additionally, every board needs to periodically assess its own performance and the performance of the individual members. And to further align the interests of directors with shareholders, directors must own as much stock as their circumstances reasonably allow, perhaps achieving this partly by paying directors only with stock.

CHAPTER EIGHT

My Other (Nonprofit) World

Penn

The University of Pennsylvania has been part of my life since I first learned to sing the "Red and Blue" as a child and attended Penn football games with my dad beginning in 1932.

Through the 1940s, as I witnessed my dad's "reeducation" in graduate school and then had a marvelous undergraduate and graduate school experience myself, Penn has been almost a second home to me. Falling in love and marrying a Penn woman whose family also had a Penn heritage. provided more glue. And of course, living near the campus has meant that the university continued to be an important part of our intellectual and cultural lives—both as a teacher in my thirties and as one who has enjoyed plays, concerts, and lectures over a long span of years.

Penn did a good job in maturing and educating me, and I am grateful. I sincerely believe that I would never have done as well as I have in various endeavors without my Penn experience. So when I became an alumnus, I also became an active volunteer in class affairs and fund-raising, just as my dad had done before me. For both of us, it was a "pay the place back" mentality.

At Drexel & Co., as we have seen, my mentor, Edward Hopkinson Jr. was a distinguished Penn alumnus and trustee. Several Drexel partners had been trustees, and at that time, Thomas Gates Jr. a Drexel partner and Penn trustee was in Washington, serving first as Secretary of the Navy and then Secretary of Defense under Eisenhower.

Therefore, when Hoppy died in 1965, it was not a great surprise to me that Wilfred Gillen, CEO of Bell Telephone of Pennsylvania and the trustee chairman at the time, invited me to become a trustee for a five-year renewable term. At thirty-nine, I was the youngest board member. Little did I expect then that I would be a trustee for all of the following thirty-one years.

It was only a month or so later that Gaylord Harnwell, Penn's president, and Markoe Rininus, CEO of Smith Kline and French and chairman of the Hospital of the University of Pennsylvania (HUP), asked me to join the hospital's board. I accepted.

The hospital complex and medical school accounted for about half of Penn's operating budget at the time. For many years the hospital had been the personal fiefdom of Orville Bullitt, a trustee. Orville had ruled with an iron hand, making financial decisions that impacted the university as a whole. Gaylord Harnwell was determined to have the president take a firm controlling hand to this huge operation. He forced Bullitt to step down and effectively stripped the hospital board of all power except for relatively minor operating matters. It was shortly after this happened that I joined the HUP board, being invited to do so because President Harnwell wanted trustee representation. Other than Bullitt, there had been no other trustees involved with HUP. I did not know this history at the time and learned it slowly and painfully over the next few years.

Becoming Chairman of HUP

After about two years as a board member, Rivinus retired and I was elected chairman. The HUP board was overly concerned with minutiae. The executive director of the hospital was occupied primarily with day-to-day operations and the board was loaded with Main Line socialite types who were not at all oriented toward the larger university. In fact, most of them seemed to view the university as an adversary that was interfering with their right to run the hospital, an attitude that was a remnant of the Bullitt era.

After about three years of this, I was sufficiently frustrated to suggest to the executive committee of the trustees, of which I was a member, that the HUP board be disbanded and a trustee committee be appointed to oversee the entire medical area. Amid much trauma, this was done and a trustee committee for health affairs was established. I chaired this committee for a short while, but these events coincided with the establishment and early years of Miller, Anderson & Sherrerd. My time was simply overloaded and I became less intensely involved in trustee activities for a while following the selection in 1970 of a new president to succeed Gaylord Harnwell.

Gaylord Harnwell, a physicist with a humanist's view of life, was a very good president who saw the necessity of intellectually improving the university. In 1953, he had succeeded Harold Stassen, who had been a terrible president in my view. Stassen was selected in 1949 after making a strong showing for nomination at the Republican National Convention. He had been governor of Minnesota, and was widely considered to be a strong presidential contender for 1952. The other strong contender was Dwight Eisenhower who had been named the president of Columbia University. The Stassen selection was a hope that we might provide the next president of the United States and gain national notoriety in the process. It was a misguided idea. Stassen ultimately faded into oblivion, but not before becoming a national joke by continuing to throw his hat in the presidential ring for years afterward.

A strong proponent of building our graduate-education capacity, Gaylord diverted resources to graduate programs and was indifferent to athletics. This combination left many undergraduate alumni disaffected, but very wrongly, in my judgment. He took us out of big-time football and back to the Ivy League. He was also the first president to make a case to the trustees for affirmative action, saying that it was the duty of the elite universities to lead the way in actively seeking minorities. If we didn't, he maintained, no others would. The trustees overwhelmingly agreed, although it took some time before alumni attitudes liberalized.

The Meyerson Presidency

By 1968, it had become obvious that Gaylord Harnwell was losing his grasp on the presidency. Tragically, the problem ultimately proved to be Alzheimer's disease, although that was far from certain at the time. In 1968, he announced that he would step down from the presidency. A search committee was appointed, of which I was a member. The committee's chairman was Bill Day, Chairman of the Trustees.

The search coincided with the hectic days of MA&S's startup and I missed several meetings, but was there for the final decision. Our first choice, even though we thought he would have an unlikely interest, was Derek Bok, dean of the Harvard Law School, a man with strong Philadelphia connections and the son of Curtis Bok, scion of the Curtis family (Curtis Publishing, publishers of *The Saturday Evening Post*). Derek was a graduate of Stanford and Harvard Law School, and had become a prominent academician. We knew that he would certainly be a candidate for the presidency of Harvard, and that the Harvard search would be underway soon. Derek saw the same handwriting on the wall that we did and declined. He became Harvard's president in 1971.

The university's expansion in West Philadelphia was viewed with hostility by the surrounding community, which had become largely inhabited by African Americans. Students and faculty were disturbed by an alleged lack of sensitivity of university officials and trustees to community needs and attitudes. Therefore, there was a desire to find a president who would relate well to the surrounding area and to the city as a whole.

A person with outstanding credentials had surfaced and seemed to be interested. He was Martin Meyerson, a man who was then serving as president of State University of New York (SUNY) at Buffalo. Martin had been a professor of urban studies at Penn in the 1950s and was well acquainted with Penn and Philadelphia. He had also been a professor of city planning and urban research at Harvard and dean of the College of Environmental Design at Berkeley. His curriculum vitae, documenting a career in urban planning and research, was lengthy and impressive.

If selected, Martin would become the first Jewish president of an Ivy League university. To the credit of the search committee and its leadership, I never heard any questions raised about his religious background. He seemed to be an obvious choice to me, the rest of the committee agreed, and Martin became Harnwell's successor in 1970.

Martin saw the need to raise the academic aspirations of the university, and worked diligently to do so. He is an intellectual's intellectual, widely read on an endless variety of subjects, and well acquainted with the broad academic community. He is also a good friend and advisor.

As I said earlier, in the early 1970s I was so busy building our business that I became less active, attending board meetings, to be sure, but doing little else. The university seemed to prosper academically. Martin did indeed pull us up a big notch. But the lot of a president is very tough. Your constituencies, faculty, students, trustees, donors, and the larger community often have very conflicting views of the institution. You must always be politically mindful of the sensitivities of each of them, yet you are unavoidably, with every major decision, spending some of your "currency" with one or more of these constituencies. A president's key decisions are often establishing priorities for the spending of inadequate quantities of financial or human capital.

After ten years or so, most presidents are not only exhausted but have also lost considerable popularity with their constituents. Martin Meyerson, despite all his accomplishments, was no exception. But before going further with this part of my tale, I must insert a major development in my life.

The Chairman of the Trustees is an office tracing back to 1749 when Benjamin Franklin was president of the trustees of the academy which became the College of Philadelphia in 1755. For eighty-nine years to 1890, there was no elected chairman. It wasn't until 1911 that the present office of Chairman of the Trustees was created, and Provost Charles Custis Harrison was elected to that post. In the years following Harrison, there have been twelve more chairmen. I was one of them.

In 1974, seeking a person with a nationally known name, the trustees chose the CEO of Merrill Lynch, Donald Regan. Don was a Harvard graduate who was well-known by the board because he had been elected a trustee after spending considerable time in Philadelphia as head of that firm's Philadelphia office.

Don was a very busy executive who, by my observation, did not put Penn at the front of his "to do list." A nice and able guy, former marine corps officer, he always seemed to me to be still commanding his troops. He had no sense of Penn's traditions and culture, and it showed. By 1978, he was ready to leave the chairmanship. Not only was he now in New York but also he was becoming interested in working on the possibility of Ronald Reagan's running for the presidency. (After Reagan's election in 1980, Don became the White House chief of staff and then Secretary of the Treasury)

Becoming Chairman of the Trustees

In March of 1978, Bob Dunlop, our leading senior trustee and retired CEO of Sun Oil Company, came to my office. The purpose of his visit was to ask me if I would be willing to be one of the trustees to be considered for the chairmanship. I was flattered but amazed. I had not been as active as several other seemingly eligible people over the previous few years. One trustee in particular, John Eckman, the CEO of William H. Rorer, a Philadelphia-based drug company, seemed to me to be the obvious choice. However, John was not well liked. He could be very cynical, blunt, and very stubborn. But by the sheer effort and hours he had expended on Penn, he deserved the post. It was obvious to most of the trustees that John both wanted and expected it.

I did not give Bob Dunlop an immediate answer, saying that I would have to talk with my wife and my partners, both of which I did. Warren was hesitant, thinking of the potential time involved, but said she would support whatever decision I made. My partners took the same approach, except for Bill Baugh. Bill, a loyal and enthusiastic Penn alumnus, told me that there was no choice—I would have to say, "Yes, I'm willing to be considered."

I did so and did not think much more about it until the June trustee meetings. I was in a development committee meeting when a messenger summoned me out of the room with the message that the executive committee wanted to see me in the Faculty Club.

I arrived, and after a few greetings, Don Regan said that they had decided they wanted me as the new chairman. Would I please accept their invitation? Well, other than the day I was asked to be a partner of Drexel & Co., I have never been so blown away with surprise. With my heart beating rapidly, I said that I accepted and would dedicate myself to the job. A single thought dominated all else: if only my dad had lived to see this!

The rest of that day is very fuzzy in my memory. I must have been knocked into a daze. Somehow I was able to tell Warren what had taken place because I know that she was present at my formal election. It took place that afternoon at the stated meeting of the trustees, always an impossibly stiff affair because it is a so-called sunshine meeting open to any members of the public who wish to come (required because of Pennsylvania law regarding board meetings of institutions receiving state funding, no matter how small). Because the trustees don't tackle controversial matters in committees, the stated meetings are simply a necessary ratification of committee decisions. Dull is too complimentary a word to describe these meetings. The details may be fuzzy but my impression was that I was very strongly supported. Trustees had wanted a Penn alumnus, and the faculty was pleased because I had actual academic experience as a teacher. I had known some of the faculty leaders as my teachers in both undergraduate and graduate school.

John Eckman was very displeased, feeling I had not earned the job as much as he had. He did not withhold his feelings, and I was sensitive to them. He turned away when I tried to speak to him, so I sent a handwritten letter expressing my thanks for all he had done for Penn. His involvement waned, and sadly, he died of a heart attack not many years later.

Over the next few months I spent many hours at the university, receiving visits from many faculty friends who wanted to tell me what they thought on an assortment of issues facing the university. I received them gracefully, doing my best to be mindful that the trustees do not run the place and must not intercede in matters delegated to the president. This was not always easy and it was not always clear where the demarcation line should be.

But first things first. We were in the middle of a capital campaign and the chairman of that was John Eckman. It wasn't long before he resigned as chairman and I assumed the job at the urging of Martin Meyerson and the executive committee.

In the spring of 1978, there had been a large student sit-in, demanding a number of things, mostly to do with Penn's alleged obligations to the surrounding community. It was a rather nasty affair and many faculty, alumni, and trustees were displeased with what looked like a caving-in to the demands. Martin took the heat.

I like Martin immensely and always have. My liking for him is most basically for his character but it is enhanced by my admiration for his range of knowledge and intellect.

I thought both then and now, a quarter-century later, that he was a good president at the right time for Penn. He made us think we should be better and believe we could be, at a time when we had what many thought was an inferiority complex. Tom Gates once said, "We don't have an inferiority complex. Rather, it's a feeling of eternal dissatisfaction." Martin made us realize the difference and use that realization to our advantage.

Martin was in his ninth year as president. I was barraged by pressures from trustees and faculty friends to seek from him an agreement to retire at the end of the following academic year. After talking with several of the more senior trustees, I met with Martin to suggest softly that he announce that he would do so. As I remember, that meeting was late in the 1979 academic year. Martin did not take kindly to the suggestion and it was only after several conversations with him that we came to a semblance of agreement that he would step aside.

My first action as chairman was to simplify the committee structure that over time had become cluttered with three ad hoc committees and over ten standing committees. The seven standing committees I established—finance, audit, development, external affairs, student affairs, investment, and nominating—have been altered only slightly since 1979. I streamlined the executive committee to consist of the committee chairmen and the president of the General Alumni Society. The latter was a very popular move that brought the alumni directly into the affairs of the university.

Endowment Worries and an Answer: John Neff

I was very worried about the inadequacy of Penn's endowment and its relatively poor performance. It seemed to me that we should have the best possible investment managers and not leave it to the individual trustees who had been doing an unprofessional pro bono job. How could we continue to have free management services yet have the best possible people doing the work?

In a flash of brilliance I thought of asking the best money manager I knew, John Neff, the manager of Windsor Fund and almost legendary as an investor, if he would do it. Yet John had no Penn connections. After talking with some key trustees, I called John and said, "John, I know this is a long shot, but would you consider becoming a Penn trustee and taking responsibility for managing the endowment?" He replied that it was a long shot but he would talk with his wife, Lil, and get back to me. He did the next day, saying that he had taken a lot from society and needed to give something back. And that's how we successfully got a brilliant value investor to donate his services to Penn.

John did an outstanding job, compiling a record that exceeded the S&P 500's returns by four full percentage points per year for the next thirteen years. The endowment was only $130 million in 1979 when he took over. It is now about $4 billion after a major fund-raising campaign and a good investment record. John also became an active, interested trustee, who donated his wisdom on more than just the investment side.

Because of a conflict of interest, Miller, Anderson & Sherrerd could not become a paid investment manager, but I recruited my partner, Rich Worley, to donate his services as both a talented fixed-income manager and as a trustee.

All went well until the mid-1990s when John Neff's style of value investing temporarily produced well-below-average results in the bull market leading to the big stock-market bubble of 1997-2000. Although he was ultimately correct, John became bearish too early, in 1997, and wanted us to take our equity ratio down to 35 percent. The investment board resisted him and he resigned as chairman. But by then we were in a transition to an internal investment department that would help choose and monitor a diversified group of outside managers.

John is now retired as manager of Windsor Fund but still an active and very talented investor. When he speaks, I still listen closely.

Martin's years as president had seen balanced budgets except for one year when a sharp surge in oil prices sent our costs soaring. Attaining financial stability while still improving the place was a tough job well done. I was determined that our budget would continue to be balanced, and it was throughout my chairmanship.

Martin sparked a welcomed renewal in arts and sciences, changing the school's name from the College to the Faculty of Arts and Sciences (FAS), thus broadening its reach and opening up more interdisciplinary possibilities

The first dean of FAS was Vartan Gregorian, an Iranian-born Stanford-educated scholar of European and Middle Eastern history, who had come to Penn in 1972. He was immensely popular with both students and faculty. Then, when Elliot Stellar retired as provost and after a search for his successor in 1978, Martin Meyerson recommended Gregorian to become provost. The trustees enthusiastically approved the recommendation.

When the search for a new president began in 1979, a large part of the campus looked upon "Greg" as the odds-on favorite.

Penn had not been as badly torn apart by controversy during the Vietnam War as many campuses, but the attitude expressed in a popular bumper sticker in those years, Question Authority, had pervaded all campuses. Civil-rights and racism issues, divestiture of stocks of companies doing business in South Africa, women's issues, and gay-rights issues had all appeared on campus. Faculty issues of compensation and participation in decision making had intensified as inflation eroded their economic well-being. The atmosphere had become highly politicized. It was in this general environment that we would conduct the presidential search.

The Controversial Presidential Search of 1980

I chaired the search committee that was charged with presenting up to three candidates to the trustees' executive committee. The search committee had a bare majority of six trustees, along with four faculty and two students. We worked diligently through the spring, traveling and interviewing with disappointingly sparse results. There were two other internal candidates: Ed Stemmler, dean of the medical school, and Tom Langfitt, the vice president for health affairs. There were a couple of very good but not great external candidates, whom I will not name because they are still active in academia, one of whom went on to become president of another Ivy League university a couple of years later.

In April or May, the search committee received a letter from a man in Western Pennsylvania who nominated his brother-in-law. Search committees get many strange letters and nominations, so this one was a bit suspect. But the nominee was the president of Tulane University, a Yale PhD and former provost of Princeton. His name was Sheldon Hackney.

Hackney came for an interview, arriving late because of fog around Martha's Vineyard where he summered. Both his experience and his manner impressed the committee. Our intelligence network began a thorough vetting of Sheldon and his references. He was very popular at Tulane and had been a very successful scholar at Yale and a good provost at Princeton. He had solidly liberal credentials of his own as a scholar of southern progressivism and was an active member of the American Civil Liberties Union Additionally, his wife, Lucy, was the daughter of a prominent Birmingham lawyer who was ostracized by the white community for having been the pro bono defender of Rosa Parks following her arrest for refusing to move to the back of a bus in Birmingham. The combination of Sheldon and Lucy, I thought to myself, ought to satisfy the most crusading of liberals. And there were plenty of them on the Penn campus.

Meanwhile, Gregorian was running for the job, as one trustee remarked, "as fast as his corset allowed." Greg is a short, rotund, teddy bear of a man who effuses personality and charm. He is also a respected scholar. I like him. He endears himself to people with the skill of a master politician. I mean that in a nonpejorative sense, but occasionally he can be quite blatant in making promises and claiming credit where none is due.

On several instances, he offended individual trustees by being obviously political in telling them that *they* were the ones who ought to be president. One personal anecdote concerned my wife, Warren, who had been named an overseer of FAS. This occurred after Martin asked me for some women candidates for the board of overseers. I gave him some names then added that Warren, a Penn graduate and Phi Beta Kappa, might be interested. He thought that was a great idea and ran with it. At a trustee party after her election, Greg threw his arms around her and told her how happy he was to see her as an overseer. Then he added, "It was my idea, you know."

Still, I regarded Greg as the favorite candidate. In early spring of 1979, it was rumored that Greg was on the "short list" for chancellor of the University of California at Berkeley. I was urged by Martin and others to speak to him, make sure he understood that he was a strong candidate, and while we could guarantee nothing, we hoped he would stay at Penn. I did so. It was either then or shortly thereafter that Greg asked me to tell him if at any time during the search process he was no longer in the running. I told him I would try to do so.

I must say that I have no idea whether or not, as some claimed, he was actually offered the chancellor's position. But the impression was widespread that he had.

By late summer we knew we were only a couple of weeks away from a decision. The field had come down to Greg, internal candidates Ed Stemmler, and Tom Langfitt, a woman who had been president of a prominent women's college, and Sheldon Hackney. They were all scheduled for interviews with the full committee. Greg was to be the last interview.

The other candidates each gave a strong performance for the committee. This made Greg's appearance seem all the more bizarre. He entered looking fairly subdued and grumpy and almost before we could ask the first question, he launched into a soliloquy. I cannot quote him accurately but in essence he said that it seemed strange to him that we needed to talk to him at all. Hadn't he adequately proved himself? What more could we possibly want to know?

It was an irrational ranting. Around the room people were afraid to look at one another and stared at the table in embarrassment. Every person there was shocked, including his strongest advocates. It seemed totally out of character with the Gregorian we knew. To this day I don't know what possessed him. Later we heard that he was not feeling well. Who knows? But he lost the trustees that day. One woman trustee leaned over to me after Greg left, and said simply, "No way, Jose."

Faculty members on the committee pleaded to have us overlook Greg's performance. But the die seemed cast.

The question for me was whether to tell Greg then, even though the executive committee was not yet involved and no vote of the search committee had yet been taken, that he probably was no longer in the running. He had told me that he would bow out gracefully with a statement that he had withdrawn from consideration for personal reasons. Yet, I concluded, no such statement would be accepted by his fans (a conclusion that was proven correct by their later actions) and would be seen as no more than what it was: that the trustees had turned down his candidacy.

Events moved rapidly from then on. The search committee voted, without having to use just the trustee majority, not to present Greg's name to the executive committee. It would be asked to consider only Sheldon Hackney and the woman candidate, both scholars and proven academic leaders who had interviewed very well. The campus knew we were close to a decision, and the press was alert and looking for leaks. The executive committee met in the Bellevue Stratford Hotel for a final interview of the candidates.

There was a serious concern about the campus uproar that would surely develop when a selection other than Gregorian was announced. It was even suggested that we might call Leon Higginbothom, a prominent African-American judge on the federal bench and a trustee, to see if we could convince him to be a last-minute candidate. It was a misguided effort to avoid controversy, but I did call him. I told him where we were in the process and asked if he would consider an invitation to meet with us. He said he had no interest in the job. I believe that Leon, hoping a Democrat would be elected in 1980, was waiting for a supreme-court nomination. Retrospectively, I am very glad he decided the way he did.

The Selection of Sheldon Hackney

The process continued with the interviews followed by long discussion and a vote. Sheldon Hackney was the selection. It remained to craft press releases and talk to the unsuccessful candidates, including Gregorian—an unpleasant task that fell to me. As I recall, the executive committee meeting was on a Sunday so we had to maintain secrecy until sometime the next day. I dutifully met with Gregorian the next morning and told him the bad news. He took it stoically, but said that we had made a big mistake.

When the announcement was made, the expected eruption began and grew and grew. The *Daily Pennsylvanian* never had as big a story to gnaw on and the Philadelphia newspapers joined the fray. There were ridiculous accusations that we had demonstrated ethnic prejudice in rejecting a bearded Iranian. Never throughout the process was there so much a hint of any bigotry. My main fear was that Hackney would be scared away. He had been warned by me of the probable campus reaction. As far as I know, he never wavered.

The faculty senate invited me to appear and explain the search process so they might judge its fairness. A faculty representative on the search committee and I went to an overflow meeting and described the entire search, detailing how arduously we had stuck to the rules.

I do not know whether or not Greg encouraged the bad behavior of both faculty and students, but he certainly did not discourage it. The nastiest possible things were said about me and the trustees, demands for changing the process were made, all, as one would expect, asking for greater faculty and student representation. The faculty senate passed a resolution asking the trustees to nominate Gregorian. The *Daily Pennsylvania* ran a story that one trustee would seek the resignation of the entire executive committee. I have no idea where the story originated, and of course, it never happened.

The final election of the new president was made by the full body of trustees at their October stated meeting. By then, some level of acceptance had seeped in, particularly as people found out more about Sheldon Hackney and his record at Princeton and Tulane.

I looked upon Sheldon as a person who might succeed in depoliticizing the campus. I think he did that over his first five years or so. He is a very sensible person with a quiet personality that is augmented superbly by his outgoing wife, Lucy.

From the beginning, Sheldon and Lucy wanted to live on the campus—something that other presidents had not done. We selected Eisenlohr Hall, a beautiful old early-twentieth-century mansion that had been chopped up into offices with marvelous old paneling that had been sadly painted over. I campaigned among the trustees for the funds to remodel Eisenlohr and restore its beauty, both inside and out. The president's living on campus has, I believe, made a great difference to students and faculty. The house is used widely for entertaining and has been marvelously furnished with antiques that were owned by the university but well hidden in nooks and crannies all over campus.

I have written this account of the search purposely without reading Gregorian's account in his biography that was published in 2003. It will be interesting to compare his version and mine.

Greg went on to become a successful president of the New York Public Library and then Brown University. As this is written he is the president of the Carnegie Corporation of New York. Curiously, I was called as a reference only once when he became candidate for these positions. I told the caller that he would be a good president, especially if he were coming to the institution from outside, not having campaigned for the job with his fellow faculty and the trustees.

As it was, Hackney spent the first few years as president undoing many promises Greg had made. Sheldon did a good, solid job as president. His strongest suit was his ability to choose very good people as managers under him. He was never shy about being upstaged and even seemed to encourage it and was always ready to give others full credit rather than claiming it for himself. There were certainly times when I wished he would be more forceful and more of an A-type personality, but I believe he was right for the time. He found a marvelous provost, Tom Ehrlich, who had been dean of the Stanford Law School and director of the Agency for International Development. Arguably, Tom was the best provost Penn had had in many years. He went on to become president of Indiana University.

I decided that eight years was enough as chairman and asked to be relieved in 1986. Al Shoemaker succeeded me and did a superb job in an era that was obsessed with political correctness, an obsession that finally resulted in a real mess for Hackney, just as he was preparing to leave the presidency.

President Clinton had appointed Sheldon to head the National Endowment for the Humanities. A Jewish student living in a high-rise dormitory was disturbed while studying by a noisy group of African-American women students outside. He leaned out the window and shouted, "Shut up, you water buffaloes!" The comment was misinterpreted as a racial insult, and the young man was hauled before the university's internal judicial system for violations of the "speech code" that had been installed by university council with Hackney's assent.

By the time Hackney heard about it, the alleged perpetrator had engaged a conservative faculty member as his counsel and the wheels of justice were turning. He was caught between a rock and a hard place. If he intervened, he would have seen the wrath of the liberal campus elite descend upon him. If he did not intervene, he knew there would be some conservatives who would be furious, but even so he didn't fully appreciate what would happen. The case became a cause célèbre in the conservative press, trustees were upset, and Hackney's nomination to head the National Endowment of the Humanities was seriously threatened. It was a sad time for the university and for Hackney, about which he has written a book. It all came out okay for Sheldon; he got his appointment. But he has a permanently black eye in conservative circles and among some trustees.

Meanwhile, we were unable to mount a presidential search quickly enough to replace Sheldon, and an interim president was appointed. She was Claire Fagin, a highly respected woman who had been dean of the school of nursing. This appointment raised academic eyebrows, but Claire carried out the presidential responsibilities well. She had dreams of greater glory, however, and while she is a wonderful and able person, she never was a serious contender for the presidency. After a year in the job, however, I think that she thought she was—or at least, should be.

My Third Presidential Search

I was a member of the search committee, the third presidential search in which I had participated. Almost at the outset I drew the task of traveling to Yale to interview the provost, former dean of the faculty and a psychology professor, Judith Rodin, a

Penn alumnus. Drew Faust, a highly regarded professor of history and one of the most popular women on the Penn faculty, flew to New Haven with me. I had no idea what to expect when we were ushered into the provost's office. Judy was full of personality, knew Penn in detail, answered every question faultlessly, and was clearly interested. As we left the office, I half humorously asked Drew why we had to look any further. But we did, not only because others had to be satisfied but also because of the requirements surrounding equal-opportunity issues.

In the end, Judy was the unanimous selection of the search committee and then of the executive committee who met at the Rittenhouse Hotel over a weekend. As I write this, she has just retired in June of 2004, after ten years in office. She will become the president of the Rockefeller Foundation. She has been truly outstanding.

Judy coalesced the alumni (always a dicey proposition at Penn), dealt effectively with severe financial problems in the medical center, was very forceful on personnel issues, did away with the speech code as her first action, overcame crime and security problems that could have been awful setbacks for Penn, and almost single-handedly revitalized West Philadelphia. As a classmate and friend of Ed Rendell, mayor of the city for much of Judy's term and now Pennsylvania's governor, she effectively integrated Penn, the area's largest employer, with the political powers of the city and the commonwealth.

Judy Rodin was the fourth president of Penn whom I have known well. Each of them has had many more strengths than weaknesses. Each was right for the time and Penn has prospered hugely as a result.

In 1997, I retired (required by university statutes) as an active trustee after a record thirty-one years. There was a big party of trustees, close faculty and medical friends, personal friends, classmates, and our entire family.

I am now a trustee emeritus and joke that the *e* stands for *exit* and the *meritus* means *I deserve it*. I can attend meetings but not vote. I remained on the investment board and retired in 2004, after thirty-eight years.

Some Thoughts about Universities

When I retired as Chairman of the Trustees in 1986, I gave a talk that attracted attention and compliments. After saying all the usual nice things, I said that I had earned the right to sound off on our university and universities in general. Here are some excerpts:

> *I think private universities need to reinvigorate their sense of privateness. Heaven forbid, I don't mean that in an elite, nonegalitarian sense. Rather, I think those who are educated here should understand that these buildings, books, labs and dorms didn't just magically appear. They were built by people of past generations who believed in private education as the standard-setter for higher education in*

general. They were built by people who had a sense of loyalty and gratitude to Penn because of what it did to form their lives.

Today, perhaps because of the high price of education and the necessity for a high level of student aid and student debt, I sense more a feeling of getting one's money's worth rather than gratitude.

It is obvious that we still have a great distance to go if American universities are to be models of social justice for the rest of society. We have made huge strides in relatively few years toward overcoming our inheritance of sexist and racist attitudes. We must, as trustees, continue to encourage and cajole our campus in these regards.

I believe we have a duty to protect the fragile structure of the university from extremists at both ends of the spectrum, both within and outside the university, who fail to make what Bart Giamatti (former President of Yale) calls "the distinction between education and indoctrination."

There remain substantial threats to academic freedom from outside universities . . . [for example] . . . an insidious movement called "Accuracy in Academia, that recruits students to monitor classes for leftist ideological content and seeks to intimidate by so-called "exposure." [and] others who would deny Federal or state monies to universities whose hospitals perform abortions or whose trustees have refused to divest South Africa—related investments.

The curious aspect of these intrusions is that, on the left, it appears under the banners of tolerance, liberality and freedom. On the right it marches under slogans of family values, religion and American ideals.

There are also threats . . . from inside the walls. I have personally been labeled a racist and worse in public by a faculty member because I disagree with him about divestment. Last year a faculty member, known for his forceful Socratic teaching overstepped the boundary between productive provocation and counterproductive tastelessness (in asking for a response to a question on a race-related justice issue from African American students, he said, "What do you former slaves think about that?"). Calls were issued for his immediate dismissal from the faculty without regard to due process. [some of these calls] came from [other faculty members] who should know better.

Trustees should be concerned about restoring and maintaining civility . . . [incivility] . . . has become tolerated . . . to a point where it seems to be an everyday occurrence. I believe that the nexus of universities is the fundamental premise that intellectual persuasion is the only responsible way to change the views of others . . . .

The role of the university as an institution . . . . is to assure that the forum is there for free and unimpeded debate and to encourage civility and the highest levels of tolerance for different ideas and views. To this end we must stand firm against pressures to have the university take policy positions on issues of the day not directly related to our educational mission.

[completing the above quote of Bart Giamatti] . . . "There are many who lust for the simple answers of doctrine or decree. They are on the left and right. They are not confined to a single part of society. They are the terrorists of the mind. But if freedom does not first reside in the mind, it cannot finally reside anywhere."

I am very proud that I have played a part in building this great educational institution. Other than my family, Penn is the most important thing in my life. It is an immensely better university, both in absolute and relative terms, than it was when we were students and when I became a trustee.

The Ford Foundation

My first contacts with the Ford Foundation were in the days when we were selling Drexel & Co.'s research services in the early 1960s. Ford was a large endowment that naturally attracted Wall Street's attention. At the time, they were still very large owners of Ford Motor Company stock, the original gift of Henry Ford. Ford was privately held by the Ford family until the initial public offering in the mid-1960s.

About that time, the foundation and the family had a serious falling out over the liberal leanings of the foundation staff that resulted in the resignation of Henry Ford II as a trustee.

In 1966, after spending five years as national security adviser to Presidents Kennedy and Johnson, McGeorge Bundy became the foundation's president. Mac Bundy was a classic intellectual Northeastern liberal. A Yale graduate and professor at Harvard, he had all the right liberal credentials except that he was a vociferous anticommunist and had even denied tenure to two Harvard faculty members who had strong communist leanings. Bundy was an integral player among the "best and the brightest" in the Kennedy White House and played a highly controversial role in the escalation of the war in Vietnam.

His presidency of Ford Foundation was also an escalation—an escalation of the foundation's presence in financing the liberal causes in environmentalism and social justice. The foundation grew, aided by the bull market of the '60s, in grants and in staff as well as in spreading its largesse internationally. From a relatively small staff, the foundation's people count grew to about 1,500 by the end of his presidency in 1979.

Mac Bundy was vitally interested in the major question of what the foundation should do with its Ford Motor stock. Modest sales had been made, but no real policy had been adopted on the stock's disposal or retention. In 1970 or 1971, my friend Bill Donaldson, who is the current chairman of the SEC, invited me and two other investment managers to dinner with Mac Bundy and his chief investment officer, Roger Kennedy. The purpose was to listen to Bundy's concerns about endowment management in general and the foundation's holding of Ford Motor. We met twice and were unanimous in our opinion that the stock should be sold, preferably gradually when the market was accommodative. This was done, and by 1974, the entire holding had been sold.

It was at about that same time that Bundy wrote a pamphlet on endowment investing, suggesting that most endowments had been far too conservative in their investment policies. The pamphlet's publication was badly timed, just before the bear market of 1971-1973, the worst since the 1930s. Bundy became a bit of a joke in investment circles for a while.

I had no further contact with the foundation until 1982 when Alexander Heard, the chairman of the board, a lovely gentleman who was the chancellor of Vanderbilt University, called me. He asked if I would have dinner with him and Frank Thomas, the president of the foundation. (Bundy retired in 1979.) I arranged dinner at the Philadelphia Club, and on a weekday night, it was quiet to a fault. We may have been the only diners. After fairly brief socializing, Alex Heard invited me to become a trustee of the Ford Foundation. They had obviously done their homework (including talking with Sheldon Hackney, who was a prominent Vanderbilt alumnus) and knew a great deal about me while I had not done any homework and knew very little about what being a trustee entailed. They wanted me to become chairman of the investment committee, a post that had been held by Bill Donaldson during his two terms (twelve years) as a trustee. It was obvious that Bill had recommended me as his replacement.

I was, of course, flattered, but I was also quite thrilled at the possibility. I told them that I was favorably inclined but needed a couple of days to think about it. I accepted two days later.

Retrospectively, I now know how little I knew about the foundation. During my first several years as a trustee, I learned in bits and pieces how Frank Thomas had become the talk of the world of philanthropy by initiating a complete redesign of the foundation's programs and staff. Strange as it seems, I was never told the complete story at one time by any single individual, and I am still not certain of all the details and nuances.

Frank Thomas clearly wanted to move the foundation toward more involvement in issues of social justice and poverty, both urban and rural, while de-emphasizing support of higher education and cultural institutions. Shortly after becoming president, in May 1980, layoff notices were given to about nine hundred people in New York and around the world. It became known as the May Day Massacre. Mac Bundy's expansion was undone in a single stroke.

It was two years after this that I became a trustee. I received a day of orientation, talking with the program officers in charge of education and culture, social justice, urban poverty, rural poverty, and international. It was very exciting to see the extent of the foundation's involvement and the knowledge of the people running the programs. It was a wholly different world for me and I felt very inadequate. With the exception of education, these were issues that I had never dealt with in my career. While this sense of inadequacy remained with me, it diminished over the twelve-year span of my trusteeship. It was a feeling that made me very uncomfortable, one to which I was unaccustomed.

The chief investment officer was John English, a pleasant, Uriah Heep-like character, who had come from a bureaucratic life at AT&T, where he oversaw the company's pension fund. An investor he was not, and he was overly cautious and protective of the people who worked for him. The materials that were prepared for the investment committee were as simple and uncomplicated as possible and revealed very little about what was going on within the portfolio. My dissatisfaction with John grew as I tried to get the committee more meaningful information.

After the stock market crash of October 19, 1987, I tried to get him to adopt a more aggressive investment stance, telling him it was time to at least bet the barn if not the whole ranch. Frank Thomas was also very cautious, so the moves we made were relatively modest. A couple of years before I retired from the board, John retired under some pressure from me, and turned the portfolio over to Linda Strumpf, a capable but quite conventional investor who carried on and at least added some investment sophistication to the process. Altogether, over my twelve years as a trustee, the investment results were very average. It was a very difficult ship to turn and my success was slight. It was a good lesson in "institutionalized investment thinking."

But my investment responsibilities were a small part of being a trustee. The exposure we received on major issues and problems was fascinating. Meetings were held for two days, a Thursday and Friday, four times a year. In addition, there were periodic trips to various parts of the globe to see firsthand the foundation's programs in action. Trustees could also schedule their own trips, either alone or with smaller groups of trustees to places of their choice to witness the grantees in action. There were foundation offices in several foreign locations including New Delhi, Bejing, Nairobi, Rio de Janeiro, Mexico City, Cairo, and Jakarta.

Warren and I participated in many of these trips, descriptions of which would consume far too much space, so I will mention only a few highlights:

> *Travel of a party of six trustees to China and Bejing in 1989, just a few weeks after President Bush's visit and a few weeks before the face-off between the agitators for change and the regime that culminated in Tianamen Square.*

This trip included an afternoon spent with the head of China's supreme court, talking about the potential creation of a system of laws rather than a system of men. We also met with the prime minister in the Forbidden City and had a large dinner given in our honor in the Great Hall of the People. A visit to Bejing University to converse with faculty leaders was followed by a trip to the countryside and a visit to a mud-brick home in a small village.

Someone once told me that China, everywhere you go, looks as if the football stadium just emptied. It's a good description of the crowded streets—crowded, not by cars but by people.

This trip provided a glimpse of the beginnings of change in China. At that time, new hotels and offices were rising in the cities to such an extent that the Chinese called their national bird the crane, referring to the dozens of construction cranes rising above the cities, side by side with the old rudimentary mud-brick neighborhoods. The electric power system was strained and we had no daytime elevator service in one hotel and had to climb up to the Great Wall because the cable cars had no power. Evidence of any change in attitudes toward human rights or democratic processes was completely absent.

In 1986 the March board meeting was held in Rio de Janeiro. The trustees broke into smaller groups to visit various places in Central and South America.

A group of four of us traveled to Mexico City and Argentina. The group included Glenn Watts, former president of the Communication Workers of America, and Bob McNamara, Secretary of Defense under Kennedy and Johnson and then the CEO of the World Bank. After seeing some of the devastation of a severe earthquake in Mexico City and the social and environmental problems engendered by the immense population flow to the city from the countryside, we proceeded to Buenos Aires. At that time, Buenos Aires looked very shabby from years of neglect but the beautiful wide avenues spoke of an eloquent past.

Argentina had lost an embarrassing war with Britain over the Falkland Islands, following which the repressive regime that had governed for some years was at last deposed. The country was trying to stabilize its economy in the face of huge foreign debts incurred and funds misspent or absconded with by the preceding corrupt, abusive, and repressive government. Thousands of people suspected of dissension had disappeared mysteriously and were presumed murdered by that regime. Stories were being uncovered about bodies being dumped from planes out at sea, torture chambers, and worse.

In addition to meeting with academics and government officials of the new democracy about Argentina's economic and social problems, we also met with the Grandmothers of Cinco Mayo. These women had organized an extensive search process to find grandchildren who had been abducted when their parents disappeared. These children had often been handed over to sympathizers with the regime who were looking to adopt children. The foundation, to aid their efforts, had funded DNA examinations to help reconnect relatives. The stories were heart-wrenching, but the DNA tests were beginning to pay off.

Continuing on to Brazil, we went on to Salvador in Bahia, and Brasilia, the nation's capital, and finally to Rio. That city, beautiful as is its setting, was surrounded by hillsides of squatter settlements called *favellas*, which we visited. These were unbelievably squalid, with open sewage ditches in many areas, flimsy shacks of corrugated metal and tarpaper, and yet containing people who were trying to get something better. We visited with several organized groups attempting to help inhabitants get title to the land. They had met with some success. The leaders of these groups were women, just as they are in many parts of the world under similar circumstances. We saw examples of how, once title was granted, the shacks were replaced by cinderblock dwellings. Yet the inequality of wealth in Brazil and other South American countries, born of centuries of political control by landowners, is a problem that will take either revolutions or many decades to overcome.

In the fall of 1993 the trustees traveled in small groups to various parts of Eastern Europe and Russia.

The purpose was to meet with embryonic grantees that were just beginning to get underway in the post-Cold War era. Our group traveled to Warsaw and rural Poland and then on to Prague in the Czech Republic.

Everywhere we went the signs of emerging democratic capitalism were evident even if rather rudimentary. In Warsaw, we met with Lech Walesa who, while no longer at the head of the government, was still an important figure. While he spoke no English and his greeting had to be translated for us, the man's powerful personality was very attractive. One could clearly envision him in the revolutionary leadership role that he had played in helping bring down the Communist regime.

Visiting the rural countryside, we saw firsthand the terrible results of bad agricultural practices that were used to force higher production by the Communists. Overfertilization had poisoned the aquifers, and drinking water had to be hauled in by truck for the villages.

One day we stopped for lunch at a small country café and Warren and I sat with fellow trustee Vernon Jordan and his wife Ann. Vernon, who was once awarded a Penn honorary degree, was a friend and confidant of Bill Clinton. Clinton had been elected the previous November. He later became known in the press as FFOB, "First Friend of Bill's."

Warren asked Vernon if Hillary Clinton was the brighter of the two and received a resounding no from both Ann and him. "Bill Clinton," said Vernon, "is one of the smartest men I ever met. If he can keep his flies zipped, he will be a great president." It was a very prophetic comment!

In Prague we met with the leadership of the newly elected legislature who were still working to understand how a democracy should work. And we were privileged to meet with the country's president, Vaclev Havel. A playwright who had been Czechoslovakia's foremost dissident and human rights activist, he spent five years in prison in the early 1980s. He almost single-handedly fomented the rebellion of the Czech people against the Communists as the Cold War came to an end. He was proclaimed the president of Czechoslovakia in 1989 and then was elected president of the Czech Republic after the creation of Slovakia and the Czech Republic as separate states in 1992.

The meeting, held in the beautiful palace that dominates the hill across the river, was quite odd. We expected a warm welcome by a warm personality and got neither. Once we were admitted through cadres of aides, the president was ushered into a room where we had all been placed at a very long table. He sat, lit a cigarette that he allowed to hang from his mouth, drank a cup of coffee, and stared at the cup while he spoke rather curtly and in Czech, not English, despite the fact that he is a fluent English speaker. He gave us no real chance to get a conversation going and eventually launched into a request for money from the foundation. He was told that we do not make grants to governments but had been working with nongovernmental organizations (NGOs) to help the country get a kick start. He was not much interested. It was difficult to picture his personality leading anything, just the opposite of our experience with Lech Walesa in Poland.

The trip was unforgettable in that we saw the beginnings of new free, democratic, capitalistic societies in the Eastern Europe that had been so dominated and suppressed by the Soviet Union and Communist regimes for some forty years.

Nothing prepared us for India, which we visited in early 1990, coincident with the outbreak of the Gulf War.

There were three couples on the trip, Ed Spencer and his wife Harriet, Bill Milliken and his wife Helen, and the two of us. Ed was the retired CEO of Minneapolis-Honeywell and Bill Milliken was the former three-term governor of Michigan. It was a marvelously compatible sixsome who were greeted and guided by the head of the foundation's New Delhi office, Gordon Conway. (Several years later Gordon became the president of the Rockefeller Foundation.)

The trip had a tightly packed itinerary. Every day was full of visits with officials or grantees, exhausting travel, careening along inadequate roads filled with oxen, people, overloaded buses, and dust, at speeds better confined to expressways. We fell into bed every night, totally worn out.

India is indescribable: The crowds, odors, dust, and dullness punctuated by bright-colored saris, poverty, beggars, ugliness, beauty—are unforgettable. If I were even to begin to write about this trip it would consume half of the book. So a couple of anecdotes will have to suffice.

In Bangalore, while visiting the university there, I was told I was expected to speak to the student body of four hundred law students. But about what? Whatever I pleased. Okay, so what do I tell law students when my only connection with the law was that I had a daughter in Stanford University's Law School? Somehow I patched together a talk about U.S. universities and their law schools, drawing entirely from what I had learned as chairman of Penn's trustees and as the father of a law student. I literally had only ten minutes to put an outline down on a scrap of paper. But it seemed to work, although I'm sure I didn't make the student newspaper's list of events of the week.

Another highlight was visiting a village where traditional birth attendants (called TBAs) were being trained by an organization founded by a woman obstetrician in Madras. TBAs, who are tradition-trained midwives, are of the lowest caste because of their contact with blood. They perform their duties, are lowly village citizens, and are completely naive about the need for sterile instruments, water, and cloths. They have been performing their duties for centuries. The infant mortality rates are very high, unsurprisingly.

The organization we visited was training these illiterate women, using pictures and diagrams, in the techniques of safer delivery. Problem cases are described, and the need for cleanliness is emphasized. The women are dressed in white saris, and are given a bag of instruments to carry. Because of their increased effectiveness and dress, they were accorded increased respect and were responsible for cutting the infant mortality rate by up to 50 percent. When the mortality rate is reduced, the birth rate also tends to go down.

Other villages we visited (there are over 550,000 villages in India) were instituting, for the first time, census techniques, measuring agricultural production, wealth, age groups, housing adequacy, etc. Illiteracy forces the use of rudimentary counting mechanisms, such as different-colored beans or types of sticks. The data were being recorded by a Ford-financed NGO and made available to various private foundations, charities, and government agencies that needed more information about village economics and demographics.

Several projects were aimed at elevating the economic status of women. India's culture insists on the primacy of sons. Often, a married couple will continue to have children until at least one son is born. The education of girls is not a priority, so women have no economic independence. The Women's Dairy Cooperative is an organization started by women and run by women, that collects, processes, and distributes milk. It provides an income to the women involved. Economic independence fosters literacy and education, particularly for daughters. It is a small but working demonstration project.

While we were in India, the Gulf War began. At its beginning, we didn't know what to expect in terms of riots or disruptions in other parts of the world. The speed at which the war proceeded preempted anything very serious, but the foundation was concerned that we travel via the safest route home. That meant not flying over the Middle East. Therefore we traveled from Madras to Singapore to Tokyo to Seattle to Philadelphia—a very long and exhausting trip. But it was very comforting to get back the old U. S. of A.

Other trips of note were to El Paso to look at the problems of Mexican immigration, the Watts area of Los Angeles to see how the community had dealt with the aftermath of severe race riots some years previous, to the black belt of the South, a swath across Alabama and Mississippi, to visit grantees concerned with the economic and social problems of the predominantly African-American population of that area, to Miami to look at the plight of the Haitian immigrants, to Harlem to enjoy the work of the Dance Company of Harlem, to Jakarta, Indonesia, and Indonesian rural villages, and many other fascinating places with interesting and sometimes tragic problems.

It was an exhilarating twelve years, but there were certain frustrations that nagged at me. The staff was composed heavily of people with either an academic or quasigovernmental background. Reports we received were lengthy, wordy, and fuzzy. Objectives were not clear, and measurement of results was either lacking or inadequate. I often felt that projects leaned too much toward the gratification of the staff.

I raised questions about accountability and measurement of results several times to little avail. I felt they needed a heavy dose of MBA know-how even though I saw that it would be heavily resisted.

Clearly, the Ford Foundation is a very liberal place. That's okay, but there was a leaning over backward to avoid any connection with the for-profit world, evidently to keep a high degree of credibility with grantees. And there was a denial of history. At the Carnegie Corporation or the Pew Charitable Trusts, the founder-donors are honored, portraits hung in the offices, and founders are even quoted. There is not a single picture of Henry Ford in the foundation's sumptuous offices. This seems very strange to me.

World Wildlife Fund

Bill Reilly, the then president of World Wildlife Fund, called on me in the mid-1980s to ask for a donation. We made a small grant from our family's Maple Hill Foundation, and I became a member of their national council. When Bill became head of the Environmental Protection Agency under George H. W. Bush, Kathryn Fuller became WWF's president and asked me to become more involved in the organization's affairs. I said that I would consider doing so after my term as a Ford Foundation trustee ended. I was elected a director of WWF for a three-year term in 1994, reelected for a second term, and while there is a two-term limit, officers can stay on for nine years. After being elected treasurer (and chair of the finance committee), I continued for the full nine years,

WWF is a first-rate organization that uses its scarce resources wisely and efficiently. But while I am an enthusiast about the outdoors and conservation, I am far from being an environmental zealot and always mindful of the cost/benefit ratios of specific proposals. Having said that, I found WWF to be most effective "on the ground," that is, in dealing with specific issues of habitat and species preservation, and least effective in the macro issues of public policy and issues such as global warming. The problem, in my opinion, is that staff become zealots and too often have knee-jerk reactions to developments in the global political arena that occupy too much of their effort.

We had some incredible experiences while I was a WWF director. Trips to Tanzania, where we were stuck hubcap depth in mud on the Serengeti until well after dark, in South America hiking through dense forest in search of a certain species of monkey, in a bay on the Baja peninsula cavorting with (and actually stroking) grey whales in their nursery, on a mountain peak in Mexico surrounded by tens of millions of Monarch butterflies in their winter haven, crossing a river in a tiny outboard at flood in Tanzania to see a herd of hippos, and traveling on the Amazon River at half flood. These were just a few of these adventures.

A group of very able, dedicated people run WWF, and I am thankful for the privilege of having been associated with them. Through our foundation, we made a major donation to a recent WWF campaign and will continue to support WWF as long as we are able.

Colonial Williamsburg Foundation

Spike Beitzel and I served together as directors of The Mead Corporation and Rohm and Haas Co. He is retired as a senior officer and director of IBM, a skilled aircraft pilot, great skier, and one of my favorite people. His wonderful mop of hair turned snow-white very early in life and is a good complement to his smiling, gregarious personality.

It all started when Spike, who was a trustee of the foundation and who would soon become the chairman of the board, invited us for a weekend at Carter's Grove. Carter's Grove is a beautiful Georgian-style mansion and estate owned by the foundation and tracing its origins to "King" Carter's plantation and his grandson's house built in the 1730s on the bank of the James River. During several subsequent ownership changes, the mansion was enlarged to its current size and shape.

The weekend was billed as simply a group of interesting people gathering for conversation and companionship. It was all of that, and Warren and I were taken with both the surroundings and our fellow guests. The purpose, not completely obvious at the time, was to introduce us to the foundation's president and a couple of trustees. We became donors to the foundation and within a few months came an invitation to join the board of trustees.

The trustees are treated quite royally: chauffeured to and from the airport, housed in the finest rooms of the Williamsburg Inn, and wined and dined beautifully. We were also put to work in committee meetings and a half-day board meeting.

The other trustees were fascinating and included Justice Sandra Day O'Connor; Jim Lehrer, my favorite news commentator; Nan Cohane, the president of Duke University; Gordon Wood, the distinguished American historian at Brown University; Charlie Brown, the retired CEO of AT&T; Abby O'Neill, the granddaughter of John D. Rockefeller Jr.; and Colin Campbell, president of the Rockefeller Foundation.

Colonial Williamsburg is an important museum of the American heritage and is enjoyed as such by about one million people annually. In recent years, it has attempted to become more relevant by being less theatrical and more accurate in portraying life as it was in the late eighteenth century. For example, only in the past twenty years has slavery been included and demonstrated to visitors as a major part of life in Colonial Virginia.

The foundation—which owns the operating businesses such as hotels, certain shops, and the golf courses—also mounts a considerable educational and research effort through a staff of historians and archeologists. While the work is fascinating, I occasionally had the feeling that we were well past the point of diminishing returns. I felt this way particularly after one session in which we heard about the analysis of the contents of eighteenth-century latrines!

I retired from the Williamsburg board at the mandatory age of seventy and urged them to elect my former partner Rich Worley as a trustee. They did so. As I write this, Williamsburg is having a difficult time. Attendance is down despite a beefed-up marketing effort, and the budget is out of balance. They face difficult choices, particularly as to whether the hotel and resort enterprises really belong as part of the assets of the foundation and as to whether the expensive research efforts should be reduced.

Pew Charitable Trusts

For decades, the Pew Charitable Trusts have been a prominent charitable foundation in Philadelphia. Established in the 1950s by the founder of Sun Oil Company and his brothers and sisters, both the investment management and grant making were done by the Glenmede Trust Company, which was organized to handle the family affairs, and was completely owned by family members.

Glenmede remains the sole trustee of the funds, but the grant making is now done by a legally separate organization called the Pew Charitable Trusts. Because there are several funding trusts, Pew was able to qualify as a public charity in 2003. The board was expanded and I was asked to become an independent director—independent in the sense that I have no relationship with Glenmede as a stockholder or director or client. There are four such directors and eleven others who do have some connection, most of them as both a stockholder and director.

In the fall of 2000, before Pew was separated from Glenmede, Rebecca Rimel visited me. By then, Rebecca was running Pew Charitable Trusts as a separate organization, but in fact, it was still the grant-making arm of Glenmede. Her purpose was to see if I would help them, as a paid consultant, to examine their investment results and the way the Pew board was organized to oversee Glenmede's investment management. I was fascinated by the challenge and agreed to do it.

The investment record had been lackluster at best, and the board's oversight, operating as a committee of the whole, was rather benignly neglectful. After all, they were directors of Glenmede and as such had thorough knowledge of that organization's activities and personnel. After several meetings with the board, I recommended that the directors establish a smaller investment committee, and add two or three outside investment experts to it so they could get a truly independent view. They bought the concept and asked me to chair this new committee. I was not really asking for the job and saw my function as being the recruiter of the outsiders and not the chairman.

Happily, I persuaded Charlie Ellis and Burt Malkiel to be investment committee members. Charlie spent his career as a prominent consultant to investment-management firms, and Burt is a Princeton professor who is famous for his book, *A Random Walk Down Wall Street* (a book that helped to stimulate the movement toward indexing investment portfolios).

Together with four members of the Pew board, we met quarterly with communications in the interim written by me. The Glenmede people were avowed value investors, but they avoided the deep, controversial value stocks that John Neff had been able to exploit, and that my low P/E work indicated were the real secret of value investing. They also tended to over-diversify so that whatever "bets" they made were very weak within the value sector. But the emphasis on value had made the portfolio *undiversified* in the context of that period.

Burt and Charlie saw the need for the portfolio to be indexed. I did not disagree in substance, but I did in degree because the index at the time was overly laden with speculatively inflated technology stocks in the Great Bubble of 1999-2000. So (with the help of Glenmede's research that saw the same problem) I worked to spread the indexing over a year's time.

In hindsight, we probably went too far in pushing Glenmede toward our policies. After all, they *were* the trustee. We had no legal power at all.

The CEO of Glenmede, Jim Kermes, saw us as a threat and brought in legal counsel from Chicago to seek an opinion (I am convinced that he knew what their opinion would be) on whether the trustee could properly delegate to an investment committee. Unsurprisingly, counsel saw us as an improper interference in the trustee's investment responsibilities.

The investment committee was disbanded. Burt Malkiel said, when I gave him the news, "You mean we were fired for doing what an investment committee should do?" I had to simply say, "Yes."

Time passed and I heard nothing. Then, a year or so later, while having lunch with Rebecca Rimel, she said she hoped I would consider becoming a director. She told me that the trusts were becoming a public charity, which meant primarily that they could seek outside monies to help further their programs. Also, the trusts would no longer be the grant-making arm of Glenmede. Rather, the Pew Charitable Trusts would be a completely separate legal entity. A short while later, she formalized the invitation and I accepted. While I am on the finance committee, I (and the entire board) have nothing to do with investments. The independent directors will confine their investment interest to the monitoring of results.

I admire greatly what Pew does that the Ford Foundation did not. That is, formulate during the grant-design process specific, measurable goals for each grant and then track them very closely. I have been a director for less than a year as this is written, but I am quite impressed with the accountability of staff and grantees in the effort to get our "money's worth." I am also impressed by the devotion of the Pew family, who compose a majority of the board, to their charitable heritage.

The priorities of the trusts are not necessarily those I would recommend if we were starting from ground zero, but I came late to the party and am watching with interest. The staff is impressive, so I am optimistic that Pew will prove to be a cure for some of the frustrations I felt at Ford.

CHAPTER NINE

On Investing

I have tried to write this section so nonprofessional investors, particularly my children and grandchildren, can understand it. I have also confined it to what I know best: common stocks.

I became fascinated with investing while watching my father's moods go up and down with the stock market. Then came my Wharton School education that got me deeply immersed in finance in general. When I joined Bishop & Hedberg in 1952, the stock market became a daily obsession that continues to this day. Once hooked on investing, it becomes an avocation as well as a vocation. And one can keep on doing it as long as the brain still functions.

The business of investing is not really as mysterious and obscure as it might appear. Once one understands that the purchase of any stock is the purchase of future earnings and dividends and that an uncertain dollar of future earnings is worth less than a dollar of current earnings, then one also understands the basis on which all financial assets are valued. There is nothing original or profound in this list of investment truisms. These are all learned in the first finance course in business school:

- The more certain a future earnings stream appears to be, the higher the price it will command.
- The more stable investors believe a future earnings stream will be, the higher the price investors are willing to pay.
- The faster a future earnings stream is expected to grow, the higher the price it will command.
- The higher the prevailing level of interest rates, the less any future earnings stream is worth relative to today's dollars that can be put to work earning the current rate of interest.

The eternal and most basic investment problem is the forecasting of future earnings when the future is really unknowable. More often than not the future contains real surprises.

Therefore, we should concentrate our attention on potential investments where the expectations are low, and try to take advantage of time periods when general expectations are low.

The only *financial* assets that can, *in the long run*, protect against inflation are common stocks. Prices of certain nonfinancial assets such as real estate, gold, and collectibles, seem to correlate more exactly with the timing of inflation. Yet, because interest rates rise during inflation, stocks usually play catch-up. It's only after inflation subsides and interest rates decline that the stocks' prices fully compensate for the past inflation.

The investment world has grown vastly in all its dimensions over the past fifty years and particularly during the past thirty years. Trading volume on the New York Stock Exchange regularly exceeds 1.5 billion shares a day with more than that traded on NASDAQ. When I first entered the business, 1.5 million shares was a big day, and often the volume would be less than 1 million shares.

The whole investment scene has become hugely more frantic. Much better and faster disclosure of corporate information, an explosion in the number of publicly held companies, the advent of futures and derivatives, and the birth of computers have all played a part, feeding on one another in a never-ending upward spiral of activity.

More than occasionally I feel frustrated by the explosion of the quantities of information and the speed at which it is thrust at us. But then I take comfort in knowing that most of it is sheer noise—meaningless, superficial claptrap that talking heads on TV and thousands of Wall Street analysts are constantly giving us. How does one have the time to sort through it all and separate the wheat from the chaff?

Needed: a Valuation Filter

To begin, we need a filter, some way to narrow substantially the universe of ideas we will consider. Some investors will look only at certain industries. Others may look only at securities that meet certain qualifications of financial quality. Still others demand a minimum projected growth rate of earnings or a minimum level of profitability. I do it by setting valuation limits that I will not exceed. If a security is valued above a certain level I will not consider it for purchase and will spend no time researching it (unless I need to do so in order to understand better the weaknesses or strengths of some other company I *am* considering).

Why am I so dedicated to valuation limits? Because on countless occasions I have seen the obvious proved: *that we cannot forecast the future.* From this, it follows as night follows day that we don't want to pay very much for this unknown future. Of course, I must still make forecasts as best I can. But I am very stingy in what I will pay for those futures that I try so hard to see. Those of us who follow this dictum are known as *value* investors.

Is there an absolute valuation limit for all seasons? No. I think in relative terms, and I try to confine my investment candidates to the lower quartile of the valuation scale at any point in time, knowing that the whole scale can go through major shifts.

I follow this *value* philosophy, as opposed to a *growth* philosophy. The latter emphasizes the search for companies with the most rapid and most highly assured future growth of earnings. If very high growth rates are forecast for a long enough period, then, mathematically, one can justify extremely high valuations. This leads some growth investors effectively to disregard consideration of valuation. And this is often what gets growth investors in deep trouble; when their growth forecast proves to be wrong, the high price they paid for it comes home to roost and large loss is the result.

The price of every stock contains a forecast of the future. Security analysts use many different methodologies to decide whether a stock's inherent forecast of the future is too high or too low relative to their own forecast. At any point in time, the price of a security embodies the expectations of the collective community of investors. Thus, if only the expected happens in the future the price will not change. One need look no further than at the volatility of stock prices to prove how often the unexpected occurs. Indeed, the volatility of stock prices is the result of the uncertain future.

You make money in common stocks by having a major disagreement with the community of investors and being correct. Every time you buy any stock, your action implies that you disagree with the consensus expectations of the company's future. The same holds true of the sale of any stock. When you sell, it's because you disagree with the current price as an accurate measure of the company's future prospects.

Investors are always seeking certainty even though it never exists. But the more certain some particular future seems, the higher the price it commands. At the top of a market, by definition, optimism prevails. In other words, the bright futures look relatively quite certain. Analysts forecast five-year growth estimates with confidence. At a market bottom, when the future seems murky, they have difficulty estimating even the next year's earnings. Also, at a market top, buy recommendations number in the thousands and at a bottom they are rare. (Sell recommendations are always rare.)

Investment quality usually refers to financial strength, market-share dominance of a company's products, and the basic stability of the business. Quality is often, however, in the eyes of the beholder. So-called quality is considered to be a protection against uncertainty. If the future proves to be rougher than expected, it is quality that can protect you from serious loss, or so the thinking goes. Thus, when pessimism is rampant, you will see many analysts and strategists flee to "high quality stocks." Balance sheets are thoroughly analyzed and business stability is sought. The opposite is true at market tops. Quality is ignored. Yet, if you examine past markets you will find that lower-quality stocks tend to do very well coming off market bottoms, usually beating the big high-quality stocks handily.

Even though investors are usually thought of as being either value investors or growth investors, all of them seek increasing earnings. Value investors just don't want to pay much for the uncertain prospect of higher future earnings.

Value Investing for Superior Results

The first serious, real-time security analysis I did was under the tutelage of Bob Hedberg, of Bishop & Hedberg—the firm I left the Federal Reserve to join in late 1952. Bob introduced me to *Security Analysis,* by Benjamin Graham, a man who had made himself a fortune investing in out-of-favor non-blue-chip stocks. He was the father of modern-day value investing, and is well-known as the mentor of Warren Buffett. My orientation ever since has been to look for "value" in the form of undervalued earnings or assets.

I carried this value bias to Drexel & Co. Perhaps best known was my work on the "Superiority of Low Price-Earnings Ratio Stocks," first published in 1962. This paper traced the annual investment results of three segments of valuation. Specifically, we looked at the ten stocks in each of the cheapest, most expensive, and the middle segments (as measured by stock prices divided by earnings, or P/Es as we call them in the business) within the thirty stocks of the Dow-Jones Industrial Average from 1937 to 1962. It showed conclusively that investing annually in the ten stocks that were the cheapest in relation to earnings produced vastly superior results. Every updating by me and others, as well as broader studies, have shown similar results.

Since 1979, using much larger universes, the evidence is strong that value investing is a superior style. No matter how you slice it, by quality ratings or capitalization size, the value pond has been the better place to fish. In historical comparisons of the Russell 1000 large-cap value and growth universes, value was markedly superior. For the twenty-three years up to 2002, the annualized returns were 15.4 percent for value vs. 14 percent for growth. And the standard deviation of these returns has been a relatively low 12.9 percent vs. 19.3 percent for the growth segment. For the nonstatisticians, a lower standard deviation means that annual returns varied less around the longer-term mean annual return. So we might be able to claim, as I do, that the value universe is less risky to deal in than the growth universe.

Yet consistency of results for either methodology is notably lacking. In all capitalization-size universes, for example, neither value investing nor growth investing has held sway for more than three consecutive years. Attempts to switch emphasis successfully from one style to another have been futile. Importantly, patience has been necessary. There have been extended periods during which, from whatever your starting point to the terminal date, you would have been significantly behind if you owned the value universe. But eventually value won out.

Why does value prove to be superior?

The cheapest part of the stock market, as measured, say, by the multiple of earnings at which stocks sell, is cheap for rational reasons. Investors, in the aggregate, are mistrustful of earnings or see no future growth or have questions about financial or business quality. Investors aren't stupid. They prove to be correct in their assessment of many (I estimate about two-thirds) of these companies. These will turn out to be dismal stocks. Not that most of them will collapse—they are already too cheap to do that—but they will drag along as below-average performers. In about one-third of the cases, however, investors will prove to be wrong. The future will be much better than expected. Some will even go from being value stocks to being growth stocks. When that happens, you can see gains of ten—to twentyfold. You don't need many of those to overcome the few losers.

The other end of the valuation spectrum, where the future is gauged to be bright, is expensive, but again for rational reasons. And here the assessment is also right about two-thirds of the time, and to be sure, the majority of these companies will enjoy the bright future that is forecast for them. But many of the stocks of these companies, because their future has already been so well discounted, will show only average or below-average market returns even if expectations are met. The only really big moneymakers will be those companies where the future turns out to be even better than the optimistic forecast embedded in the price. They are rare. But how about the one-third where the market's assessment proves to be wrong and expectations are not met? They are investment disasters. So much so that they cause the returns of the entire growth universe to be, on average, inferior.

It is much more difficult to be a successful value investor. Dart throwing at the cheaper part of the market produces, on average, only one company out of three where the assessment of the future is unduly pessimistic. But even if you hit the losers, you don't lose much on average.

Picking winners in the value universe takes a certain discipline of thought that not only shuts out or refutes the negative thinking, which made the stock cheap in the first place, but also formulates a positive story that rings true. These are stocks that are discomforting to an investment committee. Again, that's why they are cheap. The stocks are also frightening to analysts or portfolio managers because if they are wrong, the world will say, "We told you so." Investors are scared to death of being both wrong and alone. Analysts typically focus only on the many faults, and coverage may be thin.

Contrast this with picking stocks in the growth universe where you are seeking a company that you believe has an even brighter future than the rosy one already being forecast by the stock's price. The companies you look at usually have had either a comforting consistent earnings record and a persistently increasing stock price, or have had a growth story that is irresistible. Analysts all like the stock, and there are plenty of analysts to talk to and read. Management is highly regarded. Corporate strategy is admired. Your chances of being correct on future earnings fundamentals are quite good. Therefore, even if a company's business does well but its stock's price has overdiscounted the future, you can always face the loss in value and your client with the comfort of having been "right" in your assessment of the business and having had lots of company. This is usually enough to avoid the "We told you so's" and may even enable you to keep your job through a rough period.

It is easier to be in a "growth frame of mind" than always having to dispel and refute negative thinking. That's why there are more growth investors than true value investors. I would even venture the statement that the value segment of the market is less efficient than the growth segment. That is, there is less perfect knowledge residing in the collective mind of investors at any given point of time.

Know the Differences between Investing, Speculating, and Rolling the Dice!

You may think that this is unnecessary advice, but I have been amazed to find how often people really don't know the characteristics of securities they own and don't know why they own them.

Here are some rough guidelines that may help:

If you bought or are holding a security for at least three of these reasons you are probably investing:

1. It's a well-established company that you admire with a high-quality product line.
2. You expect to hold the stock for more than one year
3. It pays a reasonable dividend.
4. You expect earnings growth to provide most of the appreciation (as opposed to expecting a higher valuation of earnings).
5. You've bought it because you believe that the company is significantly undervalued relative to either its earning power or its assets

If any five of these reasons are behind your buying or holding the stock, you are probably speculating:

1. The company has been owned publicly for a short period of time or is less than ten years old.
2. The price of the stock is more than twice its sales per share.
3. Analysts are projecting earnings growth of more than 15 percent for the next five years.
4. The current ratio of price to earnings is above twenty-five.
5. You will be disappointed if the stock doesn't rise by at least 25 percent in less than a year.
6. The company has earned money in fewer than two of the past five years.

And if your stock meets any six of these criteria, you are probably throwing the dice:

1. The company has never made money.
2. Its attraction is a new product that has not yet reached the market.
3. The stock sells for more than four times sales.
4. It's a new issue in the middle of a hot market for IPOs.
5. You have little or no understanding of what the products or services are or what they do.
6. You expect to make more than 25 percent in a hurry.

I have nothing against either speculating or having the excitement of throwing dice. I do both from time to time. It's fun. It's not immoral. Speculating and gambling can provide a bit of zest to the main dish. But I know when I'm doing either one, and I know that I don't want a portfolio that is dominated by such activities. A rule of thumb? Perhaps 10 to 15 percent of a reasonably sized portfolio. And certainly it should not be one's main emphasis.

If you are really a long-term investor there is no need to shoot for the moon.

No Need to Shoot for the Moon

Only very infrequently have I had huge investment successes. But very infrequently have I experienced investment disasters. So on average I've done very well even if I have not matched some of the investment "heroes" of our era. Generally, I have believed that Vince Lombardi's football strategy of "four yards a carry and a cloud of dust" was more appropriate for me as an investor than going for the long yardage bomb. Although I have found more than a few nice winners along the way, they did not necessarily look like touchdowns—or to change the metaphor, home runs—when I first bought them. And they usually took time to mature. A good generality to keep in mind is that if you can compile better than average results in two-thirds of the years, and avoid being in the lowest performance quartile the rest of the time, you will be in the top quartile for a longer period of, say, ten years.

Investment stardom is fleeting; people who appear to be stars usually are only meteors. There are very few exceptions to this: Warren Buffett, John Neff, Bill Miller, John Nygren, Howie Schow, Martie Whitman, and my former partners, Dave Atkinson and Robert Marcin, come to mind. Interestingly, all of them are value investors or value-conscious investors. There are, however, a few entire organizations that have produced durably good investment results. Miller, Anderson and Sherrerd was such a firm during most of its history. Today, the few firms I would name are Capital Research and Management, Oakmark, Southeastern Investment Management, T. Rowe Price, and Third Avenue. But my best guess is that these names will also disappear into oblivion with time. The people will change. It's as simple as that.

Risk: What is it? How Best to Control it.

Diversification is the best risk insurance. But it also can be a cop-out. Warren Buffet has said that he considers a diversified portfolio more risky than an undiversified one in which each business that is owned is thoroughly understood and the people who run each of them are well-known and respected by the investor. Thus, enterprise investors, who own whole businesses or major parts of them, may legitimately believe that the rest of us, with relatively superficial knowledge of the businesses we own, are taking more risk, even if we own twenty-five to one hundred stocks. I believe that this thesis will be increasingly tested over the next decade. But temperamentally, I will continue to view diversification as my major risk control.

Diversification, however, can be taken to an extreme. To demonstrate this requires that you understand that every stock has two kinds of risk. The first is the risk that derives simply from being part of the stock market as a whole. As the market rises or falls, most stocks will move in the same direction as the market. Some tend to move more than the market and others move less. This characteristic tends to be relatively stable over time. Thus, for example, the stock of a more stable business such as food might be only half as volatile as the stock market as a whole while a technology company might be 50 percent more volatile. This measurement of volatility we call Beta. In the examples here the respective Betas would be .50 and 1.50. The Beta of any single stock is an unreliable predictor of volatility.

A second kind of risk derives from the risks associated specifically with the company. These might be such characteristics as financial risk, such as if the company is overloaded with debt; or technology risk, if the company is dependent on a technology that might become obsolete; cyclical economic risk; or, perhaps, bad debt risk if it's a bank or credit company.

If you hold only one stock, the risk is overwhelmingly the risk specifically associated with the company. As you increase the number of stocks you hold, you begin to diversify away the specific risks in the stocks you own and your portfolio begins to behave more like the stock market. If you increase your diversification even further, there comes a point where the portfolio *becomes* the stock market. You then own an index fund that duplicates the behavior of the stock market as a whole. (You can, of course, index to specific parts of the stock market, such as industries, investment styles, or capitalization sizes.) The point is that you can diversify away the company-specific risks in a portfolio, but you cannot avoid the general market risk.

The history of investing over the past forty years shows that most investment managers do not earn their fees either over longer periods of time or even on an annual basis. Some academics blame this on the efficiency of the market. They claim that all there is to know about a stock at any point in time is, in fact, known by all the players. While I agree that all that can be known about a company or an industry *is* known, I do not believe that necessarily translates into the correct price. The very fact that stock prices fluctuate is proof of that. There is still plenty of room for misinterpretation of the facts and for emotions to cause investors to grossly misvalue some stocks from time to time. I have believed that, at least for the management of my own assets, I can identify enough stocks that are being misgauged by other investors to create a portfolio that will, on average, outperform the stock market. It doesn't take many such stocks to accomplish that. But I don't have any illusions that I can gain a very substantial advantage over general market returns over very long periods of time.

Indexing and/or Mutual Funds

For many people who cannot spend time on their investments, or who don't have confidence in their ability to pick managers for their money, indexing is a reasonable answer. For those people, my advice is to pick more than one index, weight the portfolio toward the value indices, and overweight smaller capitalization indices.

I also believe that no-load mutual funds (funds that have no buying commission) are the best solution for most investors who will not spend the time necessary to make their own decisions. My friend, Jack Bogle, is correct in saying that a primary consideration in picking mutual funds is the expense ratio. How much are the fund's total expenses as a percent of the fund's net asset value? In excess of 1 percent is enough to erase many good results over time.

Most individual investors will not beat the market. Statistically, half should be below average and half above average. But expenses are deducted from the gross results, thus putting the average investor below the market average.

Sure, a person can get very lucky and own only a couple of big winners. That's very rare. Investors should understand that the construction of a portfolio is like putting together a symphony orchestra. All the instruments have a different part to play. And they don't all play at the same time; or at least, it's only during the rare crescendos that they do.

One final thought on risk. It is not simply the variability of returns, although that may be an element in risk. Risk for an individual investor is simply the seriousness of the consequences of losing a certain amount of money. By this definition, risk varies from person to person. You have to figure what risk you can stand. My own rule of thumb is that if you can't tolerate the loss of a third of whatever money you have invested in the stock market then you have too much at risk.

It's As Important to Be Lucky As It Is to Be Smart

I have been a lucky investor. The past two decades, spanning the period when I finally had some capital to invest, have been among the very best for investors in modern financial history. The after-inflation returns of close to 12 percent were matched or exceeded only by the years coming off the Great Depression and World War II.

Swimming against the current of low general market returns is a tough business. Keep in mind that it always will be the market as a whole that will be the primary determinant of the returns of any portfolio. Investment skills are a distant second, despite the bragging one might hear of successes. It's important to recognize the difference between brains and a bull market!

CHAPTER TEN

Friends and Family

Parents

It should be obvious to any reader that Warren's and my parents were very important parts of our lives. We were always comfortable with them and frequently included them in our social activities just as they included us in theirs.

My father was my best friend and Warren thought of her mother the same way. Not that the other parent was unloved; rather, it was more a matter of the bonding of the same sexes. Thus, their deaths were sad events and important milestones in our lives.

Tiny Shafer died of cancer of the mouth at the age of sixty-five in 1971. Her death was hard for all of us to bear. Hers was the first death in the family our children experienced. They had often been cared for by "Nonie" and had a great affection for her.

Willy Shafer died in late 1981, shy by a month of being eighty-two, after surgery for internal bleeding. That was eleven years after Tiny's death, but he was never again as complete a person without his mate.

My father, called Newt by all his family, never stopped smoking until he suffered a stroke that was at least partly due to oxygen deprivation from emphysema. He was bedridden for a year and a half, and died in March of 1978. He would have been seventy-nine the following July. Sadly, I was in Japan at the time. We were giving Buzz a graduation gift of the trip. I cried uncontrollably when Rip Scott called with the news. I could not stop thinking that I had never been as far away geographically from my dad as I was that day in Kyoto. I traveled home for the funeral but insisted that Warren and Buzz stay and complete the trip. I rejoined them a few days later in Hiroshima.

My mother suffered from dementia beginning in her late sixties. As it got worse, we determined that it would be best for both her and Dad if she were to go to a nursing home. At the age of seventy-six, she went to Bryn Mawr Terrace, a good facility near our family homes. She continued to decline mentally but lived until just short of her eighty-fourth birthday.

Our parents live on in our memories. They are often referred to or quoted by their children and grandchildren. They were neither famous nor wealthy. But they were very good people. I hope my children think of us as having been as important to them as we think our parents were to us.

Children and Grandchildren

This is by far the most difficult part of these memoirs to write. What to say about children I love; how can I tell them how I feel about my relationship with them? I'm not at all sure what will come out as I start. I have never tried to describe them to people who don't know them in ways that convey my own interpretations of their characters and personalities.

The similarities among them are few, for which we have been grateful. I believe that each of them has a respect and affection for us. I do not believe they prefer one parent to the other. They correctly think of us as a single unit, each half of which is very dependent on the other. And we, both together and individually, deal with them as distinct personalities living separate lives, seldom drawing comparisons. Our love has, I believe, been totally unconditional and has been dealt out equally among them.

These are not my children's memoirs so I will not detail their histories except for our experiences as a family, now a group of fourteen people including six grandchildren, two sons-in-law, and one daughter-in-law.

Winky Miller

Ella Warren (Winky) Miller (now Merrill) is the fourth Ella Warren, following her mother, grandmother, and her great-great-grandmother. She has always been known as Winky and even signs her checks that way. As I remember it, the nickname originated from her having one eye glued shut with mucous for the first few days of her life. Warren thinks that I grabbed the name out of the air later because I simply always liked Winky as a nickname, having known a very pretty woman named Winky in college. We long ago stopped arguing about whose memory was correct, which is probably a good thing because Warren eventually proves to be correct a very high percentage of the time.

Winky will be forty-nine in the year that I'm writing this. Self-assured, articulate, and easily sociable, I think of her as a very successful woman, wife, mother, and community leader. She makes friends easily and has a quick sense of humor. But her real strengths are in her abilities to read other people and succinctly understand what they are about. She uses these strengths to put life's issues in the contexts of the people who have created them or who are facing them. This frequently leads to very perceptive diagnoses and possible solutions.

She is admired in her community of Weston, Massachusetts, as a person who gets things done efficiently while at the same time being a mother who is active in her children's activities and a wife who runs a happy and efficient home.

Winky was a very good but not outstanding student. She is very conscientious and has always done the jobs she undertook—from being headwaiter at Rockywold Camp to Girl Scout troop leader—thoroughly, competently, and in praise-winning fashion.

The only one of the children to go to Penn, she told the others that she had taken care of that obligation for them, and they should feel freer to go elsewhere. After graduation, she left immediately for California with her boyfriend and worked in a yogurt parlor while volunteering for the Sierra Club where she wanted a full-time job. She was so good that the Sierra Club did finally hire her.

She was in California for over five years. Late in that stay, she met David Merrill while wandering through a farmers' market where he was selling apricots from the family orchard near Davis. They fell in love fast, although he had a girlfriend at the time and was slow in coming to the realization that Winky was the one.

Dave is a graduate of the University of California at Davis. He majored in soil and water—or, as he calls it, mud—and has put his education to good use as a partner in a very successful environmental consulting firm.

In the summer of 1982, Dave was invited to New Hampshire and stayed with Winky in our Betula cottage next door to Ishnewtee. He was there for only a few days, and on the night before their departure back to California, we were invited to dinner. Champagne was brought out, and Warren and I waited for the announcement that never came. The next day Winky called from Logan Airport and asked how we liked David. When we enthused about him, she said, "Good, because I'm going to marry the guy."

That was in mid-August. The wedding was scheduled for October 2, giving us very little time for the arrangements. The ceremony was held on Church Island in Squam Lake and the reception at Rockywold, followed by a square dance. It was a beautiful, unforgettable New England fall weekend. We met Dave's family for the first time and found them comfortably compatible with us.

Back to California they went for a year before deciding to pursue graduate work at Cornell. Winky got her MBA, and Dave finished work for a doctorate. It was while they were in Ithaca that our first grandchild, Ryan David Merrill, was born on June 28, 1986. Fortunately for us, Dave, who had never spent time in the East, loved it and took a job in Cambridge, Massachusetts.

I think it's fair to say that Winky was, as I was, a late bloomer. It simply took a while for her to gain the self-confidence she now has and to find out how very good she is in relating to others, quickly getting to the core of issues, and running her home.

Her children, Ryan, Jake, and Maggie, are, as are all of our grandchildren, lights in our lives. As this is written they are eighteen, sixteen, and thirteen. They and our other grandchildren are what we think of as our immortality.

Kathy Miller

Katharine, named for my mother, was born with beautiful strawberry blonde hair and insatiable curiosity. Even as a small child she demonstrated a quiet but very quick intelligence, extraordinary perseverance, and an ability to work independently. At age forty-six, she is exactly the same except that her major interest is her family and her strawberry blonde hair has become several shades darker.

Kathy is a very direct, even blunt person, and sees little need for the trappings of diplomacy. She can also be defiantly unaffectionate and stoical even though we know her emotions are very close to the surface. As a child and as a young adult, tears were never very far away

Academically, she was always at or near the top, writing honors papers with thoroughness and insight that are definitely not part of my gene set. Admitted to Harvard, she made wonderful lifelong friends, rowed on the crew, and majored in archeology. Her honors-thesis professor told us at graduation that he had seldom seen a mind and a set of hands that were as well coordinated in the laboratory.

With law school in the back of her mind, she pursued archeology for a while in Colorado, worked for the American Littoral Society, and ran a political campaign out of Washington for the leftist People's Party.

Idealistically liberal, she aligned herself with the more liberal students at Stanford Law School, eschewing the more establishmentlike activities, and being a community worker in the economically deprived area of East Palo Alto. After graduation, she chose to do work as plaintiff's lawyer in pursuit of liberal causes, such as sex and age discrimination, and even had a stint working for Native American interests in Santa Fe.

Scott Carlson entered her life after law school. When she called to say that she and Scott were going to marry, we didn't even know his name. When she told us, we all hooted with pleasure and laughter at her choosing a man with such a Waspy name as Scott Douglas Carlson.

Scott and Kathy were married in 1991 in a public park by the sea in Pacific Grove, just south of Monterey. We rented the entire Monterey Aquarium for the reception. It was a magnificent party.

During a three-year stay in New York City, where Scott studied for his master's degree in creative writing, their son, Tor Miller Carlson, was born. Scott and Kathy decided, much to our chagrin, to make their home in Palo Alto, California. Parents have no choice in such matters but to be accepting and supportive, even if we do not understand them. But we greatly miss the more frequent contact with them that would have been possible had they remained in the East. As it is now, we usually visit California at least once a year and they visit New Hampshire and/or Florida for several weeks.

They have two children, the oldest of whom is Tor Miller Carlson, a handsome, bright, and energetic boy. He seems to have the same patient attention span as his mother, being very diligent at all he does. The second child is a sweet adopted daughter named Livia, at whose birth and handing-over from her biological mother we were privileged to be present. As I write this, Tor is ten and Livia is almost four years old.

Scott and Kathy have a wonderful home. I am always moved to see our daughters as mothers and deeply pleased that they are so good in those roles.

The law proved not to be Kathy's calling and she took her education a step further by studying to become a science writer, which she does as a freelancer. As this is written, she is also president of the Palo Alto Library Foundation, devoted to the improvement of libraries for children in their community.

Paul F. Miller III

Buzz Miller is one of the nicest, kindest, considerate people I know. He yearns to be liked, bends over backward to do things for people, and yet has had a difficult life.

As a young preschool child he marched to a different drummer. His preschool teacher talked to us and suggested we have Buzz see a child psychologist. We did, and for the next six or seven years he had weekly visits. Never, however, did we get any real idea of how to deal with his problems. They manifested themselves in obsessions on various subjects, and while not crippling, were an annoyance to the rest of the family, particularly his sisters.

Never a good student, he has always learned by seeing and doing, not by reading from books or listening to lectures. But learn he does, and well.

Buzz married Marie Phillips in 1989. Marie is a dear person, but life with Buzz was not easy. We were surprised but not shocked when she asked for a divorce only seven years into their marriage. By then they had a child, Paul F. Miller IV, a charming ten-year-old redhead with an endearing manner.

They managed the divorce without acrimony, and we remain good friends with Marie, who has remarried.

Buzz also remarried, to Bonnie Wiener, in a ceremony in a Messianic synagogue. At this writing, they are ensconced in a lovely house in Media, Pennsylvania, and seem to be doing well.

To his credit, Buzz was one of the earliest of personal-computer experts. He introduced them to MA&S long before they became commonplace. As our internal computer expertise grew, he shifted his interest to the investment side where he was at a disadvantage relative to the younger MBAs we were hiring. Then he became my assistant, a job he found too clerklike, and he decided to leave and begin a business of his own as a computer tutor.

Buzz has long been searching for an outlet for his energies and talents and may have found it in videography. He pursues it with a vigor and enthusiasm that is admirable, and has produced some fine work.

I greatly admire what he has been able to do, even with some handicaps that would have sunk many people.

Ocean City, N.J., 1960; l. to r., Kathy, Buzz, and Winky, with Warren

Kathy, Buzz and Winky, 1968

The whole family with dogs, Mister and Suzie, 1975

Fooling around, 1975

Winky and Dave Merrill's wedding, Squam Lake, 1982

Winky with Jakefield Benjamin Merrill, Useppa Island, 1990

Kathy and Scott Carlson's wedding, Pacific Grove, California, 1991

Kathy holding Tor Miller Carlson, Useppa Island, 1995

Buzz and Bonnie Wiener's wedding, 2000

Mary Anne and Scotty

My mother and father would often tell my sister and me how much they hoped that we would remain close as we grew older. They had seen many examples of sibling relationships that had deteriorated and even ceased to exist. Their wish was granted. Mary Anne and her husband, Scotty, are our best friends.

It has been our good fortune that both my sister and I married people who are really loved by the other couple. Warren and I have a warm, understanding, loving relationship with Mary and Scotty—one that has become ever closer over the years.

We are four very distinct individuals—with our own likes and dislikes, idiosyncrasies, even peculiarities—have different thinking about politics and religion, yet we are as harmonious a foursome as I can imagine. We know what to expect of each other, laugh at our foibles, cheer our victories, cry over our disappointments, and respect our differences. We also are deeply in love with our mates.

Very few days pass without contact by phone or visit. Deeply interested in each other's children and grandchildren, we have traveled the globe together, owned a vacation home together, live only a half mile apart, share a love for our alma mater, and readily confide on many matters.

Once we passed the childhood stage of teasing and squabbling, I became a devoted fan of my sister, who is four and a half years younger than I. In high school and through college, my friends were also her fans and adopted her as their sister. Our father's advice to her when she was in junior high school was "If you see someone without a smile on their face, give them yours."

She heeded that advice although her smiles have too often been through tears, notably during a period of several miscarriages and later worrying about her sons who both endured the pain of divorce.

A very attractive woman, she is an amazing combination of gregarious extrovert, conversation facilitator, confidant to many people and friend of the troubled. She is good humored, fun, entertaining, very anecdotal (with an astounding memory for dates and details of past events and experiences), deeply loyal, and emotionally involved with life in all its aspects. My father called her his "blonde bombshell." She is very interested in *you*, whoever you may be.

Scotty is less gregarious but certainly not reserved, very careful and deliberate, a bit scheduled, patient, and is always enjoying his wife's outgoing sociability. He is very masculine, quite handsome and charming, and very simply, a really nice guy. After enduring the Korean War as an army cryptographer, Scotty took over his dad's automobile agency and made a success of it before passing it on to his son, Rip. Over the years he has been thoroughly involved in community activities, earning the respect of his friends and business associates.

Mary Anne and Scotty are in harmony with each other. Very seldom do they raise their voices at each other, always addressing the other as "Sweetie." They are easy to travel with because of their agreeableness. For who can stand being with a nit-picking, squabbling couple for very long?

Their lives are deeply intertwined with those of their two sons and their grandchildren, protecting them against the trauma of divorce and providing them with a comfortable second home.

The Scotts and us never crowd each other and seemed to naturally drift to mutually interesting activities or conversations. They are a very important part of our lives.

Childhood Friends

My two best friends were Johnny Wynn and Ike Kershaw. I think both of them would have classified me as one of their best friends, but they were not particularly close friends of one another. I remember spending huge hunks of time with each of them but very little time with the two of them together.

Johnny was gregarious, athletic, and interested in sports, a good student, and despite our early experience together as voyeurs told earlier, he was not very mischievous. He wore a puzzled half smile, as if he enjoyed what you were saying but didn't quite get it. Relatively speaking, his family was wealthy. They lived in a large house, a ten-minute bike ride away from the heart of town, on a quiet street. His family also had a vacation home, and went on expensive trips. He had a large bedroom all to himself with his own bathroom. He also had a phonograph of his own. In fact, he had many things long before I did, such as sports equipment and a bicycle.

Ike Kershaw was quiet, could be very mischievous, was not very interested in athletics, was very musical, played a terrific trumpet in the band and orchestra, and was interested in doing things such as building huts and tree houses or shooting BB guns at lead soldiers. As a teenager he was always in love and had no difficulty finding a girl to reciprocate. He was very handsome with black hair and blue eyes with long eyelashes. His family was in the same financial straits as mine. His father was a classmate of my mother's in high school. The Kershaws lived only a block away.

Johnny and I played soccer together in high school, raised rabbits as a business venture and generally did constructive things. When Ike and I were together, we were more playful, more juvenile. I found the company of each of them a relief from the company of the other.

It was Ike who enlisted in the U.S. Coast Guard with me. Johnny, more conservatively, waited to be drafted. Johnny and Ike were both ushers in our wedding as I was in theirs. I actually introduced Johnny to his wife who, at the time, was my secretary.

Over time, however, these friendships faded, although we could still socialize easily when we met at class reunions. We had progressively less in common, going to different colleges and then into different businesses. My deeper and longer-lasting friendships started with college and business. Three of them deserve special mention: Ed Igler, Frank Hughes, and Jay Sherrerd.

Edwin Roworth Igler

As I related earlier, I met Ed Igler at preseason soccer practice in August 1946, the beginning of my freshman year at Penn. Ed had been in the navy for three years, serving in the Pacific. He was a graduate of Friends Select School, a highly regarded Quaker school in Philadelphia, where he had played soccer.

A stocky man with a large head and handsomely dimpled face that is dominated by a prominent nose, he speaks softly and is always genuinely interested in asking and talking about "you" rather than himself. Generous and considerate to a fault, liberal and tolerant in the best nonpolitical sense, religious and reverent, a lifelong teetotaler but ready for a party, he has always been Mr. Clean to his friends, who respect him immensely.

Ed is two and a half years older than I, a difference that is magnified when one is still in the late teens. I arrived home from soccer practice and told my family that I had met a nice "older guy." Ed and I were friends from the start. His father was the Baptist chaplain at the Christian association on campus, so Ed had grown up at Penn and knew his way around far better than I did.

Ed was a big influence on me, particularly during my first two years at Penn. He was more mature and experienced, even though terribly naïve about women, had a wide group of friends, and became absorbed in extracurricular activities quickly and easily. He became a "big wheel" on campus rapidly as I watched in awe. As a senior, his classmates selected him as one of the four top honor men. He pushed me to become more involved in campus activities than I would have otherwise, and on more than one occasion was constructively critical of something I did or said.

He guided me through fraternity rushing and gently pulled me with him into Beta Theta Pi, one of the top fraternities at that time, and my single biggest correct decision while at Penn.

Shortly after starting Penn, Ed faced the shock of his parents' divorce, which he felt deeply. His father became a good friend of mine and dozens of other young people with whom he corresponded long after graduation. He was a very distinguished-looking gentleman with a large shock of white hair, was a pipe smoker (a habit that fit his looks and personality), and had a great sense of humor. He was surprisingly tolerant of my agnosticism and irreverence. Doc Igler, as we called him, was a fixture on the sidelines of every soccer game we played, rooting hard for his boys.

Ed and I spent summer weekends together, often at Ocean City, dating women who were student summer workers, usually at restaurants. Attending beach parties; double-date necking in cars; searching for cheap meals and the best cinnamon buns; beer drinking (me, not Ed); and singing at a place we called Beer, Boats, and Bait (which was exactly what the sign outside said)—we did them all and had very good time together.

In September 1952, three months after our wedding, we invited Ed to spend a week's vacation with us in Belgrade Lakes, Maine, the same place Ed and I had gone with friends after graduation in 1950 and which Ed and I had revisited the following year. It was really a second honeymoon for us yet we were willing to have a third wheel along. One night we were playing a game of hearts in the cabin and Ed and I ganged up on Warren, making sure she got most of the hearts and the queen of spades. She became more furious at both of us, but me in particular, more than I have ever seen her before or since. She couldn't understand how I, her new husband, could possibly conspire against her. We all look back on that night with good humor as the night Warren almost considered divorce only three months into her marriage!

One of the girls Ed met in Ocean City was a Theta sorority sister of Warren's, Joan Howarth. Joan was the daughter of a high-school principal in Philadelphia and was raised in a strict Methodist family. A very pretty, delightfully naïve woman, Joan and Ed were married about two years after we were. I was Ed's best man and Warren was a bridesmaid. It was simply natural that we became close friends as couples. Joan and Warren became wonderful additions to the relationship that Ed and I had established.

Over the intervening fifty-three years since graduation, we have remained in close contact. For some time, when our children were very young, the Iglers lived near us in Wayne, Pennsylvania, so we saw them regularly and watched each other's children grow through their earlier stages. They were excellent parents. Before their children reached high-school age, they were transferred to the New York area by IBM and settled in New Canaan, Connecticut.

We have traveled together and we talk on the phone almost every month between our relatively infrequent visits. One of the best things I can wish for my children is a close and durable friendship such as we have had with the Iglers.

As I write this, Ed is suffering from Parkinson's Disease that has afflicted him for the past eight years. He deals with it well and bravely as does Joan, who stands ready to help him when needed but avoids making him any more dependent upon her than is absolutely necessary.

Frank Wills Hughes

Frank Hughes, who died in 1995, was unique. A huge hulk of a man, about six feet four inches and well over two hundred pounds, Frank's presence couldn't be ignored. Nor can his absence. I miss him more than any of the many friends who have died. Seldom does a day pass that I don't wish I still had him to talk to, to swap jokes with, to sit with our feet up and a beer in our hands, and simply reflect on how great life is.

I knew Frank only slightly in high school. He was a year ahead of me. When we both pledged Beta That Pi in our freshman year, we became fast friends and remained so until he died.

He was very funny, even goofy, with a style that was totally his. He didn't *try* to be funny: he just was. Anybody else saying or doing the same things would have fallen flat. Part of it was his facial expressions, part was his timing, and part was his body movements. Big as he was, he was rather uncoordinated. He tried football, dressed for the home games, but never played. He tried soccer for one day and tripped over the ball. He had some moderate success at crew but never rowed in the varsity boat.

Frank was a born entrepreneur, always finding some little niche where he could make some bucks. In our college years, he connected with military surplus and had a decent business selling items as diverse as fatigues and surplus uniforms to shell casings (they made great lamps).

He was a born salesman and was highly successful in selling coffee-vending machines, kitchens, and railway equipment during his career. His crowning business achievement was Hughes Railway Supply, which he created out of thin air to represent manufacturers of railway equipment—from brake shoes to wheels to couplings and beyond. He would sit at his desk with a telephone headset on, calling the many friends he had made among his customers, telling them his latest jokes, asking about their families, and making them feel that he really cared about them as people (which he did).

Most salesmen deal with purchasing departments. Not Frank. He got to know the CEOs, vice presidents, and other senior officers of the railroads while artfully avoiding the kind of influence peddling that might have annoyed the more junior people who actually wrote up the orders.

Jokes and practical jokes were his stock in trade, both in his business and personal relations. When we were having difficulty with a couple of neighbors who did not like the idea of our building on the lakefront lots we had owned for twelve years, he had signs made and posted that read, "Site of future town dump, signed the Selectmen of Sandwich." Another sign read, "Reptile breeding area. Keep out."

When we finished the guesthouse on Squam Lake and proudly had Frank and Janet as our first guests, we came back from a hike one day (Frank never hiked or climbed!) to find the entire two-story central area of the house draped with clothesline and hung with underwear, bathing suits, and bras.

Frank married Lois Hooven when he was twenty-one and just finishing Penn. She was a nurse and a pleasant, pretty girl who was no match for Frank's energy. The marriage ended after about fifteen years. Frank drifted for a bit until he found Janet Mayer, a tall stately woman, also divorced. They married after living together for several years. It was a good marriage, which both of them deserved.

Frank and I talked on the phone, if not in person, at least twice a week, covering many things but always including a joke or two that he or I had collected. Our friendship had many serious moments, however, talking about his business or mine, about our families, and our general outlook on life. When he told me he was thinking of starting a business to sell railroad supplies, I told him he was crazy. So much for my business acumen!

Frank avoided unpleasantness: no unpleasant movies or TV shows or books. The world was full of humor and sweetness for Frank. He was always looking for sunshine.

At his memorial service, I gave a tribute to him that I concluded by pulling a ceramic bluebird from my pocket that had been a joke gift from him the previous Christmas. The bird had a built-in electronic song. As it tweeted on the edge of the pulpit, it sang "The Bluebird of Happiness," a song that, as teenagers, we used to stay up to hear over the radio at one o'clock in the morning.

He was a real bluebird in my life. And I think his idea of avoiding unpleasantness is not all bad! I find myself doing just that increasingly as I age.

John Jacob Foulkrod Sherrerd

I wrote earlier in this book about Jay—about his being Jack Bogle's brother-in-law; about playing pickup basketball at a playground in Bayhead, New Jersey; and about hiring him at Drexel & Co. in October 1956, the same month I was made a partner. Since that time, we have been literally inseparable, having adjoining offices for forty-eight years.

Relative to me, Jay was born with a silver spoon—perhaps I should downgrade that to a *pewter* spoon—in his mouth. He attended private boys' schools (Episcopal Academy and the Hill School) and Princeton, and took his MBA at Penn's Wharton School. He started his career having some gifted wealth—modest to be sure but, by my standards at the time, a small fortune.

We became good friends and confidants almost immediately after I hired him. From being with each other, sharing hotel rooms and restaurant meals all over the United States and Europe, we know each other's idiosyncrasies from food preferences (he loves cream of tomato soup but can't stand onions, peppers, and pickles) to behavioral habits. Comically, he told me that he walked in his sleep just before retiring in a hotel room in Switzerland that opened onto a balcony overlooking a sharp drop down a mountain!

At six feet three inches, with an athletic build, interesting face, and a pleasantly gregarious manner, Jay's presence is always attention-getting.

Jay and I do not always agree on everything. While we have the same definitions of integrity and other of life's key values, he is politically more conservative, having become so, as I did, with the coming of Ronald Reagan. While I share many of his thoughts on subjects like affirmative action (we both believe it has outlived its time and that racial progress based on claims of victimization are counterproductive), we differ on many environmental issues, and his belief in the power of free markets is stronger than mine. Even so, we share a considerable skepticism about the ability of government to solve problems.

We have traveled and vacationed extensively with Kathy and Jay and have enjoyed them immensely. Their marriage has had a rough spot here and there that Warren and I have not had, but the four of us have been and are very good friends, making an effort to have quiet dinners together every few months.

Jay is a total, confirmed, and loyal-to-a-fault Princetonian. Only Princetonians have such a high degree of zeal for their alma mater. The widespread joke among non-Princetonians is waiting to see how many minutes it takes for a Princetonian to tell you he is one by referring to their *Princeton* years (never *college* years), their *Princeton* roommate or classmate (never their *college* roommate), or some other aspect of their school that clearly tells you that the person you are talking to has a special *Princeton* background.

Once you overlook that, Jay and most other Princetonians are pretty good people!

Jay is a highly gregarious, very intelligent, and quick-minded person on most things. He can also be remarkably slow and forgetful, much to the humorous delight of the rest of us in close association with him. He has gone to client meetings and left materials on the train, and he has flown to Boston thinking he was flying to Washington. He can be totally oblivious to his surroundings. Twenty years into personal computers, he can barely use one.

But how totally lovable he is! Tall, athletic (much more so than I), and imposing, with a strong square face and jaw, he can be a frustratingly poor listener in meetings and is the epitome of the type-A personality. He is always agitated over delays, whether traffic on the expressway or flights at the airport or slow service at a restaurant. He tends to be argumentative, not unpleasantly so, but often wants more complete answers than people can give him.

All of his friends overlook his minor faults and even joke about them to his face. Where Jay comes through most strongly is with his sense of justice, of fairness, and of generosity.

We have had many humorous adventures together, ranging from hosting half-nude women at our table in a Paris nightclub and paying atrocious prices for low-grade champagne, to befriending a gorgeous bartender in a bar in the Swiss Alps and jokingly inviting her to come home with us as an au pair, to getting fairly well sloshed in a Geneva restaurant and helping an American woman seated at the next table (who worked for Howard Hughes) get luggage down from high shelves in her apartment. It was all harmless fun, and no, it wasn't as my father used to say, "I would have done the same thing; only, I wouldn't have lied about it."

We have enjoyed the sense of victory and achievement over getting our first brokerage order in London; establishing a premier research department at Drexel & Co.; and, of course, the success of Miller, Anderson and Sherrerd. He was always the incurable optimist, and I was the more cautious.

He is a better investor than I am, primarily because he is more disciplined in being able to take contrary views. Also, he is a bigger gambler than I am, sometimes almost to a fault, and loves nothing more than an occasional weekend in Las Vegas.

I love him dearly.

And Many Others

There are so many other friends I could write about, people who mean so much to me, such as Morris Williams and Rich Worley, my former partners from whom I have frequently received valuable advice (and also given some). And Jack Bogle, always intellectually stimulating and provocative, and my weekly golfing companion for many years. Or Sara Carter Vogel, whom I mentioned earlier as my assistant of thirty-one years and probably knows more about me than anyone other than Warren. And my Lower Merion High School 1945 classmates, particularly Dottie Biddle Smith and Rinky Pollock Neuhauser. Some of the best are gone; and here I especially mention college friends Brooke Friel, a fraternity brother and usher at our wedding, and his brother, Ted Friel, also a fraternity brother and piano player par excellence, and Harry Wettlaufer, a star athlete at Penn who was one of the grandest guys I have known. But those still living will excuse me for not writing more about them; else, this book becomes too long.

I must mention one good friend who has come to us late in life through our living as neighbors on Useppa Island. We first met Virginia (Ginny) Amsler when she and her husband, Ed, were looking at real estate on Useppa and asked us for some opinions and advice. Ginny is an affable, friendly, gregarious, very pretty blonde woman twenty years my junior. At first, we were puzzled by her frequent presence on the island without her husband. Our antennae went up, and we suspected something was amiss. It was, and figuratively speaking, we accompanied Ginny through the trauma of divorce. She is an emotionally fragile person, so it was quite a trip.

Several years after the divorce, she met a divorced man, Tommy Taylor, who was ill with what was probably terminal cancer. They fell in love, he moved in, and they were two very happy people, but living in the shadow of death. Tommy lived for three years and died in a room in our Useppa house that we prepared as a hospice. This was another trauma for this lovely woman. We have done a lot of handholding and tear wiping.

We have taken many exercise walks together—doing up to four miles on our small island, talking all the while (she more than I)—and have become very close friends despite a twenty-year age difference. She has been a bright, humorous, and energetic addition to our lives; and we treasure her company. We think of her as being partly a friend and partly a daughter. As this is written, another man has entered her life, and the mourning seems to have been eased a bit by time.

Mary Anne Miller Scott and Scottie, Dubrovnik, 1990

The Scotts and us, Useppa, 1984

Scottie and I acting silly, Rules Restaurant, London,1997

Ed Igler, Belgrade Lakes, Maine, 1951

Ed Igler with Warren, 1957

With Janet and Frank Hughes and Ed and Joan Igler, July 4, 1976, Squam Lake

Frank Hughes, 1990

Frank Hughes, Scottie and I, Useppa Island, 1988

Kathy and Jay Sherrerd, Caneel Bay, St. John, circa 1975

L to r., Jay and Kathy Sherrerd, Jack and Eve Bogle, Warren and I, St. Croix, 1963

Jay Sherrerd, Fritzie Flack Sands, Sara Carter Vogel, 1994

CHAPTER ELEVEN

Places for Fun, Travel, and Hobbies

Squam Lake, Useppa Island

The 1960s were a period of solid, happy family life for us. We were in a comfortable community, had many friends, our children were growing up well, our income was rising every year, and we were the epitome of the happy postwar suburban family, a veritable Ozzie and Harriet of TV fame.

Having spent my youth on the New Jersey coast, it was natural for us to take our young family to Ocean City, beginning when Winky was eight months old and starting to make intelligible noises. The following summer, with Kathy as an infant, we lengthened our stay to a full month, a summer schedule we stayed with for the next dozen years. For several years, we rented a wonderful house on the beach at Forty-fifth and Central avenues that accommodated the five of us plus my mother and dad.

Ocean City had a great uncrowded beach, good surf, and a boardwalk to visit as an occasional special treat. It was perfect for young children, and our three loved it. In 1962, a terrible storm hit the coast in March and badly damaged many beachfront homes. That summer we spent at Pocono Lake Preserve, and while we enjoyed the fishing and swimming, the shore attracted us back in 1963. But by 1965, we decided to build a swimming pool and thought we should avoid the extravagance of a vacation at the shore.

By July, as the hot summer wore on, we became restless. We called my sister who was renting a cottage on Squam Lake in New Hampshire. We had visited them the previous summer and were impressed by the lake and the area. There were no rentals available, and Mary Anne suggested we call a place called Rockywold, a family camp across the lake. After telling us there were no vacancies, Rockywold called back several days later to say there had been a cancellation and we could have a cottage called Shingled Blessedness for a week. Off we went, laughing at the name of the cottage and wondering about what we were getting into. And so began a love affair with Squam Lake that was to last the rest of our lives.

The following year, we rented Shingled Blessedness for the month of July and spent the next seven summers there, graduating to a more desirable cottage called

Ishnana. We hauled our Sunfish and Boston Whaler back and forth and looked like traveling gypsies. On one trip home, the boat trailer had a flat tire as we approached New York, and we had no spare. We pulled over to the side and spent several hours as the traffic jam passed us by. I walked two miles into the Bronx to find a service station; no one could do anything for me. Finally, a policeman found us and offered help to find someone to fix the flat. Meanwhile, Buzzy had messed his pants, and the other two were cranky. Never again, we thought. After taking the boat up the following year, we left it in a Rockywold garage for the winter.

In 1967, Scottie asked if we would like to climb Mt. Washington with him and his two boys. He talked about the dangers of the climb, how we had to carry snacks for energy, and generally made a big deal of it. Warren stayed with Buzz, and I took the girls, aged ten and nine. The morning of the climb, we left before dawn to have our breakfast at the Pinkham Notch Camp of the Appalachian Mountain Club. On the way, Winky, nervous ahead of this big adventure, was sick several times, and we wondered whether she would make it. But by the time we got to Pinkham, her nervous belly had eased. She ate a full breakfast, and we were off, up the Tuckerman Ravine Trail, a climb of about four and a half hours. It was the first such adventure for all of us except Scotty, who had done this climb at summer camp as a teenager. But it wasn't the last. Many more hikes in the White Mountains followed, but among the most memorable was the ascent of Mt. Adams via the King Ravine Trail in 1969. That night, which we spent at the Madison Springs Hut of the Appalachian Mountain Club, was the night of the first moon landing. Listening by radio, we could simultaneously look at the moon. It was a wondrous experience.

Our Rockywold years were full of good friendships and good times. The adults would cocktail until ten minutes before the dinner deadline while the children could eat earlier with their friends. Each year, as we left, Winky would cry while thinking that she would not be there again for a whole year. Squam became their second home. We sailed, read, fished, hiked, played tennis, square danced, and canoed, falling all the more deeply in love with the outdoors.

Finding property for sale on Squam was and still is very difficult. Sellers have friends standing in line so that very few properties sold ever reach the open market. In 1973, a business friend of mine, Gene Cheston, told me that he might sell a lot he had bought a couple of years earlier. We went to see it immediately, even though terrible rains had fallen incessantly for several days and the whole shoreline was flooded.

Warren was very lukewarm about owning a house to use only a month each year. She preferred Rockywold where she had no housekeeping and no meals to prepare. We decided to ask the Scotts if they would consider sharing a house and splitting the summer months. It was with that in mind that we jointly purchased a property on the entrance to Outer Squaw Cove, facing two small islands and with a great view of the water and the hills beyond. We paid $38,000 for the lot, hired a builder, selected and modified a plan, and started building as fast as we could. We all were very excited, went up in the dead of winter to see the progress, and hoped for completion before summer. We just made the deadline and moved in to Ishnewtee in late June. The construction and furnishings cost us a modest $56,000.

Winky and Kathy were both working at Rockywold that first year in Ishnewtee, Winky just having graduated from Harriton High School. Her first action was to swim to the island and take a high dive from a large rock. Then she made an Ishnewtee sign from birch bark that still hangs on the porch thirty years later. The name *Ishnewtee* was derived from my father's nickname, "Newt" or "Newtee," and our cottage at Rockywold called Ishnana. One day, when my mother, known as Nana, and dad were in New Hampshire with us, Scottie came to call, and as he approached the cottage, he asked, "Ish Nana here?" So the new house seemed naturally to be Ishnewtee. Newtee was able to spend time there in 1974 and 1975 before he was incapacitated by a stroke. He loved New Hampshire, particularly the fishing.

One day in 1975, I took Newt fishing. We were trolling because he wasn't physically able to stand and cast. We passed a dock with a woman sunbathing in a bikini swimsuit. He loved beautiful women, so I kidded him by saying that she smiled at *me*. "Hell," he said, "that's nothing. The first time I saw you, I laughed out loud." That's become a family joke.

We were in seventh heaven in the house, which is really a quite plain and modest structure with two bedrooms and a bath situated behind one open room serving as kitchen, dining and living area downstairs, and a two-bedroom loft up a flight of circular stairs. The front is all glass doors to emphasize the view. For the next few years, we worked on the grounds, transplanting hemlocks and ferns to camouflage the foundation and making the house look as if it had been there forever.

The Scotts and ourselves coexisted in the house for seventeen years and never had any serious disagreements or criticisms of the other couple. Just two years after we finished Ishnewtee, the property adjacent was offered for sale, and Warren and I bought it, thinking we wanted what Warren called a motel room to live in when the Scotts were in Ishnewtee. We built a cozy one-bedroom house with a woodstove that still is one of my favorite places. We named it Betula (birches) for the trees surrounding it.

At about the same time, we were able to buy two adjacent lots on a peninsula in Rattlesnake Cove, just around a point of land from Ishnewtee and Betula. By 1989, we could see the need for a larger house of our own as both of our families continued to expand. When we built Ishnewtee in 1973-74, there were nine of us in the two families. By 1990, there were fourteen, and now there are twenty-nine. It was time for a place of our own and time for the Scotts to buy our half of Ishnewtee.

We hired Chris Williams—an architect in Meredith, New Hampshire—to begin the design. As the project grew and grew, it became very obvious that the house would be far grander than anything we had visualized. Warren had a basic design in mind that Chris expanded upon. She became totally absorbed in the project and contributed every bit as much or more to the general design as the architects.

With the clever and artistic use of whole logs, we built an Adirondack-style camp, consisting of a main house, guesthouse, and boathouse. It took three years to complete. Camp Keekanoomp, as we call it, is a very beautiful house that has won several architectural prizes and has appeared in a couple of books on rustic structures. The name *Keekanoomp* is a combination of our grandchildren's nicknames for us: "Keekee" and "Oompah."

Keekanoomp is well used by the family. It is close enough to Boston that the Merrill family can use it for weekends. Kathy and her tribe are usually there for two or three weeks each summer, and Buzz and family for two weeks. We have many house guests, and at one time, we had twenty-four people for a weekend. Keekanoomp and Squam Lake are important parts of our lives and our children's and grandchildren's lives.

It's been said that home is best defined as where you keep your photo albums. But if so, we still have them spread among three different places: Gladwyne, Squam Lake, and Useppa Island.

Useppa Island

In 1983, Warren rather uncharacteristically said, "I think we should look for a house in a place that's warm."

We had been traveling to St. John in the U.S. Virgin Islands for two weeks each February for several years, staying at Caneel Bay, a resort built and then owned by RockResorts, a Rockefeller family-owned company. We began trips to the Caribbean in 1962, with Jay and Kathy Sherrerd, and continued that pattern for twenty years, visiting Antigua, Barbuda, Virgin Gorda, and St. John. With the children now out of the house and as we became able to take more time away, Warren wanted a place of our own in the sun. Her specific interests were Bermuda and Florida.

What I had seen of Florida was not appealing. Miami and Ft. Lauderdale, and the East Coast in general, seemed both overdeveloped and overcommercialized. But we had heard good things about the Naples and Sanibel areas on the Gulf Coast and decided to take a look in March of 1983. We told ourselves that we were looking for "Squam Lake South."

Naples left us cold. It was suburbia on canals and obsessed with golf, tennis, big boating, and shopping. And the prices staggered us. On to Sanibel and Captiva. Staying at the South Seas Plantation, an overcrowded resort at the north end of Captiva, we looked at real estate for three days and saw nothing with appeal. On our last day there, Warren saw a realtor's sign in the marina, advertising trips to Useppa Island. Remarkably, Warren remembered hearing from friends about what a marvelous place Useppa was. They had been the winning bidders at a charity auction of a week on Useppa. So after hearing that there was a house for sale on the island, we climbed onto the realtor's boat for the thirty-minute trip.

We were immediately enchanted. A natural environment full of birds, dolphins all around the island, old growth trees, an interesting history, no showy palatial mansions, old-Florida architecture—it had everything we wanted. We walked into the house that was for sale, saw a 180-degree view of water from the living room, and fell in love. Within twenty-four hours, we bought it and have never looked back.

Useppa has a ten-thousand-year history. A Santa Fe projectile point, dated to 8000-6500 BC, was found after a heavy rain in 1987. Burials have been discovered dating to as early as 2800 BC. We islanders have established a museum to show the ancient and recent history. Modern development followed a Cuban fishing village and a small Civil War fort when John Roach, the Chicago Street Railway magnate, bought the island in 1895 and built a residence and ultimately a small hotel called the Tarpon Inn. In 1911, Baron Collier bought the island and expanded the hotel and built several cottages that still stand today. I have photographs of the island in 1915 that were given to me by a friend whose grandfather came to Useppa for tarpon fishing in that year.

It is a small island, about 1.1 miles long and 0.3 miles wide. It sits in Pine Island Sound, behind the barrier island of Cayo Costa. There are about eighty families with residences, some of which are duplexes, but the "load factor" seldom exceeds 60 percent and often is only 40 percent. Uncrowded, no cars, a wide variety of people, both in terms of geographic origin and social status—it is unpretentious and very neighborly.

In 1985, the cottage next door, Honeymoon Cottage, named for the spot that Mary Roberts Rinehart spent her honeymoon, came on the market, and we bought it. Shortly thereafter, we remodeled and expanded our original cottage and connected the two houses by decking. Finally, a third adjacent cottage became available. We added it to our collection and named it Folly Cottage. Now we own the entire north point, with views of both sunrise and sunset.

We have many good friends on Useppa. When you garner a new friend later in life, when neither of you know the history of the other and your friendship becomes based only on your shared experience, it is of a very different order than old friendships from college, business, or your younger social life. You feel very close to these new friends despite the lack of shared history. In the case of Useppa, a big part of this closeness derives from the way of life on an island—the common inconveniences of shopping, the boat dependence, the social interdependence, and the occasional emergencies.

Our children, a bit wary at first, have come to love it as much as we do. Someone once asked Edna Hager, a good friend and fellow Useppan, what we did to amuse ourselves. She jokingly replied, "We count our money and have group sex." To which another friend said, "No, we don't have group sex. That would require too many thank-you notes."

Useppa has brought us many happy family Christmas celebrations and many happy occasions to have old friends as houseguests. We sail; boat; play tennis and croquet; and, as I am doing now, write or read. Useppa suits our temperaments perfectly.

In the summer of 2004, I took a writing course online from Allearn, a consortium of Stanford, Yale, and Oxford. The teacher, a Yale faculty member, was a poet. Each writing assignment was either a four—or five-page essay or a poem at least fourteen lines long. I had never written a poem before. After five rewrites, with the help of the teacher, I produced the following poem about Useppa:

Useppa Island

In a water-wrapped wilderness
A scarlet sunrise sneaks
From behind a mangrove mound
That softens the green sea horizon.

Cars and concrete,
Fast food and billboards,
Are a forgotten world
As the silence is pierced
By soaring screeching Ospreys.

The nose-brain senses the mildew rot
In the buildings of an earlier elegant age
Mixed with the sap fragrance of fresh lumber
In the newer tin roofed houses;
Homes of those who choose tropical warmth
For forming new deep friendships
And remembering years and places left behind.

For it is a place dressed in history and memories.

Tentacles of docks crawl from the shore
Where ancient peoples once threw fish nets.
Time faded whitewashed steps and walls wander,
Some with apparent aimlessness,
Their purposes, conceived by long dead designers,
Detectable only in age spotted photographs.

Calusa tribesmen and Cuban fishermen,
And other ghosts of past ages,
Attend the wine soaked dinner parties
In white painted houses,

Sail the white-capped waters,
Sit on the white beaches,
Or watch white clad croquet players
Contrast with a velvet green lawn.

A swimming pool full of child sounds,
Surrounded by tan oiled bodies
Sits beside an antique mansion
Atop a mound of bones and midden.

A century worn, surprisingly pink pathway,
Overhung by bearded oaks and hoary banyans,
Waits with quiet indifference
For the feet of another generation,
To walk in this perpetual parade,
As time both ravages and preserves
This place and its people.

As I completed the writing course, a frightful hurricane named Charley hit Useppa full force with sustained winds of 145 mph. Our most recently purchased house, Folly Cottage, was very badly damaged. The entire island was defoliated, the one-hundred-year-old Collier Inn was smashed, docks were destroyed, and several people lost their entire homes. It was, we hope, a one-hundred-year event. We are rebuilding as I write this.

Travels and Adventures

Travel with the family always emphasized the outdoors. In the summer of 1971, we were invited to join the Lovelace family, friends from California, on an expedition to raft the Kobuk River, north of the Arctic Circle in Alaska. When I proposed the trip and asked who would go with me, only Winky, then age fourteen, said yes.

Off we went by ourselves, stopping overnight in Seattle, where we had dinner at the top of the Needle and ate Baked Alaska while enjoying the city's lights. We flew to Kotzebue, where we were scheduled to meet our guides and equipment. After spending our first night camped at the edge of the gravel airstrip, we found that the guides were there but the rafts were not. The trip was almost canceled until we went in to the Eskimo village and found two men who would take us upstream in outboard motorboats.

We traveled for five days on the Kobuk River. It was beautiful wilderness with mountains to the north and miles of flat tundra extending away from the river. There were chunks of jade rock along the river bank that we brought home with us. I polished one of them and used it as a paperweight for many years then finally gave it to Winky one Christmas. We fished (Winky caught a six-pound arctic char), hiked, had some great camping sites, bathed in some sun-heated side pools, and worked our way upriver to the village of Ambler where a small plane picked us up and flew back to Kotzebue.

After Winky and I enthusiastically described our trip, I asked who would like to try something similar the following year. Everybody signed up.

Thus, it was that in 1972 we rafted the Colorado River, starting at Lee's Ferry, just below the dam, and traveling for six days down to Whitmore Wash, at the beginning of Lake Mead. Our companions were friends we had made through an informal business group and included the Lovelace family, Fred and Donna Meyer and two children, and Edus Warren and son Hootie.

This was before the many restrictions that were later placed on these trips. We could still have open fires, dug latrines, and outboard motors on the rafts. Toward the end of each day on the river, we would begin to collect driftwood that was left in the canyon before the river was dammed. The daily water level in the river would fluctuate widely, depending on the electric load that Las Vegas put on the hydroelectric facilities at the dam. We tried to time the floating of the bigger rapids to the high water levels, but at one point, our raft (we had two) hung up high and dry on a large rock, necessitating an unscheduled stop for repairs. We took time to float down the azure blue and warmer waters of the Little Colorado in our life preservers, made several interesting side hikes, learned the geological history of the canyon, and were able to find some excellent campsites, although one night was spent sleeping on pure rock.

The first night on the river, I chose to sleep under the stars with the children while Warren, who was still learning about camping, slept in our pup tent. During the night, I thought I heard a slithering sound on the nearby sand. Half asleep, I crawled into the tent with Warren, dragging my sleeping bag. She groaned and sleepily asked what I was doing. When I told her that I thought I had heard a snake outside, she sat bolt upright and said at full volume, "And you left our children out there!?"

Winky had a teenage crush on one of the guides, and the adults drank gallons of beer that we had piled high in cases on one of the rafts, dragging a dozen cans at a time in a mesh bag behind the raft to keep it cold.

Coming out of the Canyon, we went to Las Vegas for the night. The contrast between the wilderness and the obscenity of Las Vegas made a deep impression an all of us, but particularly the children. They fully understood then that their preference would always be the wilderness.

Amusingly, as we prepared to board the plane to Philadelphia, I took Buzz, who was then twelve years old, over to a dime slot machine (they don't make dime machines anymore) to gamble a few coins in my pocket. On the third dime, I hit the jackpot and dimes cascaded from the machine. After stuffing the coins in all of our pockets, we rushed to the plane while Buzz puzzled over why we would ever stop playing such a lucrative game!

I rank the Colorado River as the most enjoyable trip we ever took as a family.

By the end of the Grand Canyon trip, we were all hooked. We arranged to raft the Middle Fork of the Salmon River in Idaho the following June. Called the "River of No Return," the Middle Fork flows down through the Sawtooth Mountains in a wonderfully wild region that we accessed by small plane from Stanley to a grass airstrip. It was five days in smaller rafts than on the Colorado but the rapids seemed tame in comparison. We had the same companions as the previous year. When we left the river, we went to Sun Valley to clean up and use the Laundromat before beginning the drive westward to the Sierra Mountains.

Passing Mono Lake, a salt-rimmed lake we often see from the air when flying to San Francisco, we entered the Sierras. It was the beginning of a week's hiking and staying at the High Sierra Camps with Jon and Lillian Lovelace and their three boys. The camps are platform tents with woodstoves and a main dining tent. It also offered good camp food and a packed lunch for the next day's hike. We stayed two nights in each of three different camps, taking day hikes from each of them before moving on. Some of the hikes between camps were long, and at points, difficult. I was still a cigarette smoker and felt the combination of smoke damage and altitude. (I finally quit in 1981, just before Thanksgiving, and I consider that one of my greatest feats, succeeding only after many attempts!)

The Sierras are indescribably beautiful with sharp stone outcroppings and peaks, rounded granite hills, and awesome cliffs. It may have changed by now but the trails were surprisingly uncrowded. We hiked to about twelve thousand feet where Vogelsang Camp greeted our tired bodies. From there I took a solo hike up to a beautiful bowl with a lake in its middle to try some fishing. While I was there a powerful thunderstorm roared unexpectedly over the mountain. I took shelter in a small cave to watch the lightning strike several times around the bowl's perimeter. At one point I looked around and five feet away a marmot was sitting out the storm with me. I talked to him, but all he did was stare back.

One night at the Merced Lake Camp, we had no sooner turned out the lantern in the tent than Warren announced that she had to pee and that she would not walk the one hundred yards by herself to the john. Grabbing a flashlight, I grumpily went with her. The toilet was housed in a very small room by itself. After Warren went in and closed the door, I heard a rustling in the brush and turned the flashlight on a black bear about ten feet away. I pounded on the door to be let in to the tiny toilet space, went in, and pulled the door after me. There was Warren, seated on the toilet, with me standing squeezed in about a foot of floor space in front of her. We started to laugh until we were both in tears, then waited a while before cautiously opening the door. Our friendly bear had disappeared.

In the summer of 1973, Winky went to Outward Bound School in the Boundary Waters Canoe Area of Northern Minnesota, a maturing experience for her. By the next summer Winky was out of high school and preparing for college by earning money working at Rockywold Camp. Kathy and Buzz both went to National Outdoor Leadership School in Alaska and Wyoming respectively. From then on, college and summer work took over and the children began to go their separate ways, making family trips rare.

In 1980 the five of us went to Hawaii for Christmas and stayed at Mauna Kea, a beautiful resort on the Big Island where the body surfing was quite sporty. We went to a native Hawaiian church for Christmas Eve services, went to the top of a volcano, and visited the Pearl Harbor Memorial.

Hawaii was the last big family trip until 2001 when we spent Christmas in the Galapagos Islands. Meeting in Quito, Ecuador, all of us except Buzz and Paul flew to the islands on Christmas Day and boarded a small but comfortable motor/sailboat for a week. That night, we pulled into a protected anchorage and as we had our cocktails on deck, the crew surprised us by turning on Christmas lights they had hung from the rigging. We made all the obligatory hikes, witnessed the incredible tameness of the wildlife, snorkeled with sea lions, and on one island, saw the unlikely combination of penguins and flamingos.

On Our Own

We have been very fortunate in our business and other activities to have traveled widely. There is a large map in our kitchen in Gladwyne, marking our travels. There are dozens of pins but the world is a big place and there are notable gaps, especially Australia and New Zealand, huge parts of Africa, almost all of Russia and the other former Soviet states, Egypt and the other Arab countries, and Southeast Asia other than India, Indonesia, and Singapore. Many of our travels on business or in connection with the work of the Ford Foundation and World Wildlife Fund have already been mentioned. But we have also traveled on our own, touring Japan, barging the length of the Canal du Midi in Southwestern France, hiking in the Dordogne, exploring the lake country of Northern Italy, being tourists in the Loire Valley, hiking in Scotland, walking through Tuscany, visiting friends in Ireland, driving the Dalmatian Coast in Yugoslavia, and cruising the Mediterranean, the Baltic, and North Seas and the Black Sea. Altogether, we have visited thirty-five of the most important cities in Western and Eastern Europe and Scandinavia, excepting Berlin, Budapest, and Vienna.

In 1990, we decided to invite our closest friends, the Scotts, Iglers, and Hughes, to join us on a cruise on the *Sea Goddess*, a small but luxurious 125-passenger ship. The trip was from Venice, down the Dalmation Coast of Yugoslavia, through the Corinth Canal, stopping at several Greek Islands, then on to Istanbul, Bulgaria, Rumania, and Yalta in the Ukraine. The trip ended in Istanbul.

The Cold War had just ended. When we entered the port of Costanza, Rumania, you could see the devastation that came from years of Communist neglect. The port's cranes, work boats, and dockside facilities looked as if they had stood unattended for decades. Rust, grease, and broken equipment decorated the shoreline, and the water had a thick coating of oil. Our ship, clean as only Scandinavians can make it, glistening in white contrast to the filth around it, was pushed by a tugboat that had old tires for fenders, which left black smudges on our hull.

The town was virtually empty of consumer goods. The shops were bare shelved. If one hadn't believed the economic disaster of communism before then, this was convincing evidence. We had received official permission to travel the Danube Canal to Bucharest, the capital, where only shortly before, the tyrant dictator, Ceausescu and his wife, had been forcibly deposed and executed. But when the authorities saw the ship, they rescinded the permit, saying that the superstructure was too high to clear the bridges. It was a doubtful story, but the ship arranged for us to fly to Bucharest for the day on Soviet-made planes that looked and felt insubstantial.

Bucharest was an education in the evils of dictatorships. In the center of the city, a gigantic palace, as big as the pentagon, was being built to satisfy the dictator's ego. We have never before or since seen such vulgar ostentation. It was unfinished but the people of Rumania vowed to finish it and open it as the Palace of the People.

To compensate for the cancellation of the Danube Canal trip, the cruise line arranged for us to visit Yalta. In all of these ports, we were the first cruise ship to visit after the Cold War. And everywhere the dull stamp of Communism was evident. In Yalta and Odessa, we were always accompanied by an official "guide" keeping a watchful eye on us.

It was truly a great trip, particularly in the company of our very best friends. There were many humorous highlights but none funnier than seeing Ed Igler, proper son of a Baptist minister, sunning himself on the deck next to a woman who stripped to the waist and lay flat on her back, large breasts pointing at the sun. Poor Ed was so flustered that he didn't know whether to stare, look out of the corners of his eyes, or pretend to ignore the scene.

We made one more trip with the Scotts on the *Sea Goddess* the following year, starting in Monaco and stopping at several islands including Ibiza, then traveling the Spanish and Portuguese coasts to Bordeaux, the Channel Islands, and finally to London.

I do not want to make this a travelogue, so I will write only short summaries of a couple of the more noteworthy trips. In 1994, accompanied by the Iglers and Scotts, we toured Scotland, stopping as often as practical to take day hikes. In 1996, we invited the Scotts, Iglers, and Fred and Ruth Rozelle to cruise with us on the *Seabourn Pride*, a magnificent Norwegian-crewed ship that took about two hundred passengers. The ship started in Copenhagen and went to Helsinki, St. Petersburg, Stockholm,

Tallin, and returned to London. Five years later, we made another *Seabourn* trip, starting in Copenhagen and traveling the length of the Norwegian coast to the North Cape and twenty-four hours of sunlight. In addition to the Scotts, Ginny Amsler and her love, Tommy Taylor, went with us. Tommy had cancer and was fighting a valiant fight but he died, as I have said, in our house on Useppa the following April.

Other trips and cruises included a trip on the *Sea Lion* through the waters of Southeast Alaska, where we saw magnificent displays of whales, and one on the *Seabourn* to Morocco, Madeira, the Canary Islands, and Spain, where we visited the Alhambra and Seville. In 2000, we took our grandsons, Ryan and Jake Merrill, on a family trip sponsored by the American Museum of Natural History to Turkey and Greece, cruising from Istanbul down the Turkish coast to Kusadasi, then to Rhodes, Santorini, and finally to Athens.

Also memorable were our walking trips in Tuscany and the Dordogne. The Scotts were with us in Tuscany and poor Scotty was suffering from a very bad hip that he finally had replaced. There were some arduous parts of the walk resulting in Scotty's being almost crippled when we arrived in Florence for the trip's finale. The hotel found a wheelchair for him and I pushed it around the cobbled streets and high curbs of the city. Not much fun for either of us!

The walking trips were perfect in length, never more than six hours a day, nor less than four. A lovely picnic lunch would magically appear at noon, and the best chefs in the small towns along the way were drafted for our dinners.

Probably the highlight of all our travels was a trip in the summer of 2002 on the *Mist Cove*, a twenty-four passenger boat, through the Inside Passage of Alaska. We chartered the whole boat for our extended family to celebrate our fiftieth wedding anniversary. The Scotts and two of their grandchildren, Carrie and Stephen; Warren's sister and brother-in-law, Flip and Lew Soars and two of their grandchildren, Page and Wade Flanigan; Kathy and Scott Carlson and their kids, Tor and Livia; Bonnie and Buzz; and Winky and Dave Merrill and their three, Ryan, Jake, and Maggie.

We might say the whales or the fishing or the hiking and sightseeing were paramount, but the truth is, for Warren and me, it was the simple camaraderie of the family that made it so special.

Because of the hurricane devastation to Useppa Island in 2004, rather than spend the entire winter on a construction site, we chose to cruise the coast of South America in February 2005. Starting in Santiago, driving to Valparaiso, we boarded the *Silver Wind* for sixteen days, going down the Chilean coast, through the fjords and the Straits of Magellan, out to the Falkland Islands, then along the Argentine coast to Montivideo and Buenos Aires. We ended the trip by flying to the sensationally beautiful Iguazo Falls on the border of Argentina and Brazil.

In the time left to us, we are putting priority ratings on Australia and New Zealand, Thailand, and Vietnam. But truthfully, when we look out on Squam Lake or Pine Island Sound, we say to ourselves that it doesn't get any better than this.

Hobbies and Other Time Killers

Warren and our children laugh at my "results!" orientation. They are absolutely correct. I want fast and noticeable results. When we named a new boat on Squam Lake, Winky came up with *Rezultz* that is emblazoned on the side of the boat in large letters.

I read books and magazines fast (as long as I can stay awake!) to mine the nuggets of useful information from them, paying little attention to the details. When I undertake the study of something, I do it too quickly, trying to get at the essence of the subject and then throwing it aside when I know enough to satisfy me. This is a major weakness but can also be a strength. I get more done in less time than most people I know, and what I do, I do well, even while ignoring details that occasionally catch me up. These characteristics show plainly in my treatment of hobbies.

I am addicted to many hobbies in general but none in particular. My curiosity drives me to an obsession with new subjects that I swallow in frenzied gulps, but only up to the point where going further might make me an expert. So far from becoming an expert on anything, I am just a guy with an above-average knowledge about many things.

My most durable hobbies have been collecting U.S. postage stamps and vegetable gardening. I started both of these as a child under the aegis of my father. He started me on stamps when I was only eight or nine, aided by his best friend who began to send me first-day covers starting with the airmail stamp used on the first trans-Pacific flight. I picked up the hobby again in my thirties while spurring Kathy Miller to begin collections of her own (British America and Germany) And I have started collections for grandsons, Ryan Merrill and Tor Carlson. I watch auctions, occasionally make bids, and have built a solid collection. There is something about stamp collecting that makes me despise the look of even a single empty space in an album.

Vegetable gardening began with our World War II victory garden on an empty lot behind the house across the street. It was a big property that was subdivided into perhaps thirty separate gardens tended by neighborhood families. Working together for many hours on weekends, we had the best, the neatest, and most complete garden of them all. Dad took great pride in having a weedless, well-cultivated plot that he braggingly described either as being "smooth as the top of a billiard table," or occasionally, "as smooth as a baby's ass." Our production was awesome. Tomatoes, corn, lima beans, string beans, broccoli, lettuce, cabbage, carrots, beets, squash, and cucumbers—we grew them all and canned many for the winter to save ration coupons. We also made our own sauerkraut in a big stone crock that was kept in the cellar and covered by a board with a brick on top to avoid smelling up the house.

When we moved to Gladwyne in 1962, we asked the sellers to allow us to begin a vegetable garden on the property before we settled for the house and moved in. The garden became a family project. Everyone was drafted into preparing the soil and planting and doing the follow-up weeding. It was a test of diligence and perseverance that only Kathy passed.

Vegetable gardening is now done in New Hampshire, starting each season on Memorial Day weekend when we gather as many family "volunteers" as we can to do the planting. I enjoy it as much now as I did in 1942. It's trite but true to say that there is something very satisfying about having your own soil and hands produce your food.

When Winky was in fourth grade, she had a great teacher who had them study the solar system and universe. Dinner time discussions intrigued me so that I needed to know more. I bought a cheap telescope, read several books, and took a mail-order astronomy course. We were able to look at the planets and moon, but that wasn't enough. Warren surprised me at Christmas with a gift of a Questar telescope, the best one available for amateur use.

We conquered the techniques of an equatorial-mount telescope and enjoyed the views of twin stars, galaxies, gaseous phenomena, and of course, the planets. To have gone further would have meant serious study that was not for me. I continue to subscribe to *Astronomy Magazine* and use the telescope for special astronomical occasions, but that's enough. Interestingly, I find that very few people have gone to the trouble of learning the most basic facts and principles of how the solar system works. At a recent dinner party of otherwise sophisticated friends, I was asked to explain an eclipse of the moon that we had seen during the cocktail hour. That led to questions that amazed me by their naiveté.

I was introduced to photography by my Uncle Bill Thompson. He had a Rolliflex camera, and set up a darkroom in our basement, circa 1940. He always welcomed me as a companion, and he taught me the basics of darkroom work. I can still feel the excitement of working in the red light of the darkroom and seeing enlargements magically appearing in the developing tray. Armed with a Kodak Brownie Camera, I duly recorded my years at summer camp, family events, and eventually, with a slightly more sophisticated camera, my college years.

For a college graduation gift, my grandmother gave me a thirty-five-millimeter camera and I became a bit more serious. But it wasn't until we expanded our Gladwyne house that I had a real darkroom of my own. I took, developed, and enlarged telescopic images of the moon and planets and went to the edge but did not cross into the much more difficult deep-sky photography.

My most serious foray into photography was the building of a collection of wildflower photographs, primarily flowers of the northeastern United States. Many of these were taken on hikes in the White Mountains and fishing trips to upstate Pennsylvania. In the process, I became quite proficient at wildflower identification. Even many years later, I am always looking for wildflowers along trails and streams and river banks.

The advent of digital photography is replacing the darkroom with the computer, and I am doing my best to keep up with the technology. But the darkroom's magic was far more fun than a computer screen.

At some point, I became fascinated by the outrageous claims of cures embossed on antique patent medicine bottles and have built an extensive collection of them—first by visiting antique dealers in New England but now using online auctions.

I am an enthusiastic fly fisherman, but not to the point where I have spent time studying the insect life on the streams and tying my own flies. I love to sail but have not studied racing techniques. I am a bird watcher but would not inconvenience myself to find a rare species. I play chess but have never seriously studied the game. I taught myself to play the ukulele and planned to go to the guitar but never did. I have built an excellent collection of nineteenth-century White Mountain paintings but am far from being the expert I could be if I were not so results driven. I like to paint with watercolors but do it in spurts without taking courses to become better. I have a collection of dozens of different day lilies but have not, as most collectors do, tried to do any cross-pollination. I have climbed all the over five-thousand-foot peaks in New Hampshire and twenty of those over four thousand feet but am not interested in lesser mountains with no views.

So you see, I am really what is impolitely called a half-assed hobbyist, who knows a little bit about a lot of things and is an expert on nothing. But I sure have had fun. And Warren has been very tolerant and patient as I have moved through these many interests. She is always ready with compliments (that I usually solicit) about a painting, a photograph, or a vegetable crop.

Cocktail hour at Rockywold, Squam Lake, 1970

On the summit of Mt. Percival, Squam Lake in background, 1982

Ishnewtee, our first Squam Lake house, 1974

Teaching first grandchild, Ryan Merrill to fish, Squam Lake, 1990

With Jake and Ryan Merrill, Squam Lake, 1991

With the Merrill grandchildren, Ryan, Jake, and Maggie, 1994

Ginny Amsler and Paul Miller, IV, 2004

With all the grandchildren on East Rattlesnake Mt., Squam Lake, 2001

Camp Keekanoomp, Squam Lake, completed in 1994

Honeymoon and Conch Out cottages, Useppa Island

CHAPTER TWELVE

Some Things I Think About

God, Good, Evil, Life, and Death

In the fall of 2002, my daughter Kathy said she was intrigued by a philosophy course offered online by Allearn, a consortium of Stanford, Yale, and Oxford. It was titled "Understanding Human Nature" and was essentially a survey course, letting us taste the great philosophers from Plato though Descartes, Kant, Marx, Hegel, and on to Freud and Skinner and other modern behavioral psychologists. Classmates were from around the world, of different ages and backgrounds. Interesting discussions on the readings took place during the week, culminating with a real-time chat on the weekend.

My personal take from the course was: first, that there was little discussed that I had not thought about in some way during my life; and second, I felt confirmed and comfortable in my personal beliefs about God, life, death, and human relationships that have evolved over many years. Not that I discovered any philosopher whose thoughts were identical to mine. On the contrary, there was no one who was entirely on my track. But I found bits from almost every one of them that rang a bell with me even while I disagreed strongly on many other pieces.

At the end of the course, I was more convinced than before that there are no answers to the questions that we humans have about ourselves, our existence, and our relationships with the world around us. Absolute truths do not exist apart from science and mathematics, and even many of those truths have changed immensely over the centuries. There are only tentative personal conclusions that we each reach through a lifetime of evolving thought.

Some people are satisfied with their personal conclusions about God and life. They tend to be happy. Others may be tortured by the lack of absolute truths and seem to harbor constant dissatisfaction with the way the world seems to work. They tend to be unhappy. Count me among the happy ones who have reached some conclusions that are satisfying. I feel no need to share those conclusions widely, but I do want others, particularly my family, to know what they are and how I got there.

I start here with an outline of what I do and do not believe:

- I believe that most people are "good."
- "Good" means that they live their lives so as consciously not to harm others.
- I believe that altruism is learned and is not genetic.
- I believe that living a good, decent life is perfectly compatible with pursuing one's own self-interest.
- I believe that the primary function of religion is to promote goodness and suppress badness in people.
- I do not believe in a supreme being.
- I do not believe that Jesus Christ was divine.
- I believe that the purpose of human life is no more complicated than simply to survive as a species.

How did I arrive at these conclusions?

Some Personal History

My first memories of church are of Christmas, when I was five or six years old; a pageant at the five o'clock Christmas Eve candlelight service with Mary and the baby Jesus in the chancel, with the older boys dressed in burlap to look like poor shepherds, and the three wise men bearing gifts, with cardboard crowns on their heads.

Sunday school was part of my life. I was expected to attend and not complain. It was customary for the children to attend the eleven o'clock church service for thirty minutes before being excused for a half hour of Sunday school. I remember hearing in Sunday school the parables from the Old Testament and the story of the life of Jesus, told in the classical manner of the boy from a poor family who became a carpenter, who went on to become a "perfect" man performing miracles. I came to think of Jesus as a magician who could wave a wand and heal sick people, multiply the loaves and fishes to feed a crowd, walk on water, or turn water into wine.

These are pleasant memories. To this day I can recall the scents of the old wood paneling in the parish house and the flowers at Easter and balsam at Christmas. I can vividly picture the singing of "Silent Night" with nothing but candles lit and a large blue electric star over the altar, the churchyard in snow, and Sunday dinner at home after church. It was the big meal of the week, when we would have roast chicken or lamb or beef, mashed potatoes with gravy, and canned peas or spinach. We always had a cooked dessert such as pie or floating island. Church and religion were disconnected. That is, there was never any deep conversation at Sunday school or at home about the why and wherefore of religion. Sundays were more a social affair; a repetitive, sometimes boring time when we were obligated for some vague reason to go to church and Sunday school.

I was completely unaware that there were any other religions other than Christianity until I had a Jewish classmate in fourth grade. I had to ask my father what Jewish meant and was told simply that Jews didn't believe in the divinity of Jesus. I took Jesus for granted. It wasn't a question of belief. Jesus was a fact. Period. My Jewish friend was a curiosity, although my family never suggested that being Jewish was bad. In fact, to their credit, they always taught tolerance to us. They seemed more worried about Roman Catholics. I had several Catholic friends, and I knew they were somehow more dedicated to their church than I was. Catholicism was an integral part of their lives, far from the way I or my family felt. My grandfather and grandmother were first-generation Americans, born of English parents who emigrated here in the 1860s. As immigrants they had become Episcopalians, a natural migration from the Church of England. They had all the anti-Papist feelings and prejudices of that generation of English, and had passed them on to their children.

My mother and father never appeared to be very religious, although as Dad grew older he seemed to rely more on his faith. He said prayers each night as he went to bed. While we were young, however, I do not remember any notable demonstrations of devoutness. As a boy, Dad and his family belonged to the Dutch Reform Church in Hazelton, Pennsylvania. His memories of church included his mother rapping him on the head with her heavy gold wedding ring to get him to pay attention. I remember his saying that he was "churched out." My grandfather, with whom we lived, regularly attended the 8:00 AM communion service by himself and said a brief grace before meals. Interestingly, my sister, five years my junior, is an active church member. Somewhere during our lives we came to different conclusions about religion although we have always been very close to one another.

The Church of St. Asaph was effectively run by several wealthy families, especially the Roberts family, whose forbearers were among the very early settlers in our region. The Roberts lived in a true mansion not far from the church. We stood in awe of them and their wealth, almost worshipful. Their lives had little resemblance to ours in our small semidetached house next to the firehouse. Years later, I discovered that Mr. Isaac Roberts had given money at the request of our minister to enable me to attend summer camp, away from the pollens and dust that plagued me with allergies. Thus, I benefited from an act of real Christian charity for which I was able to say thanks to one of his sons long after Mr. Roberts passed away.

At the age of twelve, I attended confirmation class for three months prior to being confirmed as an Episcopalian. Again, it simply didn't seem to take with me, although I finished the classes, went through the ceremony, and thereafter took communion once a month during the school year. Never did I have any real religious or spiritual feelings even though I tried to concentrate and summon them. As I took communion I would look at others, appearing so pious and somber and wonder whether they were experiencing something that I wasn't. Or were they looking that way because they thought it was the way they *should* look? When they prayed, on their knees and with eyes tightly shut, were they experiencing some sense of spiritual communication with a Superior Being that I was not? Was it entirely my own personal lack of spirituality that was a roadblock to a deeper understanding?

Shortly after my confirmation, our minister (he was never called a priest, although the Episcopal Church calls them priests today) asked me and my close friend Johnny Wynn to be acolytes. We dressed in robes, lit the altar candles, processed and recessed with the choir and minister, received the collection plates and took them to the altar, helped with the serving of communion, and doused the candles at the end of the service. There was always something to giggle about, and giggle we did, as quietly as possible. We performed because we had a sense of obligation and not with any religious fervor.

It seemed strange to me that church was abandoned during the summers. Even the minister went away. Was God seasonal? I was puzzled by "Sunday Christianity," the lack of any connection between church and our everyday lives. Was religion meant to serve the religious, to make them feel better about their world once a week?

It also puzzled me that God was seen as both good and vengeful at the same time. And if he (or she, or it) is all-powerful and all-knowing, how could he have let such travesties take place as the Holocaust? Or how could he have been so full of vengeance as to let the world's population be wiped out in the flood of the Noah story? How can a vengeful God be considered a moral God? And how can he be any "guidance" if he is an immoral God?

At summer camp, we would occasionally have bull sessions about religion and I always found myself arguing the agnostic position, even though I didn't know what the word meant at the time. In college, during fraternity-house discussions, I again was the one who questioned the existence of God and the purpose of religion. I have no idea how I arrived at the positions I took on these subjects; they simply seemed to be there. I was never concerned that I was subjecting myself to hell and damnation for thinking the way I did.

When Warren arrived in my life, I found that she had not had the same degree of "churching" that I had. She had been sent to Sunday school by her parents who never attended church. She was struck by that and was puzzled over the aura of magic that seemed to surround Jesus. I remember her telling me how she had explained to herself the miracle of the loaves and fishes: Jesus had set the example of sharing, and others followed so that there was enough for all. But both of us were puzzled by religion. We felt obligated to have a church in our lives but we were both agnostics. I should add that Warren was a bit more fearful about denying a God than I was. She decided to be confirmed at St. Asaph's and attended confirmation class. I was then serving as an usher on Sundays. The church was only a very short walk from our little apartment over the dry cleaners.

Warren was confirmed, took her first communion, and never returned for her second. We both became inactive and have been so ever since with the exception of a short experiment with Quakerism some years later. We seldom talk about religion. We both are comfortable with what we believe and don't believe. Our thinking has evolved over the years, and I will try to relate that evolution. I speak for myself and not for Warren because, while we have similar views, they are not identical.

Many Questions and a Few Answers

As an adult I never could accept an image of God in a human body. It simply seemed ridiculous to me, in view of what we know scientifically about the world, to think there was some spirit dwelling in a humanlike body—probably a big body, as pictured in old religious paintings. Over the years I have asked myself many questions such as: Is there a being at all? Is there a spirit at all? Is it external to the world? Part of the world? Part of the universe? Was God responsible for the Big Bang? If God exists, what was there before God? Is there reward or punishment after death? Or are there rewards to the living, as in "virtue is its own reward"? What is the power of prayer?

I have formed personal answers to some of these questions that satisfy me, while recognizing that each of us has to come to his own answers. Some of them are, in my opinion, irrelevant. I don't try to answer them. For example, why should I care whether God created the Big Bang? When I do try to have answers, do I think my answers are correct? No, because I don't believe there are any "correct" answers. They simply make me comfortable with myself.

Do some people believe in God because they are afraid of the consequences of not believing? Assuredly so, in my opinion. And why not? If there is any possibility that there is a God who insists on belief in him or her or it as a condition of entry to heaven, then the safest course is to believe. It is the comfortable way. If we cannot prove God exists and we cannot prove God doesn't exist and if there is a possibility that there is a penalty for nonbelief, then why not believe?

So how do I get around this quandary? By choosing to believe that if there is a God, he loves us all unconditionally. But merely making such a statement acknowledges that I am not sure that God is a myth. True. It's not possible to be *sure*; but I am nevertheless *comfortable* in being an unbeliever.

I do not know whether many or few people fake their beliefs. But I think that it is very important to be faithful to one's self. I remember when I first thought, while saying the Apostles' Creed, that I really did not believe what I was professing to believe. I stopped saying it and have never said it since.

Recently, I came across an essay by Thomas Paine and was struck by what he wrote 235 years ago:

> *I do not believe in the creed professed by the Jewish church, by the Roman church,*
> *by the Greek church, by the Protestant church, nor by any church that I know of.*
> *My own mind is my own church.*

But it is necessary to the happiness of man, that he be mentally faithful to himself. Infidelity does not consist in believing, or in disbelieving; it consists in professing to believe what he does not believe.

When a man has so far corrupted and prostituted the chastity of his mind, as to subscribe his professional belief to things he does not believe, he has prepared himself for the commission of every other crime.

Respect for Others' Beliefs

Let me be clear that I have absolute respect for religious beliefs of others. When I was young, I argued frequently about religion and could not understand how some people could believe as they did, particularly my Catholic friends who seemed so dogmatic. I feel differently today. Religion is a very personal set of beliefs. Faith is not explainable. Those who have it are to be envied in some ways. To many of them, life is a series of events governed by God. That is a very comforting view, a view that denies complexity. But it is different from my view, which holds that we are responsible for ourselves and our actions; that accidents occur, both good ones and bad ones, that are not willed by a God. My personal view is not incompatible with religion or faith. Where I differ from those who believe in free will while professing religious beliefs is that I believe there is no real purpose to the world and human existence. We are an evolutionary accident.

I know people who have devoted their lives to being Christians. I respect and admire them immensely. One couple spends half of each year helping a black township in South Africa pull itself up educationally and economically. We know young people who spend their time teaching in poverty-ridden communities, and health workers who are totally dedicated to improving the lives of fellow human beings. Some of them do it with religious fervor. Others do it because it offers some satisfaction in their quest to improve a very imperfect world. In my lifetime, such people have been too rare and have had a disproportionately beneficial effect on the world around them. Nothing I say here should be interpreted as disparaging to them.

Flirtation with Quakerism

When Warren and I were in our thirties, with three young children, we decided that they should have some exposure to religion to enable them to come to intelligent conclusions for themselves as they grew older. Our impression was that the Society of Friends (Quakers) had demonstrated over three hundred years that they practiced what they preached. That is, they seemed to be the least hypocritical of any sect we had observed. Long time champions of civil rights, religious tolerance, improved justice systems, prison reform, and liberal education, Quakers are a notable presence in the Philadelphia area. After attending several meetings, we sent the children to First-Day School at the Radnor Meeting and began regular attendance ourselves. It was a stimulating, although not spiritual, experience for me. Meetings were hard work. Sitting, concentrating, listening for a spiritual message to share with others, was far from relaxing. For me it was also far from successful. Following one meeting, Warren was in tears, confessing that it was very stressful for her.

We concluded that becoming a Quaker was too difficult. Sadly, we did not have the degree of dedication to ideals that seemed to be required. It was not that we did not believe in those ideals. Rather, as we freely confessed, we were too occupied by other matters in our lives to spend the time and money that would be required of a good and active Quaker. We stopped attending after two years. But we both maintain tremendous admiration for the Quakers and their activities in support of their beliefs.

The most valuable thing I gained from my exposure to Quakerism is a definition of God that I have clung to ever since. At the time, I was still puzzling about the existence of God, so this came as a relief. Each Sunday, the meeting was followed by a "forum" in which some subject, ranging from international politics to religious topics, was discussed. One such session asked each of us to submit a definition of God. The purpose was to demonstrate just how diverse such definitions are. They were indeed diverse. As the definitions were read, one leapt out at me. It was "God is the sum of all the goodness that resides in the hearts of men." Eureka! Not an image, not a mystical spirit, but an idea that contained the core of what I believe. The concept that God is the goodness in human hearts and that it may be intensified through education, and yes, even religion.

God, an Invention of Man

At the heart of the evolution of my reasoning has been the belief that humankind invented God because people desperately needed explanations of how we got here, why there are stars in the sky, why storms and pestilence are "sent," what happens after death, why so many of us are poor and only a few rich, and the many other mysteries of the world. During my education, I gained the strong opinion that religion, needed as it was to explain poverty, misery, and one's lowly position in society, was exploited by both secular and religious leaders to gain and maintain power. As Karl Marx put it, "Religion is the opiate of the masses." I also came to appreciate how many wars have been fought and lives lost in the name of religion. I always greeted cynically the thought that "God is on our side" in a war.

I came to believe that religion has an important purpose in our lives. That purpose is to modify behavior and to bring out the goodness in human hearts in such a way as to create a society that is more orderly and livable. True, wars have been fought and torture employed in the name of God and Jesus, but without religion as a base for morality, conditions might have been a great deal worse. It seems to me that the Ten

Commandments, thousands of years after they were first written (by some person or persons, in my view, not by God), are good rules by which to govern society. With the exception of the command not to worship idols and not take the name of the Lord in vain, the commandments are moral, not religious, directives. In Judeo-Christian societies, they became backbones of legal systems.

Science and God

Science has now explained many mysteries. Darwin and those who followed have explained that evolution is purely accidental. Animals don't adapt to environments. It is only through the accidental appearance of certain genes that enable the strongest to survive. "Survival of the fittest" is hardly a compatible thought to gentle religious beliefs such as "the meek will inherit the earth."

I suppose that there will always be ultimate mysteries. How did the original mass that exploded into our universe in the big bang get there in the first place? Was it part of some master plan? Why and how do those accidental genes appear? While no person has the answers to these questions, I reject the notions that they will never be found and that there is only one explanation: a Creator or Superior Being.

For me, the belief in a Creator is the easy way out. Had generations of scientists let literal creationism prevent them from persevering to discover how the human body works, how plants grow, or how an atom is composed, we would still have a life expectancy of thirty-five and spend much of our lives hungry. Are the discoveries of science also part of some master plan that is revealed to us only over millions of years, in little pieces? I cannot prove otherwise but simply choose not to believe that.

Indeed, I have wondered why scientific experiments are occasionally stopped or impeded by religious beliefs. Currently, important work with stem cells is being severely hampered by "religious" people who hold that human life is so precious that we should define it as beginning with conception. Many people, in the name of the Holy Bible, choose to believe that Darwinian theory is wrong. There seems to be a fear on their part that scientific advances might degrade morality or lessen the level of religious conviction in the world. Of course, the latter has been happening for many generations. As I write this, only in America, among the predominantly Christian nations, is professed belief in God holding its own.

The Purpose of Prayer

As I have observed people who profess religious faith, I have noticed that many of them use religion for personal comfort. They seem to pray mostly for themselves and their loved ones; for events that would affect them either to happen or not happen, even for them to make a foul shot in basketball. I am not saying that prayer is bad or useless. In fact, it is a marvelous stress control and method of strengthening the will, just as is transcendental meditation. If prayer makes people feel better or gives them some added strength to face crises or accomplish some task, it serves an important purpose.

One can, of course, pray for bigger things, for a certain path of world events or for wisdom to be imparted to world leaders, which may give the person praying a sense of participation, a sense that he or she is not sitting idly while Rome burns. Again, one may feel better about oneself and the world for having done so. But is there really power in prayer to change the course of events other than what might be accomplished by giving people an elevated sense of what they themselves can do, an added strength to do something? I don't belittle that as a goal of prayer. Prayer can impart strength and determination that can change the course of events through personal actions. That I do not doubt. As for prayer that hopes to change something not in one's own domain, I believe it is an ineffective exercise even though possibly benefiting the mental well-being of the supplicant.

Jesus, Yes! Religion, No!

I believe that Jesus existed as a person, a highly unusual person for his time and culture. He preached a different message from what the Jews had heard before: love one's neighbor, demonstrate love, kindness and generosity, forgiveness, turn the other cheek and you will be rewarded with participation in the Kingdom of God. His words were regarded as revolutionary and dangerous, for which he paid the ultimate price. In my view, Christianity has taken these simple messages and garnished them with legends, ceremonies, created hierarchical organizations around them, and even twisted them toward forms of intolerance, e.g., the Inquisition or the current tendencies of the Christian Right to be intolerant of different views of life. Wars are fought between people with different interpretations of Jesus.

In 1978, I was invited to visit Israel by some Jewish friends. The purpose of the trip was to generate support for Israel among the non-Jewish community. It accomplished this purpose, although I increasingly feel that the war of the terrorists is partly our fault for having not pushed the Israelis hard enough to forge compromise agreements with the Palestinians.

In Israel we visited many Christian sites, including Bethlehem, the various New Testament sites in Jerusalem, the hill where Jesus is supposed to have preached the Sermon on the Mount, the Sea of Galilee, and the temple where Jesus upset the tables of the money lenders. I admit that these visits created a spiritual feeling in me, an almost supernatural reverence. I attributed those feelings to confronting the places I had heard about as a child, and toward which I had ascribed a magical image many years ago in Sunday school.

The message that Jesus brought was designed to improve the way people relate to one another. I do not believe one must think of Jesus as divine or believe in the supernatural legends that surround him to accept his message. Jesus was a philosopher who spoke wisely about life, was martyred, and then glorified in ways I think would horrify him.

Afterlife?

I have come to believe in a definition of immortality that offers me satisfaction. When I was very young, I imagined a picture of heaven that was cartoonlike. It was in the sky and everyone was dressed in white and had the same faces and bodies they had on earth. They could look down upon the rest of us on earth and some special ones had wings. One could arrive on this idyllic scene only if he or she obeyed the Ten Commandments and the Golden Rule. When I became old enough to discard this image, I had some trouble finding another that satisfied me. What I know and read about human biology and physics brought me to question an afterlife and the whole concept of heaven and hell. I began to notice how often my father spoke of his dead parents, particularly his mother, and how he seemed to emulate her, at least in the image of her that he provided. After Dad's death, I found myself passing on to my children and grandchildren pieces of his wisdom and humor. I do the same thing with memories of dead friends whose faces I can see so very clearly and whose voices I can hear in my head.

I began to reflect on how good people have a lasting effect on the people close to them and the institutions they touch. As I did so, I came to know that I had not only genetic inheritances but also a heritage of ideas, values, morals, and views of life that were held by generations past. We send out concentric ripples, like a stone cast into the water, that have effects on everyone we touch, effects that are lasting and may be passed from generation to generation of friends and family. The better we are as people, the greater and longer lasting our influences will be in making others, including the unborn, better people as well.

Thus, I believe my own influences on family, friends, and others I have known, perhaps as members of organizations and institutions, will live after me. That sounds quite conceited, I realize, and I do not mean it that way. All people, regardless of personal accomplishment, have it within their means to teach by example such qualities as outward honesty and inward honesty, loyalty, generosity, tolerance, optimism, bravery, and love. These may or may not be genetic, but regardless, they are at least reinforced by learning. The better the teacher, the more lasting the lesson. This, I believe, is what immortality is all about. It's not a concept that will satisfy some people but that's not my design. Each of us must come to grips with his own questions about immortality and find his own answers. There is no absolute truth.

Christian values are good values. I have tried to abide by them and feel good about myself for doing so. Society works better, even if still very imperfectly, because of them. I subscribe to them wholeheartedly, but without believing in the necessity of a God to worship, or a religion to clothe them with ceremony and hierarchy.

Evil and Its Consequences: A Doomsday?

What about evil? It exists and prospers in certain places at certain times and in certain people. Is it inconsistent to say, on the one hand, that human beings are basically good and yet recognize that evil coexists with goodness, even in the same person or persons?

I don't think so. All of us experience temptations to break the rules, laws, or mores that we acknowledge as being crucial to a functioning society. Most people resist most of the time. Why? Is it simply a matter of being afraid of the legal or social penalties? Or is it a more fundamental human characteristic than fear, perhaps an innate desire to live in a safe society that tries to nourish our children as they proceed along paths to maturity? Are we "hard wired" with a morality that tends to aid our survival as a species?

I believe that we are good because it serves our quest as a species for survival. We establish laws, rules of morality, and religions to reinforce good and suppress evil. To be sure, we are not always successful, and from time to time, we find the necessity of more extreme measures, such as wars; wars that appear contrary to our quest for the survival of the species but which often can be shown ultimately to be a suppression of evil.

The human costs of evil are immense and growing as world population crosses 6.5 billion and as the technologies of war and terrorism become potentially more horrific. I easily become pessimistic when looking at the historical trend toward a greater and greater ability of our species to self-destruct. But seeking survival doesn't guarantee it. Species that have become extinct did not want to die!

My point is that there is no more evil in the world today than in the past. But the costs of evil have escalated exponentially. Neither a God nor any other force may save the species from ultimate extinction. All we can do is try to keep postponing doomsday.

This sounds more pessimistic than I intend. I believe that self-destruction is a possibility, I also believe that we can, during many generations to come, avoid that end by harnessing the inherent goodness in mankind. But it will take more than prayer, more than God. It will require enlightened, strong leadership in the major countries of the world, strong economies that make further inroads into poverty, expansion of international trade that creates political and economic interdependence, and major breakthroughs in the quest for racial and religious tolerance.

The triumph of good over evil is not assured. But I believe it will happen. Why do I believe that? Because I want to believe it.

Postscript

My daughter, Katharine, after reading this told me she and I were in substantial agreement about religion. She differs in two major respects. First, in defining God. She thinks it is inconsistent to define God as the goodness in us without defining the evil that resides within us as the devil. Well, I have no problem calling evil the devil. But why must I define God in the first place?

I think the answer is that no definition is necessary in an absolute sense. I sought one because I need it to rationalize my atheism within my own mind. "Aha!" one might say, "So you too *need* a God even though you profess no belief!" Perhaps I need not call goodness "God." I could simply profess a belief in the inherent goodness in us. That's okay, I can stop there. But I find it useful to find some positive relationship between the widely held beliefs of others in God, the power of prayer and immortality, and my own beliefs. That is, not state all my beliefs in the negative; what I *don't* believe rather than what I do. I admit to some negative statements in this discourse but have tried to look at the positive contributions of others' beliefs, either to them as individuals or to society.

Kathy's other point of disagreement was on immortality. She asks, "Doesn't the evil that men do also live after them," e.g., children who are abused often abuse their own children. Perhaps we are neither wholly good (angels) nor wholly bad (demons). What lives after us? Only the good?

Kathy and I agree that the purpose of the concept of afterlife as I have defined it is to positively affect morality and behavior so that one will be rewarded by being remembered favorably, so that the influence one has had on others will last. The idea of a literal afterlife, going to heaven, has the same purpose—to enhance behavior during life.

Indeed, evil also has an afterlife but it can be a beneficial one. The memory of Hitler has served to create awareness in us of what can be produced by certain economic and political circumstances and may make a recurrence of such a person less likely.

Politics and Political Philosophy

When I cast my first presidential vote for Harry Truman in 1948, I was importantly influenced by two forces. First, were my father and mother, both political liberals in the context of that day, and second, was a course in economics I was taking at the time. The professor made considerable effort to make us understand the issues of the day in economic terms. They also happened to be the way he saw the world, i.e., with liberal eyes. Regardless, it was my first serious attempt to analyze the issues in anything other than superficial ways.

By the time I finished my education in economics, I saw myself as a progressive liberal on social issues and as one who saw government playing an increasing role in economic issues, including income redistribution and other poverty "solutions." To most people in 1948, the Cold War was just beginning to become a major concern, so there was no real issue for me other than being strongly in favor of the Marshall Plan and foreign aid to the devastated countries.

In 1952, I was an enthusiastic supporter of Adlai Stevenson against Dwight Eisenhower. Stevenson was an intellectual politician, a rare combination we have not seen since. Eisenhower proved to be a magnetic personality in a period with very few disturbing problems and won my vote for a second term in 1956. He swept the country quite broadly, taking all but nine Southern states with 57 percent of the popular vote.

When John Kennedy was nominated in 1960, he charmed me and brought me back to the liberal camp. While I thought he handled foreign policy and the Cuban missile crisis well (after a terrible start with the Bay of Pigs disaster), on economic issues, he was a mixed bag. On the one hand, he saw the merit of cutting taxes to stimulate growth, and in turn, garner higher tax receipts. But when he tried to browbeat the steel industry into not raising prices in April of 1962, I reacted negatively to such an intrusion in the free market. In retrospect, I see that it was then that I began to become more of a free-market advocate.

Nevertheless, when Barry Goldwater was nominated by the Republicans in 1964 to run against Lyndon Johnson, I was so horrified by what then appeared to be his internationally belligerent and domestically conservative positions that I changed my registration from Independent to Democrat. Johnson took 61 percent of the popular vote that year. Interestingly, however, Goldwater went on to be a respected and statesmanlike figure, and with time his conservatism became almost middle-of-the-road as the whole political spectrum shifted to the right.

I have remained a registered Democrat, but have continued to vote as an Independent. Intensely disliking Richard Nixon, I voted for both Hubert Humphrey in 1968, and George McGovern in 1972. I still believe that Humphrey could have been a great president. I was privileged to meet Humphrey twice, once during his campaign and once in the White House when he was vice president (where I very briefly also met Lyndon Johnson). Humphrey was the last Democrat I supported enthusiastically. The popular vote in 1968 was essentially tied, with only 0.6 percent plurality for Nixon. But that was the year that the South, strongly resistant to Civil Rights pressures, deserted the Democratic party, with Wallace taking the Deep South and Nixon taking the rest of the South. Talk of a "new majority," a Republican majority, became widespread. It seemed to be true in 1972, as McGovern, a terribly weak candidate, garnered less than 40 percent of the popular vote, and took only Massachusetts, Rhode Island, and the District of Columbia.

Still disgusted over the Watergate scandal that forced Nixon to resign, and attracted to the honesty of Jimmy Carter, I continued my streak of Democratic votes.

Then along came Ronald Reagan, whose economic policies and firmness with the Soviet Union attracted me. In the meantime, we had seen Carter's complete ineffectiveness, particularly in handling the Iran hostage affair. We also had seen the power of free markets in responding to the higher OPEC-caused oil prices of the early 1970s with reduced consumption and a greater supply.

But another set of facts was emerging about the "fatigue" of the liberal social policies of the previous twenty years. Welfare rolls continued to swell, inner city education was failing despite higher budgets, and both businesses and individuals were chafing under the increased web of bureaucratic regulations. Reagan struck the right note when he said that people wanted government to "get off their backs." He also said, "Government's view of the economy could be summed up in a few short phrases: If it moves, tax it. If it continues to move, regulate it. If it stops moving, subsidize it." This rang very true to me in 1982, and he got my vote then and again in 1986.

Retrospectively, I believe that Reagan will be judged as an important president, one who had a few strong ideas and pursued them doggedly, and who probably pushed the Soviet Union to defeat in the Cold War.

I met Reagan twice. The first time was when he was running for reelection in 1984. He was in Philadelphia with Senator John Heinz to greet people who had provided financial support to the campaign. But the second meeting was more intimate. He was barely a year out of office and had come to Philadelphia to speak at Penn's 250th anniversary celebration. Walter Annenberg, a faithful and very rich supporter, had issued the invitation and the Annenbergs invited us to dinner along with about twelve other people. Warren and I were the first to arrive and found Reagan alone on the sun porch. In chatting I said that he must feel very good about the Berlin Wall coming down and the Cold War ending, which became obvious only after he had left office. He said that, yes, he was proud, but then launched in to a string of jokes about the Soviet Union, noting that he collected them. We could not get him to talk seriously about anything.

At dinner, Reagan showed his wonderful ability to charm and entertain by relating the "real story of the Gipper" as Nancy watched adoringly.

When George H. W. Bush ran against Bill Clinton in 1992, neither candidate attracted me, and as a protest, I voted for Ross Perot, an independent third-party candidate who garnered 17 percent of the popular vote.

I thought Bill Clinton was an unorganized, womanizing, yet charismatic person. I did not vote for him for either term. But he dragged the Democrats to the center and demonstrated that they could win by doing so. Now, in 2004, I wish we had a centrist running instead of two candidates who are at opposite ends of the philosophical spectrum.

George W. Bush has distinctly different views from mine on many issues but I am in basic agreement with his philosophy of minimal intrusion by government in the private economy. I believe that the experiment Bush is furthering of low taxation on capital is worthwhile seeing through for at least a decade. Perhaps we will learn whether low taxes on capital are, as advertised, stimulatory to economic growth. As this is written, I am very concerned about the huge disequilibrium in world trade and finances that has the United States running huge deficits both domestically and internationally, the latter caused by the immense gap between our imports and our exports. Just how that gap will eventually begin to close will determine a great deal about the direction of both the U.S. and global economies.

I see George W.'s views on abortion and his occasional implications that he is speaking for God, rather than to God, as not only abhorrent but also in direct conflict with his favoring minimal government intrusion. Yet I voted for him in 2000 and again in 2004, feeling the opposing candidates were weak alternatives that were not acceptable at a time when winning the struggle in Iraq and against terrorism were so vital.

In this year of 2004, it seems to me that the Democrats have a long road back to power. Since 1968, with the exception of the ineffectual Carter Administration, which I view as having won the White House only as the result of the Watergate backlash, the Democrats have been in control of both the White House and Congress for only two years. They have become, as a friend of mine, Paul Isaac, says, the Grievance Party, representing the downtrodden and the otherwise "self-ascribed aggrieved minorities of all types, the disadvantaged, the social critics, the international idealists, and those who want different economic and social policies enforced by the state." The positions they have taken simply don't play well in Middle America, let alone in the South.

The Republicans have become the party of self-ascribed morality, appealing to old-fashioned but solid middle class values and to people with strong religious beliefs. As and if they continue to push their religiously based positions into politics, we are setting ourselves up for some divisive constitutional battles. One can only hope that the great center of the political spectrum will find an effective spokesperson who will give it cohesion and energy to become the major voting bloc that must be courted by both the left and the right.

Before leaving the subject of politics I want to emphasize that I am deeply patriotic. I believe that those of us who lived through the years of World War II tend to express our patriotism with more openness and intensity than recent generations. I know that patriotism can take many forms, and I do not impugn those who may express their personal patriotism differently. However, when someone suggests that the United States has serious flaws relative to other nations, I get red-faced and furious.

At the Core of Character: The Eternal Verities

Without integrity, one is not a whole person. I believe that people who lack integrity know it. They have simply decided to ignore their consciences. One's conscience does not lie. To ignore it is not a subconscious decision.

Integrity is not only dealing honestly with others. It is also and primarily dealing honestly with one's own values and intellect. As Polonius says to his son, Laertes, in *Hamlet*,

This above all: to thine own self be true,
And it must follow, as the night the day,
Thou canst not then be false to any man.

But easier said than done? Can any human, subjected to the interactions of everyday life and the necessities of being politic and diplomatic, ever perfect a complete consistency of intellectual honesty? I doubt it. I know that on several occasions, I have acted with political expediency in order to achieve ends that I believed met the test of morality. But to my best knowledge, I have never taken any action or said anything that I knew was not true and that might be harmful to an individual or group of individuals.

I do not want this to be a sermon on morality. Matters are not always divided into simple rights and wrongs. Beyond that, our minds have an amazing ability to rationalize, see extenuating circumstances, or justify means by the ends in order to win arguments with conscience.

I believe that as humans, we instinctively understand the difference between cruelty and kindness, honesty and mendacity, courage and cowardice, tolerance and bigotry, work and idleness, love and hate, loyalty and fickleness, education and ignorance, humility and arrogance. Psychiatrists are now hypothesizing that evolution has hard-wired some of these values into us. That is, we have survived to become the superior species, not only because of superior intellect but also because of a genetic value system that has enabled us—despite frightful outbreaks of cruelty, hatred, and war—to coexist with billions of other creatures like ourselves.

On the Importance of Hard Work and of Earning Your Way

I believe that hard, long, and bone-tiring work is a character builder. Actually experiencing how furnace hot a factory floor can be in a July heat wave, how long an eight-hour day seems when you are doing a boring job like mail sorting, or enduring a ten-hour day cutting lawns in ninety-five-degree heat—these make you appreciate what many people must tolerate every day. I am glad that I did these things, but having done them makes me very grateful that they were just for the two-month span of a summer job.

What is Success?

Clearly, success is not becoming wealthy or achieving an important status in your profession or community. These are the results of success, not success itself.

I believe success is minimizing the difference (what I call the personal "gap") between what you know your potential is and your actual performance. Closing the gap should be one's paramount objective in everything one does, from nurturing a happy family and instilling in them a solid set of values, to academic work, to a career. This is a very high standard and certainly not one that I have achieved. In fact, not many people do.

It is a goal worth having. One knows when he or she has performed up to his potential. But what a rare feeling it is. And what a great feeling it is! That's because self-respect is highly dependent upon minimizing the gap. To do so will always mean that you have exceeded the expectations that others have of you.

At the beginning of each school year, I gave each child a one-on-one talk, saying that it was not the grades that were important, it was knowing that you did your best. Years later, when Winky was a graduate student at Cornell, I discovered that those talks had been disturbing to her because it was very seldom that she thought she had done her best. She was right; it is rare that you have conviction that you could not have done better, but it's something to strive for. I don't think I left her with any permanent scars!

Meritocracy, the Uncompromised System

Straying from meritocracy produces mediocrity and should be done so only for the strongest possible reasons. When schools, businesses, or other enterprises cater to the less capable and devote fewer scarce resources to the more capable, the average skill level created is reduced.

Today, for example, in universities, we are constantly being bombarded by the educational advantages of "diversity." I agree strongly with that *if and only if* the average academic quality of the students and faculty is not reduced to achieve the diversity.

I first was exposed to the idea of affirmative action when I was a young Penn trustee. I listened carefully as President Harnwell spoke to us about the necessity of elite schools taking the lead in admitting black students even if we had to lower our standards a bit to do it. I was in total idealistic agreement. The Ivy League did take the lead and the ice was broken for minority admissions across the country. Most larger businesses, after legislative and regulatory prodding, also made and continue to make genuine attempts to build diverse workforces.

Much was accomplished in the past forty years to reduce the ugliness of racism and sexism in our institutions, much more than might have been expected in only a generation and a half. But the speed at which it took place also brought us to the point where the competition is intense for what is an increasing but still limited number of qualified minorities. While that is good, it has also built expectations based on a theory of victimization. Reduce the standards today, this theory states, for those who have been victims of past discrimination, and eventually the need for reduced standards will disappear.

In the meantime, other qualified students are being denied admission slots, and those admitted under affirmative-action programs are increasingly looked upon as people who are where they are only *because* of race. Let me qualify my opinions on these difficult issues—those of us who have not had to endure racism have been too quick to dismiss the probability that our view of the world, while it may not be racist to us, is a view that inescapably is that of white elitists.

Have the benefits of diversity been worth the compromise of meritocracy? I believe the answer is a definite yes, but I also think it's time to consider reducing the degree of compromise before "victims'" expectations leave a permanent mark on our attempt to be a meritocracy. Of course, many of us, myself included, have believed in some preference for alumni children. If administered without care, such preferences may compromise my meritocratic ideals. And the fact is that large donors, alumni or not, *are* able to gain favor in admissions. It's unrealistic to believe that will change. But I believe that's okay if legacy status is used *only* to express preference over others of equal ability.

It's too easy for a Wasp male to express concern about the splintering of America. There are countless groups seeking recognition and pursuing their special agendas, e.g., Hispanics, Latinos, African-Americans, Italian Americans, Asian-Americans, gays and lesbians, born-again Christians, Jews, Muslims, and many more. Each of them has succeeded in heightening their own sensitivities to the extent that it is difficult to begin legitimate debate without engendering outraged cries of racism or cultural or religious bias.

Civil discourse must be an integral ingredient in building a diverse democracy. As I write this, in the midst of the polarized atmosphere of the 2004 presidential election, my hope is that we can discuss issues with civility and respect. But achieving that appears to be a long and difficult road.

Advice to a Grandchild

In 2004, our oldest grandchild, Ryan Merrill, left home for the University of Colorado. Ryan is a terrific boy but has never been an adventurer, so this is his first really independent experience. I couldn't resist giving grandfatherly advice in a letter that is an exposition of my values as an eighteen-year-old might be able to see them. Here is the letter:

Dear Ryan,

In a few months you will begin what should be one of life's greatest adventures in starting college. The place you choose will have a profound influence on your life. It's the place where you will grow up. You will make your closest friends and perhaps find your life's mate there. You will learn how little you know about the world and you may find a few teachers who will shape your intellect in ways that importantly determine what you accomplish over the following fifty or so years.

Or it may be simply four years of drifting, drinking beer, and having fun. It's up to you. You will get out of college only what you are willing to put into it. Regardless of whether you choose a school close to home or far away, you will be alone in making your decisions and you will experience new, intense feelings of freedom and independence. What you do with these new feelings will affect your future life in many important ways that may not yet be clear to you.

The Quakers believe that all people are endowed with an "inner light", what is sometimes called a conscience, which speaks to you. It doesn't make mistakes. When that voice tells you that you can and should do better, or that you should or should not do something, listen to it. Only if you do, will you feel really good about yourself.

Whatever you do, I sincerely hope you will keep some strong guidelines in mind:

First, never compromise your integrity. Sadly, cheating is very widespread in colleges today. You may be tempted to "go along with the guys" and cheat or help others to cheat. Listen to the inner voice within you that says, "no", if this happens. You will always respect yourself more, and others, who may coax you to do otherwise, will also respect you more. True friendship never demands you to disregard your conscience. A good test is to pretend that what you are about to do (or not do, as the case may be) will be in a headline in your hometown newspaper. Would it make you ashamed or proud?

Second, get your priorities right. Academic studies come first. Always. Be unabashed in your curiosity, both in and out of the classroom. Extra-curricular activities are there by the dozens to choose among. Not just sports, but many others, from debating societies to hiking and skiing clubs, to groups that come together for some common interest, such as politics, business, or a language. Get to know what they are, and then choose to be engaged to the maximum extent consistent with your academic priority. Parties and social life are also an important part of college, but make damn sure they are not at the top of your agenda!

Take every opportunity offered to get to know your professors. Some of the best teaching is done outside the classroom. This is not easy in a big university, so you must actively seek such opportunities. Chances are very good that you will find some subject that really interests you. When you do, dig deep, and don't be timid with your questions.

As you choose among social alternatives, such as fraternities, or simply groups of friends, try to pick people who share your priorities. If you decide to join a fraternity, see how it ranks academically, and choose from among those that have the higher academic standings. It will be important to associate with people who, while they need not be intellectuals or book worms, respect the scholarly side of things.

Third, be a believer in moderation. Getting drunk is disgusting for others as well as yourself. Stay away from people who are not moderate. Dope and drugs are equally disgusting. Nobody ever lost the respect of others by avoiding them entirely.

Fourth, be kind and considerate in your attitudes and actions toward others, particularly women. It is likely that women friends will become a more important part of your life. Who knows? You may even fall in love with your future mate in college. I did. You have been very fortunate to have some marvelous women in your life; a great Mom, two loving grandmothers, and a sweet sister. Be sure they can be proud of the way you treat other women.

Finally, get involved with the world. This year you will vote in the presidential election. Your vote carries with it the responsibilities of citizenship in the greatest country in the history of the world. Get to understand the issues and have opinions on them. Debate the issues with friends. You will find that you can learn a lot in bull sessions about politics, religion, and even sex!

You have been reared in a marvelous, loving family. You have great parents and siblings, and very loving grandparents. From what I see, you have a good set of values. You have a good education that is going to become more complete. I can't think of any reasons why you might screw it up. So don't.

Be your own best friend. You can look at the person you consider your very best friend, and see ways in which he could change to make you like him better. Often you don't feel comfortable telling your friend about what you see as his shortcomings. But you can tell yourself about your own shortcomings and do something about them. You will become a better friend of Ryan Merrill.

Always remember how much many people love you and are very proud of you. If you ever feel in need of help, ask them for it promptly.

I know that words alone from a parent or grandparent may not sink in fully. But it has made me feel good about both you and me to have written this.

I love you,
Oompah

A Good Place to End

This advice to a grandchild may be a proper ending. After all, that's really what we are about: passing on to younger people the mores, ideals, and ideas that, we have learned, are important in achieving a productive and happy life. Not only passing them on but also trusting that they will build on them, improve them, and even change them if it becomes intellectually and morally imperative to do so.

As one ages, one naturally tends to think more and more about the past. I now have had probably at least 85 to 90 percent of the total experience I will have as a human being. But nevertheless, I am excited about the future that only my children and grandchildren will know. If only our urge to survive as a species spurs us to the sensible use of technology for the broad benefit of our species, the world can be a better place

I fervently want, wish, and hope for a future for my children and grandchildren that is better in terms of peace and prosperity in the world. On a personal level, I want them to know the love of a mate, the company of good friends, and the sense of accomplishment I have known.

My life has been far better than any dream I might have had in terms of companionship, accomplishment, satisfaction, health, and happiness. I have trust that it will continue that way for however many days I have left.

I deeply love my friends; my family; and, yes, myself!

What more can I possibly say?

INDEX

Printed in the United States
56922LVS00005B/55-57

9 781413 499582